OUR
GLASGOW

Memories of Life in
Disappearing Britain

PIERS DUDGEON

headline
review

First published in 2009
by HEADLINE REVIEW
An imprint of Headline Publishing Group

First published in paperback in 2010
by HEADLINE REVIEW

1

Cataloguing in Publication Data is available from the British Library

ISBN 978 0 7553 1714 1

Typeset in New Baskerville by Avon DataSet Ltd,
Bidford on Avon, Warwickshire

Printed in the UK by CPI Mackays, Chatham, ME5 8TD

Headline's policy is to use papers that are natural, renewable and
recyclable products and made from wood grown in sustainable forests. The
logging and manufacturing processes are expected to conform to the
environmental regulations of the country of origin.

HEADLINE PUBLISHING GROUP
An Hachette UK Company
338 Euston Road
London NW1 3BH

www.headline.co.uk
www.hachette.co.uk

Contents

Maps of Glasgow   vi

Chapter 1   From Legend to Enlightenment   1
Chapter 2   Character   19
Chapter 3   The Great Change   56
Chapter 4   The Women of the Tenements   94
Chapter 5   Street Magic   134
Chapter 6   Class War   179
Chapter 7   Conflict   212
Chapter 8   Glasgow at War   241
Chapter 9   Glasgow on the Move   282
Chapter 10   New Lamps for Old   320

Acknowledgements   348

Sources and endnotes   353

Index   369

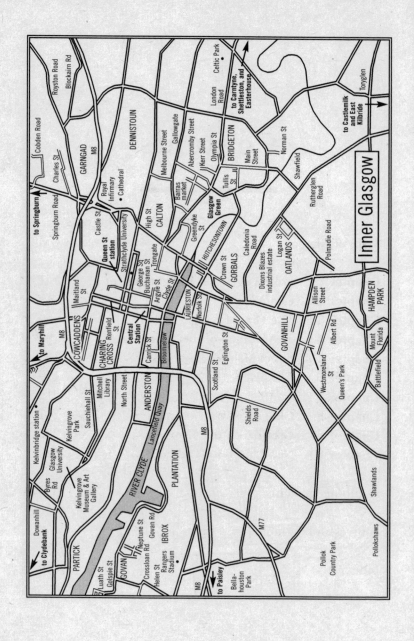

Inner Glasgow

Royston Road
Blockairn Rd
Cobden Road
Charles St
to Springburn
Springburn Road
GARNGAD
M8
DENNISTOUN
Castle St
Royal Infirmary
• Cathedral
Melbourne Street
Gallowgate
Abercromby Street
London Road
to Carntyne, Shettleston, and Easterhouse
Torglen
to Castlemilk and East Kilbride
Celtic Park •
Olympia St
Kerr Street
BRIDGETON
Norman St
Queen St station
Strathclyde University
High St
CALTON
Barras market
Greendyke St
Glasgow Green
HUTCHESONTOWN
Tullis St
Main Street
Shawfield
Rutherglen Road
to Maryhill
M8
Maitland St
George St
Buchanan St
Trongate
Argyle St
Clyde St
Crown St
GORBALS
Caledonia Road
Dixons Blazes industrial estate
Logan St
OATLANDS
Polmadie Road
COWCADDENS
Renfield St
Central Station
Carrick St
Broomielaw
LAURIESTON
Norfolk St
Scotland St
Eglinton St
Allison Street
GOVANHILL
Albert Rd
HAMPDEN PARK
CHARING CROSS
Mitchell Library
North Street
ANDERSTON
Lancefield Quay
Shields Road
Westmoreland St
Queen's Park
Mount Florida
Battlefield
Kelvinbridge station •
Sauchiehall St
RIVER CLYDE
M8
PLANTATION
Kelvingrove Park
Kelvingrove Museum & Art Gallery
Byres Rd
Glasgow University
M77
to Clydebank
Dowanhill
PARTICK
Luath St
Colpsie St
GOVAN
Crosshoan Rd
Neptune St
Helen St
Govan Rd
IBROX
Rangers Stadium
M8
to Paisley
Bella-houston Park
Shawlands
Pollok Country Park
Pollokshaws

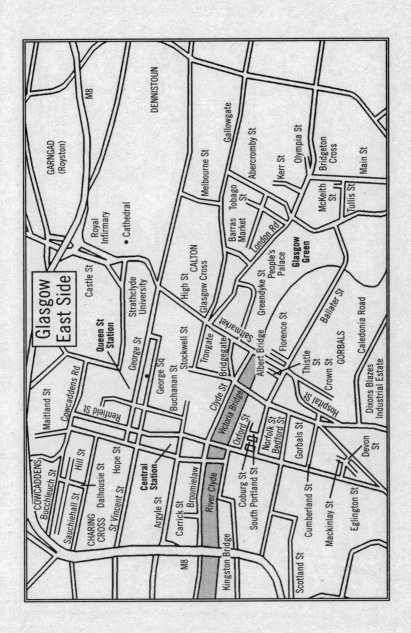

CHAPTER ONE

From Legend to Enlightenment

L egend has it that Glasgow was a Christian foundation. In the sixth century, so the story goes, St Kentigern (known with more street cred as St Mungo) founded a monastery beside a burn called Molendinar, less than a mile north of the River Clyde, some fifteen miles upstream from its estuary. The 'second city of the Empire' started here.

Fourteen hundred years later, a young Bill Paterson was growing up in Dennistoun in Glasgow's East End, where, as fate would have it, 'only a couple of blocks away from our back green' was visible 'the only surviving stretch of the Molendinar', otherwise 'obliterated and entombed' by the Industrial Revolution, which a century earlier had all but squeezed Nature out of the original settlement.

The Molly, what was left of it, was by then 'a turgid and deeply unhealthy creek', but Paterson and his friends liked nothing better than to follow its every twist and turn, as it 'slopped out of a culvert' here and 'meandered stinkily on a dogleg course' there, past waste ground and ancient bleach works, before 'disappearing into another culvert under the cinder football pitch'.

'In these few hundred yards,' recalled actor and writer Paterson in his autobiographical account *Tales Beyond the Back Green*,[1] 'the ancient Molendinar gave us a whole continent to explore, a whole world of downright unhealthy adventures and the source of many as yet untold tales . . .'

It was as if these boys, if only they could find its source, might alight upon 'the fountainhead, the very heart of the "dear green place"', as Glasgow has become known. The search so inspired Paterson that he became convinced that—

> It was beside this limpid stream that St Mungo set up the monastic settlement that one day became Glasgow Cathedral and that nurtured a town that crept down the hill towards a river called Clutha. The burn slipped into the broad salmon-filled waters, turned west and headed for the Atlantic via Rothesay. Some time over the years the Clutha became the Clyde and the great city of Glasgow flourished.

It is most certainly true that here, on the banks of the Molendinar, were sourced not only the spiritual, but also the intellectual and pathological founts of the city. For not only was Glasgow Cathedral founded here in 1197, but also

Glasgow University in 1451, and the Royal Infirmary nearly 350 years later.

But while it is incontestable that the Church played a vital role in the development of mediaeval Glasgow – not only building its cathedral and founding its university, but also obtaining for it the status of burgh, making it an independent centre for trade – it is likely that Glasgow itself did not begin with the coming of Christ, that there was some kind of settlement here long before Kentigern arrived, possibly as early as Neolithic and Bronze Age times. For, just a short walk south, there was a well-established ford over the River Clyde much used by trappers in their journey between the West Highlands and the West Lowlands, and the rabble has always felt at home here, their secular preoccupations good enough reason for the ascetic Mungo when he turned up in the sixth century to push on up the hill and build his spiritual retreat a respectable distance away.

Linking these two sites – high and low Glasgow – was a track, transformed today into the High Street which runs from Cathedral Square, down into the Saltmarket, where there is an important meeting of the ways known as Glasgow Cross.

If a geographical anchor to the city is required, this is surely it. Here, even today, you cannot fail to detect vibes of the mediaeval hubbub, a sense of Glasgow before industrial revolution gave the city its principal reputation for shipping, engineering, textiles, and left-wing intransigence.

Glasgow Cross not only pulls together High Street and Saltmarket, it funnels two other roads – Gallowgate and

London Road – from east of the city into the wonderfully named Trongate, which, as seductively as it slips off the tongue, today supplies access to the pleasures of Glasgow's West End.

Approach the Cross for the first time after dark, when the lights of the seven-storey mediaeval Tolbooth Steeple cast their eerie majesty all around. Lead in from the city's East End, from the area of 'the Barras' market, as iconic a nest of vipers as Petticoat Lane has been for Whitechapel in London's East End.

Gallowgate and London Road conspire to delimit the area of the famous market with Moir Street, which leads us to the site of Glasgow's guiltiest secret from the darkest days of the Industrial Revolution, the notorious 'pens' or 'back loans' hidden behind the on-street tenements, each with as many as four closes (entrance areas) to between four and six minuscule dwellings on each of three landings. In one of these, the infamous 'Pudding Pen', as many as a hundred souls once resided in conditions unimaginable to modern man.

Trailing further east along London Road finds Bridgeton, or 'Brigton' as it is spoken, heart of the East End and once a Protestant Irish stronghold, home to the infamous 800-strong Billy Boys, a gang which, within living memory, marched regularly with their Orange Order band to Glasgow Cross and played 'God save the King', in order to reaffirm their loyalty to a Dutchman dead these 300 years.[2]

All roads lead to Glasgow Cross, a time-slip of a place where countless criminals last saw the light of day (hence Gallowgate). Stagecoaches from Edinburgh and London stopped here. Its 'plainstanes' [flagstones] were a place of public proclamation. The Steeple was once part of a larger building housing not only the tolbooth, but the city's administration and a debtors' prison, self-run by its inmates with regulations, such as this, fit for a Glasgow-style gentleman's club:

It is firmly and irrevocably agreed upon that the members of these rooms shall not permit the jailor or turnkeys to force any person or persons into their apartments, who are thought unworthy of being admitted [and . . .] Every member, when liberated, shall treat his fellow prisoners with one shilling's worth of what liquor they think proper . . .

Nearby, a Mercat Cross, one of many across Scotland signifying an important trading place, is the symbolic centre of the city, and surely its historical heart.[3]

The Mercat Cross was a declaration of commercial intent, but for centuries the city's inaccessible position in the north-west did little to encourage trade. Indeed, Glasgow might have remained a cathedral and university town for many years to come, a St Andrews in the west, had it not been for the discovery that there was land far to the west worth colonising. Suddenly, with the discovery of America, Glasgow found itself no longer planted on the western edge of the world, on the shores of the mighty ocean that stretched to no one knew where. It was now 'across the Atlantic' from a new continent with which, in the eighteenth century, it built up a prosperous trade.

The merchant community grew rich on the tobacco trade with North America. By the 1760s, the city was the foremost tobacco trading port in Britain, bringing in almost half of all the tobacco imported into Britain. Records show that in 1715 two million lbs were imported; in 1741, eight million; in 1771 – the official peak – forty-seven million, though much more was also smuggled in illegally, to avoid customs tax.

When trade with America was eclipsed by the War of Independence (1775–83), resourceful Glasgow merchants found new markets in such places as Canada, the West Indies and later India. Tobacco was a major revenue generator in the city, producing the so-called Tobacco Lords, who, dressed in red silks and top hats, would strut their stuff on the plainstones (flagstones) of Glasgow Cross along with the town crier. Among them were the Speirs, the Cunninghames and the merchant James Glassford, who owned the palatial Shawfield Mansion in the heart of the eighteenth-century city.

Tobacco was largely traded for textiles and cloth, especially linen from the handloom weaving communities of the East End 'villages' of Bridgeton, Calton, and the Gorbals. The tobacco was then mostly re-exported to European ports.

It was in the days of the Tobacco Lords that Glasgow began to 'make the Clyde', widening and deepening it by means of walls and jetties, transforming it from a shallow salmon stream into a navigable river, work that took 150 years to complete.

In the process of time, the city became not only a great international sea port, but the centre of a great shipbuilding industry, which changed Glasgow once and for all.

Industrial revolution was first visible in the textile industry, which in 1750 was still domestic, but a significant commercial proposition. Men and women worked their spinning wheels and handlooms at home in the country-side. Agents sorted out the sale of cloth at market. But soon these spinners and weavers would be uprooted and herded together in factories in the city, losing their centuries-old craft skills to the more efficient but less refined perform-ance of steam-driven machines.

The transition from a rural, craft way of life to an urban, factory-based one was a massive change for the people involved. The move threatened to lose not only their time-honoured skills but a whole philosophy of life to future generations. Thomas Hardy wrote of their time; Charles Dickens wrote of the new industrial world they were drawn into. The rural handloom weaver had been in tune with the countryside. There was empathy with its seasonal rhythms and an unconscious sense of its beauty as fundamental to life. From nature and the rural community these people drew the deep-truth values that characterised a tradition they were not simply a part of, but helped to define. In many ways, the story of their industrialisation is the story of the rural worker's attempt to hang on to some of this tradition in the face of appalling odds, while the later work of environmentalists is an attempt somehow to redress the worst excesses of the revolution.

People were moving from a holistic culture in the lap of nature, where women worked alongside men and if things got tough you could at least grow your own food, to a materialistic, male, machine-based one, with thousands working in close quarters in factories, and later in chemical and engineering works, the docks and shipyards, often using dangerous materials and generating tremendous noise, filth and heat, for little personal gain at all.

Up to the late-eighteenth century, yarn was spun from raw cotton on a spinning wheel. Weaving cloth by hand was, in its simplest form, a matter of securing parallel lengths of yarn (the warp) vertically into a structure (the loom) and then feeding more lengths crosswise (the weft) through them – the weft yarn going under and over each warp yarn successively. The weft yarn was contained in a shuttle, a bobbin-like device which led it under and over the warp. To charge the shuttle with weft yarn, the weaver *kissed* the shuttle – drew the weft thread from the cop (a roll of thread wound on a spindle) by sucking it through a small hole at one end of the shuttle.

The series of inventions that triggered the Industrial Revolution in textiles worked on these ancient processes. They included the flying shuttle, the spinning jenny, the water frame, the spinning mule, the steam engine and the power loom. The flying, or fly, shuttle was invented first in 1733 by John Kay. It ran on wheels and could be pulled rapidly across the loom with a cord. Then, in 1764, James Hargreaves invented the spinning jenny, which could spin more than one strand of yarn at once. All the inventions were geared not to enhance quality, which had always been the weavers' great pride and was always better achieved by skilled hand, but to speed things up. The rat race, as Clydeside activist Jimmy Reid would, much later, proclaim, had begun.

There were other inventions to increase output, the most important of which was the power loom – a loom powered by steam or water wheel. The first to be patented was by William Horrocks in 1802. It was, however, the new spinning machinery that first led to the factory system. Suddenly, spinners no longer owned their own wheels. They had lost their autonomy and independence. No longer did they work in their own homes at their own pace, but in their employers' factories at the machines' pace. With the advent of the power loom the earnings of handloom workers collapsed, as they tried, ultimately unsuccessfully, to compete with the power looms in the factories. There were worker riots in some parts of Britain, as weavers began to grasp just what these changes really meant.

But nothing was going to be allowed to stand in the way. By 1829, most of the 10,000 people at work in Scotland on power looms, were situated in Glasgow. It was this that kick-started the city's industrial revolution, because implicit in the development of the new textile machines was a need for metal components, ironworks and engineering shops. The Carron Ironworks, near Falkirk, was established in 1759, and access to this and the Monkland coal fields, which fuelled the iron furnaces, was facilitated by a decision in 1769 to build the Monkland canal, an undertaking that would take some twenty-five years to complete.

Another key moment was the invention of the 'hotblast' process, a method of pre-heating air and blowing it into a blast furnace. Patented in 1828, it greatly reduced the time and therefore the cost of producing pig iron. If you were an entrepreneurial spirit and wanted to get on, you got into coal and iron founding and engineering, ideally into an integrated colliery-ironworks business. That, by the 1830s, was what the money-men in Glasgow were encouraging.

In the following decade, the transportation of raw materials and products was greatly enhanced not only by the canal, but also by the advent of the railway. Capitalising on their new engineering expertise, the greatest centre of railway manufacturing in Europe was created at Springburn, to the north east of the city centre. At their peak the Springburn works employed 9,000 men building and repairing steam engines, carriages and wagons, and living in tenements nearby, a community with one of the richest local histories in Glasgow. Once, one of the great sights to be had in the city was a locomotive being hauled from Springburn to Finnieston Quay for export.

Meanwhile, the development of the steam engine by such as mathematician John Napier and engineer Duncan McArthur, and the success of Henry Bell's steamboat *Comet* in 1812, laid the foundations of the Clyde's shipbuilding industry. Within twenty years almost sixty steamboats were plying on the river. In 1834, the marine engineering partnership Tod and MacGregor began building iron-hulled ships, facilitating vastly more ambitious projects.

Simultaneously, on the back of the railway and shipbuilding industries, other industries prospered, such as boiler-making, joinery, carpet-making, and navigational instrument production. Many other businesses rose up, not simply to furnish the trains and ships, but to take advantage of the transport they facilitated to all corners of the earth.

By the twentieth century Glasgow was a compact, cosmopolitan, port city with a developed economy which generated a wide range of jobs. Most activity was confined to about two miles of waterfront, on the north bank of the Clyde from the Broomielaw (now Kingston Bridge), past Queen's Dock (which included a timber terminal) to Elderslie Dock, and on the south bank from the Broomielaw, past Kingston Dock and Prince's Dock to George V Dock.

There were major granaries and fruit lairages on the north bank just east of Queen's Dock, and another major dock at Rothesay, just beyond the city boundary, which concentrated on ores and chemicals. Four 100-ton-plus capacity cranes serviced these docks, including two at Queen's Dock where the massive locomotives from the Springburn locomotive works would be lifted on board ship for export to various ports throughout the Empire.

The docks and quaysides were busy with the constant loading and unloading of ships up to the 1960s. Dockers lived in close proximity to their labour, in communities such as Tradeston and Gorbals, Broomielaw and Anderston, apparently in close communities with tight bonds of kinship.

Family ties and contacts were of vital importance for Clydeside shipyard workers in particular. Families formed the basis of the skilled boiler-making gangs, and apprenticeship was typically a father's legacy to his son: 'Getting me a trade, that was my inheritance.'

The personal relationship between a boy's father and the foreman – 'someone he trusted; someone he had dealings with' – was considered by eighty per cent of the men interviewed to be directly related to their introduction to the trade.[4]

Beyond the docks the city grew up as a centre for shipbuilding, metalworking and engineering and these traditional 'heavy', male-worker industries continued to dominate until after the Second World War.

The Glasgow Museum of Transport lists sixty-four shipyards as being once in existence on the Clyde, and fourteen still existed within the city boundaries in the mid-1950s. Many of the most famous seagoing liners were launched from the Clyde yards, including the Cunarders, *Queen Mary*, *Queen Elizabeth* and *Queen Elizabeth II* ('*QE2*') – in 1934, 1938 and 1967 respectively, the latter two both from John Brown's shipyard in Clydebank. Bill Alexander, like many others in Glasgow even fifty years ago, remembers the Clyde as an exciting hive of industry that seems to the youth of today as belonging to another world:

> Oh! The thrill of sailing down the Clyde, staring in awe at the skeletons of great ships yet to be launched. The sound of the great hammers on steel hulls, the flash of welders' torches or the fireworks display of the grinders' tools.[5]

At the beginning there was a heroic dimension to what was going on. The concept of the heroic had permeated the literature of the nineteenth century, boys' stories especially, and explorers were the glittering heroes of the day. Gallant tales of the search for the Northwest Passage over North America, expeditions to the Arctic, the Antarctic, the exotic Orient and the dark continent of Africa, had provided a steady stream of adventure that thrilled British society at every level throughout the century, at once capturing the imagination and stoking the Imperialist dream. The Industrial Revolution was seen to be at the very heart of this heroic endeavour, the Empire ideal which, in 1841, was defined in a series of lectures, *On Heroes, Hero-Worship and the Heroic in History*, by Thomas Carlyle, a Scot who lived down the road in Dumfries.

Everyone, it seemed, was swept up in the heroic enterprise, and the rural workers' traditional pride in their work survived the transition. It is a consistent thread running through industrial workers' oral memories and autobiographies, as is the stress men placed upon themselves 'never being idle'. They carried the worker tradition, which made no distinction between work and life, out of the old world into the new. Work was something more than a job. This work ethic is apparent also in accounts of workers in other industries from the mid-nineteenth century, and by weaver poets like Henry Yates and Richard Rawcliffe, who experienced the great change between manual and mechanical labour personally in England's industrial north. In his poem 'Heroes', for example, Rawcliffe extols the ethic that drives his class of working men:

The man who glories in the right:–
In honest toil 'neath virtue's wing;
He struggles hard from morn till night,
And calmly bears affliction's sting . . .

Work is important in itself, irrespective of the money earned. Rawcliffe calls upon operatives in the weaving industry to work out their contracts even in the face of personal monetary loss. Work was a virtue to be cultivated and remained so in Glasgow even into the twentieth century. Glasgow was a city with a deeply engrained work ethic. In an economy dominated by heavy industry Glaswegians worked hard for their daily bread . . .

'Labour is a law of life,' commented an Irish cleric in 1937 in a eulogy to ten Irish migrant labourers – 'martyrs to duty' – tragically killed in a bothy fire in Kirkintilloch near Glasgow in September 1937.[6]

In his memoirs, Glasgow-born MP David Kirkwood, who rose from apprentice engineer to Independent Labour Party leader and Labour MP, noted of Clyde shipbuilding workers:

These men – the finest, the most expert craftsmen in the world – had lived their lives in their work. Their joy as well as their livelihood lay in converting the vast masses of Nature's gifts into works of art, accurate to a two-thousandth part of an inch.[7]

They worked it out, the shipwrights, the plate-makers; and the many steel plates of these massive ships did fit and the ships were launched with due pomp from the Clyde, the best advertisement for the Empire you would ever see.

It was remarkable how they built ships. It was all through experience . . . Once you got it up there, and you got it tae fit – and it did fit – it was a great satisfaction. That's when tradesmen gets the satisfaction, when everything works. Because you put a lot intae the job. And everybody else, you

know people who don't really know the job . . . You've got
tae be a mathematician an a'. You've got tae dae sines,
tangents, and a' the different degrees. At that time there
were no, there were no calculating machines. All you had
was a log book, a wee log book. You got your, you know,
your numbers and you calculated.[8]

Pride in one's work in the shipyards was the single most
important moral element in a Glasgow worker's life and
gave rise to its own poetry, as here, in 'The Yairds', by John
F Fergus:

I've wrockt amang them, man and boy, for mair nor fifty
    year,
I canna bear to quit them yet noo that I'm auld an' sere,
The Yairds is just the life o' me, the music's in my bluid
O' hammers striking strong an true on rivets loweing rid;
I'm auld, I ken, but, Goad be thank'd! I have not lost my
    pride
In honest wark on bonny boats that's built upon the Clyde.

This ethic – this 'willingness to work' – was just as evident
among unskilled workers, often in atrocious conditions, as
this 71-year-old retired sheet metal worker with a lifetime's
hard graft behind him, observed:

The filth that we worked in right fae fourteen years of age.
And being a man with no education, the only thing you had
was the muscle in your arm and what experience you got
with metal, and a very willingness to work. I would go in
and say to people, 'Yes I'll do that in that time.' And

15

whatever it took to do that [job] I would do it. Silly now,
looking back through the years, you know.[9]

At length, the terrible conditions of the shipyards and the
harsh living conditions in the tenements provided for the
workers to live in, did awaken these 'heroes', as Rawcliffe
termed them in his eponymously titled poem, to their
exploitation, but at first even poverty was exalted for itself
and given a place of respect, as in 'The Honest Poor', a poem
by the Dumfriesshire-born poet Hugh Gardiner Graham,
written in the 1860s, a period of terrible depression:

> There's honour in the poor man's breast more dear to him
>   than gold;
> There's loving kindness in his heart; there's truth and courage
>   bold . . .
> There's resolution in his soul to brave life's toilsome way . . .

But in the end, cast into poverty and misery to make a
handful of industrialists rich, the worker enslaved by the
Industrial Revolution finally began to speak out, as here, in
weaver William Billington's seminal poem, 'Fraud, The Evil
of the Age' (1883):

> With what unutterable shame and scorn,
> Humiliation and indignant rage,
> The bosom of the honest man is torn
> Who contemplates the evils of this age—

Almost a century later, the Glaswegian trades union leader
Jimmy Reid would define precisely what those evils were,

what the changes foisted on the worker by the money-men of the Industrial Revolution, obsessed by savings of time and cost, really did mean:

> We are human beings and people insult us when they talk about our participation in the rat race. Reject the insidious pressures in society that would blunt your critical faculties to all that is happening around you, that would caution silence in the face of injustice least you jeopardise your chances of promotion and self advancement. Because this is how it starts and if you start before you know where you are you are a bullied paid up member of the rat pack. The price is too high, it entails the loss of your dignity and human spirit, or as Christ put it 'What does it profit a man if he gain the whole world and suffer the loss of his soul?'.[10]

From the earliest days of the unions, those who rebelled were swiftly dealt with, as Boyd Calder, who grew up on the Clyde immersed in stories of his grandfather working as a riveter's 'holder on'[11] in the early years of the twentieth century, recalls:

> My father told us that my grandfather was involved in a rent strike in Springburn and as a consequence was put on a blacklist. He found it very difficult to get a job after that. I suppose he was marked down as a troublemaker. We heard tales of him walking miles to stand outside the gates of some yard at hiring time, only to be turned away, time and time again.
>
> The family had to go on 'the Parish',[12] but with many rigours attached. Anyone accepted for Parish help was

stigmatised through having to wear Parish-supplied clothes, boots etc. It really was quite a stigma and brought shame on the poor people who were desperate enough to go for help from the State. My grandmother died when my father was only thirteen and with a family of seven they found it very hard to get by.

At the end of it all, in 1971, when the government's intention to – in secretary of state Nicholas Ridley's words – 'butcher the yards' slipped out, 'the slaves established the right to work', as Sam Gilmore, one of the leaders of the famous work-in at the Fairfield yard in Govan, put it. The work-in was a return to Richard Rawcliffe's notion of 'the man who glories in the right', as much as it was a political statement, and they proved it at Fairfield's by refusing to down tools. Determined to honour the many contracts they had, the men occupied the Govan yard. The government and the employers had figured out how to stop the strikes but not how to put a stop to work, and the workers, who gained support from all corners of the earth and all classes and raised millions to keep the effort going (including £5,000 from John Lennon), won. The yard stayed open.

CHAPTER TWO

Character

Who were the men, women and children on whose lives the Industrial Revolution in Glasgow marched forward?

The first influx to really swell the city's population occurred between 1750 and 1821, when it grew by 459 per cent, due in part to migration from Ireland and the Scottish Highlands and Islands. These intrepid souls, from the south and north respectively, set a trend for immigration that would continue unabated to the present day, involving an almost constant stream from Ireland and intermittent injections also from Italy, Eastern Europe and Asia.

Glasgow was virtually alone in this in Scotland. It was all

rather confusing to Deirdre Chapman, a girl from Scotland's restrained and predictable, one-dimensional Protestant East, when she arrived in the city in the 1950s:

> When I got here in the fifties my landlady was Italian and her maid-of-all-work Irish. There were wayside shrines all over the landings and stairs and they went to Mass before I was up. In the east I had never knowingly met a Catholic, and in history and in geography classes at school I had had problems believing that Highlanders and Islanders were fellow countrymen. Such wild tragedy and exotic scenery had no place in the tidy controlled environment I knew. But here were girls with names like Donalda who could sing in Gaelic and had aunties on Barra, and other girls in cashmere twinsets who lived in remote suburbs and had grandfathers that were Russian Jews.[1]

Many would perhaps hesitate to include Highlanders and Islanders in a list of exotic influences in Glasgow but the waves of Scots flowing to the city from the north were long treated as immigrants by the locals, who spoke a different language and appeared quite different. Most arrivals from the Highlands spoke Gaelic, rather than Scots or English, and the mirth that the Highland dress provoked among Lowland Scots has been well documented in popular culture, with Andy Stewart's song *Donald, Where's Yer Troosers?* sung worldwide.

> Although I was born in Govan (which makes me a 'Keelie'!) both my parents, like many others in the area, were Islanders. Hebrideans from Skye in their case. As a

consequence I spoke Gaelic as my mother tongue in the home, long before I spoke English (or should that be 'the local patois'?). Many other children in Luath Street and Howat Street and the others nearby had a similar background, and we could switch languages in our play without thinking about it. We were proud to be Glasgow Gaels.[2]

Sociologist Dr Seán Damer sums up public feeling towards them:

To say that the Glaswegians' original attitude towards the Highlanders was hostile would be to put it mildly. Generally, they were seen as uncouth savages, and basically feared . . . They were referred to quite simply as the 'Irish', as was their language, until well into the eighteenth century. This reference to their historical origins was meant to be abusive, to classify the Highlanders and their language as foreign.[3]

However, the Highlanders soon found a place in society – as often as not, in the police force. The sturdy men of the north were generally superior in stature to the city-dwellers of the lowland west, and towered over most locally born law enforcers. At one point in the nineteenth century, these Highland giants were said to account for nearly half of the Glasgow police – though only ever around ten per cent of the Glaswegian population – and the ubiquitous 'teuchter polis' became a well-known fixture of city life. The triumph of the Glasgow police as world champions at tug o' war in 1900 confirmed the legend of the powerful Highlander in the city's folklore, and burly officers became popular as protectors of public order. Nonetheless, a distinct Highland identity was retained, and as recently as the 1930s the Central Station bridge over Argyle Street was known to many as the 'Heilanman's Umbrella', due to the number of Highlanders that congregated there to socialise and catch up on news from the north.

The larger wave of migrants from Ireland related well to the Highlander due to the similarities between the Irish and Scottish Gaelic languages, but this had no bearing on their reception by the main body of people in Glasgow.

Asked whether it was harder for Asians to settle in Glasgow in the 1950s than it was for the Irish, who had the same skin colour as the Scots, one migrant – politician Bashir Maan who came to Glasgow from his native Pakistan in the early fifties – answered from personal experience: 'It was not as hard [for the Asians] as for the Irish, they suffered too much.'[4] So hopeless were attempts to integrate initially that in 1798 Catholic and Protestant Irish buried their differences in a United Irishman's Rebellion against the British Government, which resulted in their exclusion by both Scottish Episcopalians and Catholics.

Catholics in Glasgow were treated by many as uninvited intruders, ostracised by the Protestant Glaswegian majority for bringing their families and religion into an already crowded metropolis – though this had little to do with religion. The Catholics were associated with the Jacobite Rebellions that had plunged Scotland into civil war in the eighteenth century, and were seen as disloyal to the United Kingdom. Many Irish Catholics were opponents of the British monarchy and government, mainly for nationalistic reasons – the struggle for a free Ireland was foremost in the minds of many, and disgust over the seventeenth-century Ulster Plantation and subsequent atrocities persisted.

But the Irish Catholics would not be put off. There was a sense among them that they were coming home, as Owen O'Leary recorded in Cliff Hanley's *Glasgow: A Celebration*:

> For starters, the very name Scot came from Ireland, and I have never in my life worked out why some people in this Northern piece of sceptred isle real estate should be shirty about the Irish in Glasgow when, for God's sake, we invented the place.
>
> What I am talking about is the invasion many centuries ago by the tribe the Roman scholars called the Scoti, who sailed across the water in coracles or something of the kind, from the actual Emerald Isle, and displaced the Picts, whose only contribution to civilisation was some kind of heavy-duty tattooing.[5]

From the eighteenth century, the Irish arrived in Glasgow in droves, both Catholic and Protestant. The Protestants were more simpatico spiritually with the 'proddy' lowland Scots in Glasgow, and livened things up by bringing with them a fierce loyalty to the Orange Order, so that by 1835 there were twelve Orange Masonic lodges in the city.

The Protestants initially found work in the weaving villages of Calton and Bridgeton. Historian Michael Moss calculates that about thirty per cent of the area's weaving population were of Irish origin by 1819.[6] Once the factories, ironworks and shipyards got going, they invariably moved into the better paid, skilled and supervisory positions in these industries. Reflecting the labour picture in their Irish homeland, Irish Catholic migrants, meanwhile, first found work as labourers in farms to the west of the city, and then as labourers in the docks, shipyards and other industries. It would be on their backs that the heavy work of the Industrial Revolution would be undertaken.

The building of the Monkland Canal in the late-eighteenth century was just the kind of work for which Glaswegians saw Irish Catholics as fit. This main artery of the new industrial city, which also ran passengers to and fro on horse-drawn barges from 1807, was of magnetic interest to children from the Dennistoun, Riddrie and Blackhill areas, often to tragic effect: there were so many cases of children drowning in it that the Monkland got itself the nickname of the 'killer canal'. But for young Bill Paterson, it was the industry that the canal brought to the area just to its north – in the region of what is Royston today – that really fired the imagination:

You might be surprised to know that there was ever a canal there at all, you'll probably know it better as the M8 motorway, Townhead interchange, but if I tell you that the one big bad thing that shaped the Molendinar that we knew and loved was a place called Blochairn, you might just nod your head in recognition. Blochairn was one of Glasgow's biggest steelworks and it thundered and roared day and night. If it had the image of hell on earth we loved it all the more, because it spawned some truly gruesome tales. Our neighbour Mr Baird, who despite claiming to be 103, had a job there, and night after night the back green kids would gather round his ancient fireside and hear some of his tales. We would spin out a measured two inches of Highland brew and listen to stories that curdled the blood. Stories of hard-working men being squashed to pulp between falling sheets of steel, of apprentices vaporised in vats of molten metal, or heads and limbs sliced off by red-hot girders. Now we knew why the Royal Infirmary was only half a mile away.[7]

The Irish Catholic labourer was invariably the victim in these blood-curdling stories for when, with the opening of the canal, this area – known in the nineteenth century as the Garngad – became a vortex of industry the Irish Catholic made it a home from home, as Paul Kelly, whose grandfather arrived in Glasgow towards the end of the nineteenth century, discovered:

In 1894, the northern part of Garngad consisted of four parallel streets, each running in a south to north direction. Starting from the west, the four streets were Turner Street, Villiers Street, Bright Street and Cobden Street. These four parallel streets were enclosed on the north by Charles Street and on the south by Garngad Road. Both Charles Street and Garngad Road still exist today, though Garngad Road is now called Royston Road. In the late-eighteen hundreds, these six congested streets of north Garngad could be described as a 'Little Ireland'. About ninety per cent of the households in Turner Street, Villiers Street, Bright Street and Charles Street were headed by a person born in Ireland.[8]

People think of the Gorbals as Little Ireland, and it is true that this 'village' just south of the Clyde became another of the favoured settlement areas, largely for Irish Catholics, from the 1840s, but the title was first given to the Garngad, which was one hundred per cent an Irish Catholic 'state':

> The place I went to secondary school, Royston, had once been called the Garngad. Almost entirely Roman Catholic, it had its bloody street-battles with Protestants and its holy-day marches celebrating old victories. Lest anyone doubted this was also political, for decades, the first thing you saw entering the area was enormous graffiti declaring, 'YOU ARE NOW ENTERING FREE GARNGAD'. The IRA would have been delighted.[9]

If there is any difficulty in picturing nineteenth-century labouring-class ghettoes such as this, let the shock of Indian journalist B. M. Malabari at the squalor and poverty here in 1890 speak for itself:

> Men and women living in a chronic state of emaciation, till they can hardly be recognised as human, picking up food, what even animals will turn away from; sleeping fifty, sixty, eighty of them all together, of all ages and both sexes, in a hole that could not hold ten with decency; swearing, fighting, trampling on one another; filling the room with foul confusion and foul air. This is not a picture of occasional misery; in some places it represents the everyday life of the victims of misfortune . . .[10]

Besides inadequate housing and chronic overcrowding, the industrial environment of the Garngad was poisonous.

Besides Blochairn, there were chemical works employing thousands of men. Respiratory and pulmonary disease was rampant, and the Provan Gas Works, opened by Glasgow Corporation in 1904, did nothing to help.

South of the Clyde, another hellish industrial landmark of the time, and key employer, was Dixon's Blazes in the Gorbals, an ironworks with five blast furnaces that lit up the sky for miles around, founded by William Dixon, son of the owner of the Little Govan colliery. A century on, Gerard Coyle, who lived nearby in Pollokshaws Road from 1952 until 1974, remains in awe:

> I remember it well because at night . . . It was called Dixon's
> Blazes because these two big sort of tanks . . . it looked like,
> I don't know what you called them but the flames used to
> be released from them . . . quite spectacular! I don't know,
> they would shoot up maybe twenty or thirty feet, I
> suppose.[11]

Where there was drama, there was danger. Where there was danger, there was work; but it could cost you your life. Turner's asbestos factory at Dalmuir was a case in point, as this former employee recalls:

> After a period of unemployment, I said, I'll take the first job I
> get. I walked down the Dumbarton Road to Clydebank – we
> were living in Clydebank at the time – walked into every
> shop, through every doorway, and I eventually came to
> Turner's Asbestos [Cement Co.] . . . I'll never forget till the
> day I die the first impression of that place. It was like walking
> into Dante's Inferno without the fire. It was just Hell!

The noise was unbelievable. The size of the machinery was awe-inspiring you know, awe-inspiring. Three big machines took up the whole width of the factory. They were a sheet machine, and a pipe machine, and then another sheet machine. Dust was flying through the air everywhere, clouds of dust. And there were wee men walking about – I ended up dain it for the first two or three days I was there – sweeping the floor. Nae masks, just overalls. Clouds of stoor [dust] everywhere it just filled the air, and it was settling just as fast as they were sweeping it. And then it was dumped. Shovelled intae wheel barras, takin' out tae the side of the Clyde and dumped down at the grounds of what's the hospital down there now . . .

Tae be heard – I know it sounds crazy, but you had tae shout in a whisper. That was the strange thing, you had tae get in-between the pitch of the machines and you could be heard. But if you shouted at the top of your voice you couldnae be heard, and if you spoke at a normal tone you couldnae be heard. You had to get in there somewhere, and where you wernae as loud as the machinery you could actually be heard. Believe it or not, not above the sound but under it.[12]

This worker and his wife eventually contracted asbestos-related disease, the latter from washing his dusty overalls on a regular basis. Many a lagger died from asbestos-related disease. Glasgow has one of the highest rates of mesothelioma – the deadly asbestos-related cancer – in the UK. This took a great toll upon the bodies of workers and on the lives of families and loved ones; just one indicator of how the traditional, heavy industries left a grim legacy and cast a very long shadow many years after the factories and shipyards closed down.

Asbestos was also heavily used in the construction industry – which, then as now, recruited large numbers of Irish Catholics. The Red Road flats in Petershill, just north of Royston, the highest flats in Europe when they were built in the 1960s, were riddled with the 'magic mineral'. The Red Road joiners were nicknamed 'white mice' because they were covered in the stuff, and years later the death rate among them from asbestos-related disease was astronomically high.

While Protestants had a long-standing and near-total monopoly on skilled employment in Glasgow, discrimination consigned the Irish Catholic labourer to the most arduous and dangerous employment, and life itself was a lottery. 'Catholics need not apply' was a common enough sign or slogan. The attitude persisted long after statutory anti racial discrimination regulation – for example, through the practice of asking at interview or in job application forms about which school the applicant had attended.

Attempting to hide one's religion when seeking employment was almost impossible as schools in Glasgow were – and often still are – segregated along sectarian lines, as Sam Gilmore, a Catholic, recalls:

On application for a job the first question was, 'What school did you go to?' The Catholic schools were all named after saints, so that was a dead giveaway. That always struck me as funny.

The difficulties faced by a young Catholic trying to find a job were considerable. Hugh Savage, born and raised in Bridgeton in Glasgow's East End, remembers the discrimination he faced as a young man during the interwar years, and his frustration at the system in place:

> The first week after my fourteenth birthday I started to work my way around the factories in Brigton looking for a job. It was my first experience of discrimination. I began at the Acme Wringer Company, then Templeton's Carpets, Tullis and Martin's Leatherworks and so on. In all I must have gone to nearly twenty factories, and they all said the same, 'What school did you go to?' There was I with my new short trousers and shoes, my best woollen jersey and shirt and tie, a wee boy looking for his first job, and all these people could think about was what religion I was. Probably that was the first time I became angry. Not with the bigots that were denying me a job because of religion, but with the whole stupidity that divided people in their way through life.[13]

Even for those Catholics able to surmount the obstacles they faced, employment could be short-lived once a man's co-workers established his religion. Sam Gilmore again:

> Catholics didn't eat meat on a Friday. For the new guys on the job, Friday was the day. They're eating their sandwich and everybody is looking to see what's inside it. No way could you eat meat. If you were Protestant and you happened to like cheese you made a point of not eating it on a Friday, in case they thought you were a Catholic.

Lagger Hugh Cairney recalled how jobs prior to the 1950s were clearly demarcated by religion, and how impossible it was even to apprentice to a trade:

> When my father was a young boy, sixteen and that, looking for work, if you were a Catholic in the shipyards you didnae get employed. You got employed as a labourer or something like that but you didnae get employed to learn a trade, and the only thing at that time going was the [asbestos] insulation, you can go to that – we werenae a trade, we're still no' a trade . . . So that's why the majority of Catholics – our industry have been a majority of Catholics for the simple reason they couldnae get trades.[14]

So, what on earth made Irish Catholics flock here from the mythically beautiful Emerald Isle? The answer is that by the mid-nineteenth century there were worse living conditions in Ireland even than this.

After the fungus *Phytophthora infestans* appeared, rural Ireland was all but destroyed. There had been warnings aplenty that a nation should not depend upon one crop alone, and when the potato harvest failed in 1845, 1846 and again in 1848, people were left with nothing to eat and no way to make money to support themselves. Many wandered the countryside, begging for food or work. Many starved to death. Famine took a million lives in Ireland. Reports from observers make sobering reading. William Bennett's *Narrative of a Recent Journey of Six Weeks in Ireland* was published in 1847:

Many of the cabins were holes in the bog, covered with a layer of turves, and not distinguishable as human habitations from the surrounding moor, until close down upon them . . . We spent the whole morning in visiting these hovels . . . My hand trembles while I write. The scenes of human misery and degradation we witnessed still haunt my imagination, with the vividness and power of some horrid and tyrannous delusion, rather than the features of a sober reality. We entered a cabin.

Stretched in one dark corner, scarcely visible, from the smoke and rags that covered them, were three children huddled together, lying there because they were too weak to rise, pale and ghastly, their little limbs – on removing a portion of the filthy covering – perfectly emaciated, eyes sunk, voice gone, and evidently in the last stage of actual starvation. Crouched over the turf embers was another form, wild and all but naked, scarcely human in appearance. It stirred not, nor noticed us.

On some straw, soddened upon the ground, moaning piteously, was a shrivelled old woman, imploring us to give her something, baring her limbs partly, to show how the skin hung loose from the bones, as soon as she attracted our attention. Above her, on something like a ledge, was a young woman, with sunken cheeks . . . who scarcely raised her eyes in answer to our enquiries, but pressed her hand upon her forehead, with a look of unutterable anguish and despair.

We entered upwards of fifty of these tenements. The scene was one and invariable, differing in little but the number of the sufferers, or of the groups, occupying the several corners within . . . It was my full impression that one-fourth of those we saw were in a dying state, beyond the reach of any relief that could now be afforded; and many more would follow.

After this, the horrors of the Garngad didn't seem so bad. Those who could, left Ireland in search of a better life. The Garngad's St Rollox Chemical Works,[15] Millburn Chemical Works, and Tharsis Sulphur & Copper Works were high on the émigré's list of possible employers. Work was plentiful where there was danger to health, and special rates applied; the downside was that many workers died. As Owen O'Leary bemoans:

Ireland was the lost continent, full of accordion music and football and whisky priests, till the eighteen-forties, when the sodden English imperialists invented the potato famine – the very first Westminster try at curing the Irish Problem.

So a lot of those that were left, left . . . And I will not hesitate to admit, because I am an honest man when you catch me napping, that a lot of us, my sainted grandfather included, couldn't read or write. All we could do was build canals and railways if you threw us a potato scone and shouted Paddy and used the whip.[16]

There was, nevertheless, pride and a sense of adventure in many a clannish Catholic-Irish heart. Maria Fyfe was born in the Gorbals in 1938. Her grandfather was the first in the family to find his feet in Glasgow:

Dad was proud of being an O'Neill. His father was born in Kilrea, the small village in County Londonderry where Martin

O'Neill, Celtic's former manager, comes from. The place is
hoaching with O'Neills: it's a name as common as
MacDonald in the Highlands. My granddad O'Neill's name
was Daniel, but he was known back home as Daney, and in
Glasgow as Celtic Dan . . . Daniel made a life for himself in
Glasgow, most probably finding digs with an Irish family . . .

Immigration from Ireland to Glasgow peaked in the
middle and second half of the nineteenth century, with
more than 1,000 people arriving each day during one
period in 1847. The 1851 census showed that around a
third of the entire Glasgow population was of Irish
extraction, and after centuries of mixed marriages very few
Glaswegians could today claim that no Irish blood flows
through their veins.

Longtime Glasgow resident John Hamilton describes his
own family's arrival from Ireland around the turn of the
twentieth century, earmarking the docks, rather than the
more dangerous chemical works, as place of work:

My family have been in Anderston about a hundred years.
They left Ireland because of the usual: lack of work, and
poverty. Some went to America, some went to Scotland or
England, Liverpool. When they got off the boat they'd look
for a house, then find a job in the shipyard or local docks.
Quite a lot of the Irish went to the docks – it was poor pay
in those days, grotty, heavy work – and the only ones who
would take it were the Irish. And they didn't even get it
regularly; they had to queue up each day. If you weren't
working that day you'd to go back the following day and the
boss would say, 'you, you and you'. They eventually made it

a good job – it became a father-son job. Most of them
found they'd done all the hard work, the heavy work.[17]

The call-on procedure meant unpredictable, hard and
often dirty work, certainly, but it could be rewarding, as this
retired sheet metal worker recalls of his one and only,
fifteen-month period of being a docker:

My stepfather was a docker, and I said to him, 'What about
getting me a start at the dock?' And he wasnae very happy
about it, but he did. And in 1953 I got a start. And he
didnae want tae know me. He says, 'Well, you wanted it,
there it is.' And I got sent to Queen's Dock. And there was
6,000 men in Queen's Dock, and they had a system . . . You
had a black book. The covers were black so they called it a
black book. And you had a fifteen-minute free period, where
you could get a job on your own. And if you didnae get a
job on your own you'd to hand your book into the control
officer, and he would make up so many gangs of so many
men – eighteen or twenty, whatever it was. And the first day
I went in . . . 'green'.

These foremen, they all stood on a platform that went
round the hall about eighteen inches high. And the first
morning, I saw this man: 'Give me your book, son. Follow
me.' And this was the big time – Alex O'Connor was his
name. He was the big time; 'heavy ganger', they called him.
And they got the cream of the work. And we went to a ship
up at Stobcross at the far end of Queen's Dock – where the
ferry came from Govan over to Stobcross. And we lifted all
the hatches off and the beams, and it was oranges and what
have you. And the crew wanted it cleaned up. It was a four-

hour shift to do that. And eh, about eleven o'clock we put all the hatches back and that was it. The man gave me my book back. He says, 'That's you now. You'll get another job at one o'clock.'

And I went in at quarter to one and here was the fee booking. And a big Irish chap says to me, 'Are you looking for a job, lad?' 'Yes.' 'Give me your book.' And he took me round to a hut round the back of the old tunnel that was there and he handed me a shovel. And there was another three lads. One got a shovel along with me, and the other two got brushes. And they walked us along to the Dublin cattle boat where the cattle . . . You had to take all the barriers down and hose them. The urine was like that at the bottom of it. And a favourite trick of these dockers . . . I smoked at that time . . . 'Have a cigarette.' And when you lit the cigarette with the ammonia . . . Oh, it took your breath away.

Anyway, that was my first day. I got that cleaned, and I went to step on a tram car . . . 'Get off this tram.' We used to go home with some weevils when you were at the oil cake. They looked like fleas. And I remember a lady tapping me on the shoulder and saying, 'You've a large flea on the back of your neck, son.' It was these weevils. They never stayed, they were harmless.

Anyway, I stuck that for fifteen months. I earned a thousand pound bar a penny. And the old man says to me, 'If you live to be a hundred you'll never earn a thousand pound again at the dock.' It was an oddball, you know . . .[18]

In the shipyards there were three kinds of worker: the black squad (lowly pieceworker – the boilermakers:

riveters, platers, caulkers – paid according to what they had contracted to do), hourly-paid workers with a trade (electricians, engineers, etc.) and staff (timekeepers, pay clerks, draughtsmen and under-foremen). Then there were the foreman and managers, known as 'hat men' because they wore a bowler hat as opposed to the worker's flat cap, or bunnet. There was no safety clothing until the 1960s, but there were unofficial uniforms: hourly-paid workers wore an open-necked shirt with perhaps a scarf or cravat; office workers, timekeepers, draughtsmen and under-foremen wore collar and tie (collar and tie job):

> You could tell when the men went into the yard what they were working at, you would see the electricians and the engineers going in in boiler suits, nice clean overalls, and you would see the black squad coming in and they would have any sort of old clothes – old patched trousers with a dirty cardigan, an old jacket with the elbows out, a muffler round the neck, and maybe an old bunnet.
>
> Moleskin trousers were the favourite with riveters because they were hard wearing. They got so thick with oil they were like leather. You bought a pair of moleskins for your work, they had to last you six months. When you took them off at night they could stand up themselves, nobody ever washed moleskins. When a riveter came home he just dropped them off and put them into the press until the next morning. Moleskin trousers and a grey flannel shirt to soak up the sweat was the attire for the summer time. In the winter time it was all sorts of gear, all sorts of old jackets and cardigans, all patches, we were like walking ragbags.[19]

Riveters fastened plates and beams onto the ship's skeleton by hammering red-hot metal rivets to make a watertight connection. A manual riveting squad consisted of four members: a left-hand riveter, a right-hand riveter, a holder-on and a boy rivet-heater. Before the introduction of welding during the Second World War, the way in which riveting was performed changed little from the nineteenth century.

> You had a furnace and the boy put five or six rivets in the fire, he had a bag of rivets at the side of his fire, he throws the hot rivet to the holder-on and he picks up the hot rivet, sparking hot, and puts it through the hole, rams it through with a back-hammer. The riveter drives it in with alternate blows on the outside of the shell, and that way you fill up every hole with rivets.
>
> In the bulkheads you could be bent nearly double and riveting heavy beams and plates. That was twice as hard as ordinary shell riveting. You had to work just as fast because the rivet had to be hammered while it was red-hot.
>
> Men would be riveting eighty to a hundred feet up, sometimes higher. We would be working – swinging hammers – on two wooden planks, sometimes only one, without any guard rail. The plank would be bouncing as they worked. We'd have been safer trying to work on a tightrope.[20]

Shipyard folklore has it that a particularly gifted riveter once banged a rivet in so hard that it flew across the Clyde and killed a sheep on the far bank. But the jokes came later. For a young apprentice come with earnest expectation to join the shipyard community and learn a trade, it could be a scary first day, as this seventy-two-year-old retired boilermaker plater recalls:

How long was your apprenticeship?
Five years in these days. You done your five years. But you had to . . . You were sixteen till you were twenty-one. And you finished up you were a boilermaker/plater, and after that you were either a plater, a caulker, or a burner.

So did your time start when you were sixteen?
I was sixteen.

But you left school at fourteen.
I left at fourteen.

What did they do? What was their job at that age?
At that time you het rivets, or you worked with other tradesmen doing, doing . . . certain jobs. Maybe cutting steel, cutting bars at the . . . what we used to call it . . . the shears like, you know. I was fortunate. I was never sent tae the heating like. And after that I think it was up to the foreman what job you were put tae . . . You got a chance at caulking and that, and welding.[21]

All around the new recruit was noise – the thunder of running machines, the screeching of worked metal, the cries of mistakes and mysterious intentions, and all this often in the half-light of a ship's hold.

When I went into the shipyard at first I didnae like it. I was stuck in the bowels of the ship, I couldnae believe it, they were throwing red-hot rivets to each other. It was dark and

striking because of the oil lamps they used . . . I thought I was
in Hell. I was only sixteen at the time and I couldnae stand it
but I got used to it, it was a matter of getting used to it, you
had to suffer it or be out of a job.[22]

In the late 1930s, the shipyard day began at 7:50 a.m. and
finished at 5:30 p.m., five days a week, Saturday was a half-
day. The horn would sound to call the men to start and
stop work, and there'd be a whistle on Friday evening – the
'pay whistle'. There are plenty of people around in Govan
today who can remember the daily scene at the Fairfield
yard. Recalled Tommy Stewart and Sydney Smith:

Crowds of men walked down the streets when the horn
blew and the yard emptied. Down Ederpark Street, Golspie
Street, along the Govan Road to Linthouse and in the
opposite direction to Govan Cross.
    They walked with their thumbs hooked into their gallasis,
or arm openings, in their waistcoats with four small pockets
which held cigs, matches, French chalk and bits of pencil.
They all wore caps, even boys of fourteen and fifteen. Their
dark clothing and dirty faces merged with the surprisingly
dull buildings – not until close up [were] their eyes and teeth
recognisable.[23]

It is the classic shipyard scene. At full working, Fairfield
employed 5,000 men. The sight of them pouring out on to
the streets of Govan is one that is imprinted on the
memory plate of one of the Glasgow village's more famous
sons, Manchester United boss Sir Alex Ferguson, who
named his house Fairfields after the yard for which his

father worked, and called his first racehorse Queensland Star after a ship his father helped build at the yard:

> When I was born on December thirty-first, 1941, the production of the yards was more important than ever because of the Second World War, but shipbuilding and the Upper Clyde had been synonymous for more than half a century before that time . . . At the end of a shift those streets would be filled with thousands of hurrying men, nearly all of them wearing the cloth caps they called bunnets. It was an unforgettable sight, that tide of bunnets. I remember waiting at the gates of the yard where my father worked, eager to recognise him among the mass of grimy, heavy-booted figures clattering towards me, or looking down from the back window of our tenement onto the main artery of the Govan Road to pick out his distinctive walk so that my mother could put his food on the table.[24]

Alex was never himself employed in the yard, but his brother Martin was. The family lived on the corner of Govan Road and Neptune Street. The great tidal wave of bunnets suggests full employment, but even in the good times the black squad, like the dockers, suffered the lottery of the call-on.

> There used to be a daily market. If you were a riveter or whatever you used to go down in the morning and wait outside the foreman's office and he would say, 'You, you, you', and give you a start.
>   Sometimes the foreman would walk up and down the lines of men waiting for work without saying a word, not

even a grunt – which most of them were capable of. That meant that there was no work for you that day. They were just reminding you that they had all the power and you had none.[25]

These workers were also subject to the indignity of the piecework system, pay according to work done. For example, if you were a riveter, a counter came along and counted the number of rivets you had hammered home, before you were paid.

They paid you maybe twelve-and-six [12s./6d.] per hundred or twenty-five shillings a hundred, or whatever it was. You had to put in thousands of rivets to make up your wages at the end of the week.[26]

Sometimes there was a negotiation for a whole gang between a charge-hand and a rate-fixer, and it became a question of who was stronger – manager or worker. This boilermaker charge-hand tells how tough it was to hold out for the best deal for his men:

I was a charge-hand. When the new jobs came out you knew nothing about it. You had tae figure out how you were going to dae the job. And you had to put a price on it because you'd rate-fixers there.

So the rate-fixer comes in and he starts to negotiate . . . You know, the rate-fixers, they didnae want tae give you nothing like . . . So, there was one time there that I blacklisted a job . . . This was a tank we were building and I wanted twenty-two pound for it. And the firm wanted to give me five pound. I had a squad of about twelve men, and I says, 'Naebody touches that job.' Well, I'm the charge-hand so I've got to make decisions.

I says, 'Naebody touches that job, cos they're no going to pay us.' I says, 'We're going tae work on a job there and this job's going to last for a while and we're going tae get nothing out it.'

You tried to prove your point. I put everything down on paper, how it's all worked there, but you don't show that tae the rate-fixer, because you're only learning them more about their job. You knew more about the job than they did. They knew nothing about the job.

So, after that, when I blacked the job there, the gaffer came and tried tae force you, saying, 'You'll need tae dae this.' I said, 'I'm no dain' it.' So you went from there to the head rate-fixer and they tried to put you through it again, to force you.

I said, 'No, I'm no accepting it.'

Now, while that was going on the five pound started going up tae ten pound, then it went tae fifteen pound and I still held out. So, therefore, it stopped at that. They said, 'Right you are.' Then the manager's sent for. He says, 'Well, I think you're getting a reasonable price there, but you're just being stubborn.' I said, 'Oh?' I said, 'I've got men there that are working under me and I've got to make their wages.' I said to him, 'If you go for a suit you can buy a suit for . . .' – I think it was twenty shilling in these days – 'you can go and buy a suit for twenty shilling, or something like that, or you can get a suit for maybe three or four pound there.' I said, 'Why dae they sell one suit at twenty shilling and they sell the other suit at four or five pound? Workmanship!' I said.

'If you want tae get workmanship done, you've got tae pay.
Either that, or the men will just hang the job up, and the job
will never be right.'

So, after all that, it finished up I got my money. It took
about three months.[27]

All this was along with the hard, physical, dirty graft. The
sheer toughness of the work environment was unlike
anything that anyone had ever experienced before the
Industrial Revolution slipped into gear.

Some of the conditions that these men were working in was
really atrocious . . . When you see the conditions in the Clyde
it was like fighting an atomic war with a bow and arrow, you
know. You hadnae a chance. In the yard there, if you were
working at the stern of the ship . . . The only way you could
work round the rudder post, and round the screw and that,
was when the tide went right out. And when the tide did
come in and then went out it left all this residue. All rotting
fruit that had fallen off ships, and dead dogs and what have
you. And the men had to go down and work amongst that
you know. And you can imagine the conditions in the middle
of winter.[28]

John Brown's on Clydebank had a terrible reputation for
cleanliness in the toilets, so much so that I had heard the
comedian Billy Connolly, who worked as a welder in
Alexander Stephen's yard, draw on his experience of them
in a sketch. I asked Sam Gilmore, who knows Connolly and
was working in the yards at the same time as he, what the
truth of it was. Gilmore had found a way to circumvent the

prejudice he was up against as a Roman Catholic and
became a shipyard electrician and senior shop steward:

> Conditions were terrible in the yards. There were absolutely
> no cleaning up facilities. When you went up to the toilets,
> you got two shreds of paper – like that [he signified a
> lavatory sheet two or three inches square] – and you went in,
> and before long [seven minutes, I discovered was the allotted
> time] they were rattling the door and you know your time
> was up!
>
> John Brown's yard was even more primitive. They had a
> big trough running the length of the toilet and a wooden
> plank that you sat on, with holes in it. So people used to go
> to the toilet and they'd make wee boats, and they'd start off
> at the top and put a wee light to it. They'd float it down
> with people sitting there, and the next moment, 'Aargh!'
> That was John Brown's.

The shipyards compared with no other industry for the
sheer filth, as Hugh Cairney, a lagger from the late 1940s,
recalled:

> When I started working it was disgraceful, I mean you shared
> your cabin, whatever – you built the cabin yourself practically
> – you shared it with the rats and everybody else. That was in
> the shipyards, but I got oot of the shipyards and went to the
> oil refineries . . . and that was completely different frae the
> shipyards. I think I only went back about once or twice in my
> career, back to shipyards again. I didnae particularly like [the
> refineries], but [you were] oot in the open and . . . it was
> different. You had things like boiling water – you went in

and you had a hut, you had boiling water, you had a tea man, which you never had in the shipyards. Yeah, they've got them in the shipyards noo', but in they days you never had them, so you had to go and try and find a burner or a fire or a riveter's fire and try and boil your can up, you know?[29]

As safety precautions were nil in the yards, death by accident was also common. In the 1930s one of Glasgow's finest writers, Edward Gaitens, described a young lad taken into a Clyde shipyard by his father witnessing an accident that killed one worker and injured another. Amazingly, the work continued as the bodies were removed:

The father removed his cap, bowing his head; the boy copied him. 'My, there's been a man killed already! It's terrible. Terrible!' The boy looked up asking, 'Do they not stop the works when a man's killed, Da?' His father answered, 'No, the work goes on, son. The work goes on!'[30]

Ralph Glasser – born in the Gorbals, his parents Russian Jewish immigrants – recalls listening to the men at Dixon's Blazes relating:

Grim anecdotes of terrible things – of men crippled for life, or killed outright. The concluding words of one of these tales gave me nightmares for a long time, 'there was nothing left of the poor bugger but his feet'.[31]

Residents of Govan shared with me a catalogue of disasters, the first occasioned to a man who fell through the roof of the blacksmith's shop at Fairfield's yard during the war, when painting the glass roof with blackout paint.

He landed a few feet from me. I had only started a few weeks before. He fell into a large metal box holding lime used for softening steel. He was lifted out, covered in white lime powder and black paint . . . quite dead.

Then there was a mountain of a man – six foot, eighteen stone – [who] was decapitated when a Fairly Float was accidentally released from its housing and struck the back of his head while [he was] working at the side of the ship on the guardrail. His mate standing next to him was unhurt but suffered severe shock and never worked again . . . I also know the man who had the job of going into the water to recover the severed head.

And a young lad, engineer and keep fit fanatic, excellent swimmer . . . skylarking about the mooring ropes during their break, slipped from the rope straight into the water feet first and never surfaced . . . no trace of the lad could be found. It was low tide . . . he had stuck in the mud and drowned just feet from the surface. The Clyde being so dirty in those days there was no visibility beyond two inches into the water.

I can never forget a man caught in a drilling machine and thrown over the machine minus his arm. His mates rushed him to the ambulance room, where there happened to be a doctor . . . this only happened every six months . . . The patient was on the operating table of the Southern General within seven minutes.

The doctor then asked us to show him the scene of the accident and help him look for the man's arm . . . perhaps it

could be saved. We could not find it anywhere, until I
noticed what appeared [to be] a bundle of rags at the top of
the machine spindle. It was the arm wrapped into a tight roll
entwined with the man's boiler suit and shirt sleeve.[32]

What's clear is that facing the appalling conditions and danger of the work not only failed to alienate the industrial worker, it actually enhanced character and self-image. Values rose up within the shipyard community to become its characteristic expression: a survivor-sense of self-worth, a resolution born of never getting something for nothing, a work ethic driven by a tight-lipped, dogged pride, and want, but above all by a macho spirit, too.

Working in manual labour was regarded within the community as the pinnacle of machismo, and such workers looked down with disdain upon clerical workers and those who did not work with their muscles. It's a feature of Meldrum, a shipyard rigger in Hugh Munro's 1961 novel *The Clydesiders*:

'The bastards', he whispered. Inside him distrust of sedentary
men smouldered to madness. His fists bunched . . . The
rigger found himself gazing vacantly at the crowns of two
clerks perched on high stools . . . He felt no kinship. To him
they were two sheltered specimens of a soft breed whose
activities could hardly be classed as real work and whose
semi-indolent existence was supported entirely by the sweat
of hard-grafting chaps like himself . . . Arrogant behind his
own dirty face he saw their clean ones as an affront. And
automatically hated them.[33]

Similarly, Danny Shields, an unemployed riveter and George Blake's main character in the Clydeside interwar novel *The Shipbuilders*, looked down with disgust upon his son when he obtained a job as a cinema doorkeeper, derisively noting that he had 'never done a stroke of real man's work in his life'.[34]

Tolerating danger and risk-taking at work were perceived to be manly attributes. If, as a novice apprentice, you witnessed a fatal accident, you soon forgot about it amid the monstrous sights and sounds, so proud were you being there. As Edward Gaitens put it, you strutted on, 'cloaked in rare distinction'.

The whole business of being an apprentice was bound up with self-image. Sharing the experience was a vital element of the juvenile friendships which developed beyond the yard on the streets of Clydebank. Apprenticeship was the key to gaining acceptance into the fringes of street-corner society. It was on street corners that reputations were first made and challenged. The ideals of 'hardness', which guaranteed respect in the harsh environment of the shipyard, were equally important outside it.

I went in as an apprentice riveter because all the other boys at our corner – we stood at Miller Street corner – were apprentice riveters. If you wanted to meet anybody at night you met them at the street corner. A big group of us, about sixteen to eighteen, would meet at the corner, so they called us Corner Boys. Corner boys were considered loafers and hard men.

All our gang were black squad apprentices. We had quite a good time discussing things in the yard after working hours, what happened in the yard was discussed at the corner that night and then we would make our way to the dancing.[35]

The machismo and challenge of work and conditions, the example of their peers, and the knowledge that they were involved in the defining industry of Glasgow, their birthplace and second city of Empire, all served to give the shipyard the appeal of a brotherhood to which the boys longed to enter, even if it took a while to acclimatise to the more brutal elements:

I was sent to work with a man called 'Baldie' . . . there was a suggestion of a monkey about him. He was very strong, and I never knew him tired. Although I was no prude, I had been shocked at first by the blasphemy and obscenity of the workmen, but that feeling soon wore off, and when I started as Baldie's mate I had acquired considerable proficiency in the use of bad language.[36]

As an apprentice you could expect a first-day initiation drama to test your bottle, such as the rubbing of boot polish and other unpleasant substances into your genitals. At fourteen, at dinner time on his first day at the Fairfield yard in Govan, apprentice Tommy Stewart was invited to a game of seesaw:

There were three huge empty cable drums from two to ten feet in diameter. The boys could jump about them, run on top of them causing them to roll along the dockside, like any circus acrobat.

The seesaw was a plank thirty feet long on one large drum.

Working this seesaw – a few boys on each end – it worked great. The seesaw lifted them fourteen or fifteen feet in the air.

It came to my turn, I suddenly found myself alone on one end and this thing was whipping up and down fast. I was a little apprehensive, but OK. I was really enjoying it, when suddenly it stopped, with me about fifteen feet in the air . . . A few of the boys ran forward and by keeping the other end on the ground and me in the air, they turned the whole contraption ninety degrees and I was suddenly overhanging the water of the Clyde by about twenty-five feet.

It was a long time before the horn went and they rolled the drum from the edge of the dock . . . and lowered me gently to the ground . . . There wasn't a word said. I aged a lot that day . . . when I returned home that night [I was] no longer a tough guy.

Undoubtedly, working in these conditions did toughen men up and desensitised them to danger. Such values were passed from father to son and from journeyman to apprentice, and some revelled in the 'hard man' or 'he-man' image, showing pride in the scars from work injuries. Beyond the yard, part of the image was, of course, being able to hold your drink, an area of expertise in which steel workers mounted a convincing challenge:

About one steel worker in every ten could stand up to them successfully, which was one reason why the furnacemen

were looked up to in the world of heavy industry. That they
got the biggest pay packets was another reason. They also
had the biggest thirsts and that too was a prideful
possession in that part of the world . . . A legend grew up
about the steel smelters.[37]

Hard drinking and heavy smoking have always been 'strong
symbols of virility and machismo in Scottish culture'.[38]
Wages were sometimes distributed in the pub, where it was
very difficult not to conform. As shipyard worker Joe
Curran commented in 1964: 'Even the man that didn't
want a drink was more or less forced to have one.'[39]

It was a very macho culture . . . It could also be quite violent
too. But it was, you would say, very much an old-fashioned
west of Scotland man's world, definitely . . . You had to be
able to look after yourself . . . had to be prepared to stand up
and say you were prepared to fight . . . if you backed down,
that would be it. Everyone, everyone would stamp on you
from then on, so you had to do that. But once you'd done
that, that was OK.[40]

Conformity was essential, but one particular element in the
social mix transformed everything. Brutality was mitigated
by black humour, and 'patter' – the repartee, the tale-
telling of great feats, of accidents narrowly missed or of
gruesome deaths and mutilations. Injured men would earn
cryptic nicknames – such as 'bracket-head' for the shipyard
worker who was injured by a falling object from above.[41]
Asbestos workers joked that they could never be cremated;
others that they rushed to eat an injured man's sandwiches

after he was taken off to the Infirmary. It was quick, very funny, never malicious, unmistakably Glaswegian. It was the community you were joining at your coming of age as Jim O'Donnell, who served a four-year apprenticeship as an insulating engineer and worked in the industry all his life, recalls:

> Oh good comradeship you know, you always get good
> squads, good patter, och aye it was – it was a great job . . .
> Oh I loved [it] . . . even the noo' when you go on to sites and
> you've got a good squad of guys, your day goes in, you're
> working away . . . [42]

This sheet metal worker used to working at Hyde Park, one of four Springburn locomotive works, one day found himself working at the Fairfield shipyard and saw at once where the talent for patter came from:

> When I went tae the yards I was amazed. I said, 'How can
> men stick jobs like this?' It was filthy and a', like you
> know . . . You know yourself, the men are a' going aboot,
> and you've got to go off, climb [maybe forty or sixty feet
> sometimes] off a – when you're right down at the bottom of
> an engine room there – and you've got to go ashore to go
> to the toilets and that. Och the me! They're no going to do
> it! So, you know what was going on [laughs]. And some
> of . . . You had people there that was cleaning the mess up.
> They were involved in a' that and a'. And I said, 'How can
> people stick that?' It was unbelievable, like, you know. And
> if they hadnae that . . . way of life and the patter and that,
> nobody could have stuck the job. Billy Connolly, you know,

> he was true enough. He must have took a lot of copying
> and . . . Cos that's how the patter goes on, you know.

I've noticed while moving about this city that nothing is let go, there is always a hook that someone will hang something humorous on, given half a chance. It must have played a huge part in people's lives during the Depression. Maria Fyfe took up the point:

> I think people appreciate wit and humour here very much. Some of it, like Billy Connolly, comes out of the shipyard experience, jokes spread around. The *Herald* is good for carrying every day its diary, you know little stories of someone making a sarcastic comment or a joke about something or someone. The one that sticks in my mind is when some shipyard workers were sitting playing cards and not getting on with their work, and one of the men with a bowler hat comes round and gives them a ticking off and they ignore him and he says, 'Do you know who I am?'.
>
> Can you guess what's coming? One says, 'Hey Jimmy, this silly bugger doesn't know who he is!'

I tell Maria that I am reading Connolly's biography, written by his wife, that his is like a 'breaking free' type of humour: 'Connolly had this need to break out; the impression one gets is that he would have been deeply disturbed had he not had the nous to break free from the spiral of unhappiness that had been constructed for him.'

Connolly first lived with his sister and parents in a two-room apartment in Dover Street, on the north bank of the Clyde in Anderston. When he was very young his mother walked out on the family and he was brought up by an aunt who beat him and a father who sexually abused him. He seems to have found his real family in the Alexander Stephen shipyard, where his instinct for survival and repartee met and even on occasion topped the practised and merciless ribbing of more seasoned workers.

His wife, the comedienne and psychologist Pamela Stephenson, tells how one of his first jobs was to make tea for twelve, older, fellow welders, who conned him into subsidising the fee they paid him for making it – 2s./6d. a week each – by fixing him up with a suit at Tailorfit and making out they were paying it off weekly at the same rate. The elaborate hoax went on for two years before Connolly realised what was going on.

The humour of the shipyard was the changing-room camaraderie that perhaps rugby union players know best of all sportsmen: ruthlessly ego-pricking, mercilessly piss-taking, but characterful, warm, and clannish. It rescued Connolly and released him to be himself, as anyone who has seen him perform can tell.

> [The shipyard] was an extraordinary society of men, and in a way Billy's first family.[43]

Said Tommy Stewart, who worked alongside Connolly in Alexander Stephen's yard:

> We used to go in, in the morning, and we laughed until we came out. Everything was a joke. Not like that nowadays.

CHAPTER THREE

The Great Change

In 1851 Hugh MacDonald, a writer and poet born in Bridgeton in 1817, observed Govan, on the south bank of the Clyde, as something of a rural idyll:

> In the vicinity of Govan there are a considerable number of elegant villas, embowered in cosy garden-plots, screened amidst hedgerows and trees, and generally occupied by well-to-do citizens [of Glasgow], who can afford to combine the pleasures and profits of the city with the charms of rural retirement. These are in many instances so situated as to command a view of the river, with its steamers and sailing vessels ever passing and re-passing on their watery way; while the countryside around, with its fertile haughs, gentle

undulations, belts and clumps of trees, all chequered with
the verdant fences of the thorn, presents many a sweet
snatch of landscape of the fairest English type. The village
itself, as seen from the margin of the Clyde, with its
handsome church and elegant spire – a facsimile of that at
Stratford-on-Avon . . . – has an exceedingly fine effect, and
has often tempted into action the imitative skill of the artist.

MacDonald went on to delineate Govan's character as a
charmingly higgledy-piggledy congregation of houses, a
place that had been permitted to '"hing as it grew", each
individual proprietor biggin' where it best pleased himself,
and without the most distant regard for the opinion or
convenience of his neighbour.'

It is, in fact, the most curious and eccentric little townie that
we know, and always wears, to our fancy, a kind of half-fou
[drunk] aspect. At two places, the Pointhouse and the Ferry,
it comes rambling down towards the river; but, as if startled
at its own temerity, it staggers rapidly away back, zigzagging
into nondescript lanes and wynds, the irregularity of which
would break the heart of any individual whose bump of
order had an extraordinary degree of development. It has a
predominance of thatched houses too, as if, in its sturdy
independence, it was determined to retain its straw bonnet
in defiance of the innovating state.[1]

Sturdy it may have been but defiant it was not. Rather,
Govan was positively welcoming to 'the innovating state',
which was about to change its old-world image beyond
recognition. By the turn of the century, T. C. F. Brotchie

recorded, it was 'one of the great workshops of the world':[2]

> Within its boundaries, it is impossible to get beyond the
> sound of the hammer. From early morn till late at night, we
> hear the continuous hum of industry.

Change to every aspect of Govan was almost instantaneous. In 1894, just thirteen years after MacDonald's idyllic description, Morris Pollok, the owner of Govan's silk weaving works, lamented that it was 'justly regarded as one of the dirtiest and most unhealthy districts in Scotland'. The very rapid expansion of the shipbuilding trade had thrown into the district 'a population considerably in excess of the house accommodation, and the amount of overcrowding which existed was something very extraordinary'.

> It is by no means uncommon to find in a very small
> apartment a man and his wife and six lodgers, and it is not a
> very wonderful thing to find more. There are sometimes
> nine; nay, within the last few days I have been told of a case
> where there was a man and three children and fourteen
> lodgers in a room and kitchen . . . part of the men worked
> during the day and part during the night, so that as one
> squad turned out another turned in.

Just 9,000 people lived in Govan in 1864, when Pollok was shaking his head in dismay. By 1907, there were 95,000, and the tenement building programme launched to house the burgeoning population had barely kept pace.

It was a similar story in the Gorbals, a 'village' a few miles to the east along the Clyde, its population peaking at around 90,000, its tenements reputed to be 'one of Europe's worst slums'. Once again, prior to the industrial onslaught, after an earlier, darker history as Glasgow's leper colony, the Gorbals had been a suburb of great promise, as Glasgow-based writer Ian R. Mitchell, records:

> In the early years of the nineteenth century the burghers of Glasgow looked across the river and saw, adjacent to the village of Gorbals, a prestigious example of Regency town-planning rising on the southern bank of the Clyde. The aristocratic names of its streets reflected its aspirations: Bedford, Eglinton, Norfolk.[3]

From the late 1940s until 1958, Charles McLaughlin lived at 60 Mackinlay Street, just south of this area, and remembers the 'large houses which the upper class had moved out of. They had been subdivided. They were magnificent, sort of Georgian-type houses, they should have been preserved.'[4]

But in the Gorbals it was mostly the same story as in Govan: seamless rows of tenements. Further east, in Bridgeton, where the late Hugh Savage was born in 1918, it was the same story again:

> Street after street of smoke-grimed tenements, with the occasional red sandstone one where we thought the toffs lived.[5]

In her historical account of day-to-day domestic life in the tenements from 1910–45, Jean Faley, who was brought up in a tenement house from 1942 until 1958, points out that:

'Almost seventy per cent of Glasgow families before the First World War lived in [tenements]; and in 1951 the proportion was still as high as 50.6 per cent.'[6]

The owners of these tenements were not only the local Corporation. Some were owned by housing associations, but most were privately owned. Hugh Savage was amazed to discover in later life that many of the owners lived abroad, 'some as far away as the Argentine'.

As is clear from surviving tenements that have been restored, many of these monuments to the Industrial Revolution are, in fact, very attractive sandstone buildings, extremely well constructed, most of them the colour of Bath stone. Some are reddish, as Savage points out, but in the old days the more significant distinction was whether a tenement close, the common entrance to the apartments in the building, was or was not *tiled*. Tiled closes, known as 'wally' closes, were very much to be desired.

A typical tenement might have twenty closes, each opening onto three storeys of mainly one- or two-roomed apartments ('hooses'), three to six on each landing, accessed by a staircase. There was cold running water only and one earthenware toilet for all the occupants on each floor. These toilets were racked up on a tower tacked on to the back of the building.

The ground-floor, street-side entrance was known as a close mouth, leading to a dusty, rather than grassy, communal area at the rear of the building, the back court. This rear area serviced a number of closes and was compartmentalised by lowish walls known as dykes, topped in pre-war days by railings, and including middens and wash houses.

Inside a wash house were two round, iron-hooped wooden tubs with handles sat on a long low table in most wash houses. There was a safety-plank nailed to front and back, because a tub of hot suds on a table slittered with soft soap could be lethal. A cold water tap was set into the wall and an iron boiler, built round with brick or stone, sat over a fire-place. There was a 'dolly' and dolly-barrel for dumping out the grime and sometimes a big mangle in the corner. The ritual began early, winter and summer, with someone going down to fill the boiler and kindle the fire under it. Most of the family took a turn at that chore.[7]

The middens, where households dumped their ashes and other waste, were of brick construction, usually joined to the dykes between the back courts, in most cases adjacent to the communal wash houses. They were approximately 9ft x 9ft with a 7ft-high roof, and a wall across the 4ft entrance about 30 inches high. This served twelve to sixteen households.

The owner of the building was never in evidence. He rented it out through a factor, a manager; effectively no more than a rent collector. The factor was responsible for organising repair and maintenance, but this was seldom done. He was not a very popular person, and the panto-mime and music hall comedians helped people get their feelings about him off their chest in countless jokes. The problems of the tenements, which were beyond any factor to solve, were iniquitous overcrowding and poor sanitation.

It is not uncommon for eight, ten, or twelve persons to be herded together in a single room. There are 1,750,000 'houses' without baths [in Glasgow], and 105,000 [with] no internal sanitation.[8]

In the Gorbals, people live huddled together 281 to the acre . . . five and six in a single room that is part of some great alattern of a tenement, with seven or eight people in the room next door, and maybe eight or ten in the rooms above or below. The windows are often patched with cardboard. The stairs are narrow, dark at all times and befouled not only with mud and rain. Commonly there is one lavatory for thirty people and that with the door off.[9]

Families were brought up, some of them in single rooms, and how the women coped with that is beyond my comprehension. My parents were considered to be lucky because we had a two-room and a kitchen and an inside toilet, but even to have a room and kitchen was a luxury at that time. And there were a lot of people that were bringing up a family in a room and kitchen and also had lodgers. Nowadays, I don't think we can understand what that actually meant and the pressure that meant on the housewife herself or the mother.[10]

Single room houses were known as single-ends.

A one-room home about 14ft x 14ft plus an area for a set-in bed, it had one supply of cold water through a brass faucet, which ran into a black metal sink, with a drain plug hole. There was no inside toilet.[11]

Savage describes these as 'hovels . . . Some of the single-ends hardly measured eight feet by four feet. They had set-in beds which in some cases slept two adults and four children.'

For Sam Watt, James Baxter and Cathy Page, all raised in Springburn in the 1920s and '30s, these closet beds typified an unbelievably cramped and intimate domesticity.

> In the kitchen there was a hole-in-the-wall bed. That's where my mother and father usually slept. See in the old houses it was just a square hole in the wall. And it was what they called a bearer with wooden planks across it. And the two straw mattresses sat on top. That was their bed.[12]

> These were often built as bed-closets, that is, beds in large cupboards with a door; but in accordance with the recognition that ventilation was crucial to health such confined spaces were outlawed in 1900, when the Glasgow Building Regulations Act decreed that, 'No dwelling house shall contain an enclosed bed or a bed recess which is not open in front for three quarters of its length, and from floor to ceiling.'[13]

> When you look at it now, ye know, you wonder how people were sort of able to fit in! I mean the places were spotless, ye know, they really were. And the size of the room! We had the five of us. And it was a masterpiece of organisation at night.[14]

One step up from the single-end was the two-room house. Marion Smith was born in 1906. Her father was a brass moulder in the Atlas locomotive works in Springburn. He worked on the brass parts of the engines, which were sent all over the world, transported to the docks with outriders and police escorts. Her mother came from Dennistoun, 'rather more posh than Springburn', and had had a good education; she played the violin.

Our house had a coal fire in a stove, which had to be blackleaded with a paste mixed up in an old saucer, and then buffed up, and finally shone to a gleaming finish. There was a piece of velvet kept for the purpose. The steel trimmings were shined up with emery cloth. As my father was a brass moulder, the mantelpiece, above the stove, was gleaming with brass adornments, all made in the works. This was one of the perks of the trade . . .

There was linoleum on the floor, which was polished, and a small hearth rug in front of the fireplace. The kitchen chairs were wooden, and the kitchen table was covered with a sort of oilcloth so that it would be wiped over with a damp cloth . . .

There was an inbuilt coal bunker and a wooden dresser alongside. Just imagine coal being tipped into a bunker in the middle of the living room! There was a black iron sink with a single brass swan-neck cold water tap. Cupboards for pots were underneath the sink, and the cupboard for food was alongside at right angles. This was always referred to as the 'press'. There was a set-in bed at right angles to the fireplace . . .

We had gas lighting, quite new then. Inverted gas mantles, Veritas-make, and a glass shade. We also had a paraffin lamp. My dad was the only one allowed to touch it, trim the

wick, and fill it. It was on a stand and quite elegant, another
wedding present . . .

In the room was a green plush suite, two easy chairs,
small chairs and a couch. There was also a set-in bed there:
four children slept in it. The others slept in a 'hurly', which
was a fold-up bed which pushed underneath the hole-in-the-
wall bed. Believe it or not, eleven of us were housed in two
rooms until I was twenty-one years old.[15]

Privacy was not a feature of life either in a single-end or
two-room house, but decency was generally preserved, as
Robert Douglas, born at the start of the Second World War
in Maryhill, to the north-west of the city centre, describes
in his account of a typical morning:

Ma must have been up for a while; she already had the fire
on. I took my pyjama top off and went over to the sink. A
kettle of hot water was waiting. I ran some cold into the
white enamel basin with its blue rim then poured enough
hot in to give myself a good slunge.

'Turn 'roond, Ma. Ah'm gonny dae ma "below-the-belt"
bits.' She obligingly turned her back to me, changed the
wooden spoon she was holding to her other hand and
carried on stirring the porridge. I got to work with the
facecloth.[16]

An alternative was a shower and then a dip at the public
baths, as Doug Heath who grew up in Springburn in the
1950s, remembers:

Saturday morning was our day to take a plunge. We would carry our 'swimming trunk burritos' (a towel wrapped around our swimsuits) and head to the baths. As soon as the door opened, the aroma of Brylcreem and chlorine was unmistakable. We would get changed, then take the obligatory shower with carbolic soap.

It was always fun to dive for big copper pennies. The ones with Britannia on the back.

Every public bath facility had a vending machine. There was nothing like a scalding cup of chicken soup after swimming a few lengths of the baths.

After chatting up some of the local mermaids (usually unsuccessfully), it was time to dry off, put on our street clothes, re-make our swimming trunk burritos, then head to the local baker's shop.[17]

With large families the norm, it was common for twenty or more people to be using one toilet. In fact, thirty or forty was not that unusual. John Wotherspoon, born in 1920, has grim memories of how this could impact on tenement life:

We stayed on a five-door landin', so that there could be anythin' up to thirty-five, forty people usin' that toilet, so you were aye queued up for it, so if you were caught short – and in these days the lack of food and everythin' it affected your bowels, you know, diarrhoea and such like – you had a terrible job, you know, if you were caught short, somebody in the toilet and you were waiting to get in.[18]

Such a situation could have disastrous results, as Robert Douglas records:

> 'Jeez!' The place was minging. One of the neighbours must have been in shortly before me. I opened the small, steel mesh-covered window above the toilet. A breeze straight from the Arctic blew in. As I peed I leaned forward, one hand on the wall, to bring my face near to the window. Better freezing than being gassed.[19]

Chamber pots were an alternative, their emptying veiled in the name of decency.

> If a woman was coming down the stairs with a chamber pot under her apron in the morning you just didn't see her. No one ever told you not to. But when she didn't have the chamber pot it was, 'Good morning, Mrs McGuire,' or whatever, and you did recognise her.[20]

Poor sanitation, indoors and out in the back courts with open middens, inevitably attracted vermin.

> One day there was a commotion in the street. Large rats were running up and down and men were killing them one after the other in front of us kids.[21]

To Frances Kathleen Walker, who was born in 1938 and emigrated from the Gorbals to Australia in 1963, this would not seem unusual:

Can I say now that it was hell living in Mathieson Street? My father was in the RAF serving in India but he rarely sent us any money. We were seven in one room. We had one cold water tap when the pipes were not burst and shared one toilet with all of the close. At night when all the beds were down the only things that could move were the rats and, believe me, they ran all over us. The rat-catcher came one night and in our single-end he caught fourteen. I almost lost my leg to a rat bite. It took months to heal. We never had enough to eat – to be honest, we were starving. I have a few photographs of us slum kids in the back courts – we look like tinkers.[22]

In his autobiography, *Born Up A Close*, Hugh Savage explains that middens were sometimes set against the ground floor windows of a close, 'so there were all kinds of vermin, the houses were rat-infested'.

Middens played a significant role in the life of the tenements. Unemployed men and children would rake through them for anything of value, men would empty them in the dead of night, which fact played on a child's imagination in extraordinary ways.

Rubbish was carried from the houses and flung over the low wall into the midden, most of it loose . . . I believe they were emptied once a week by men during the night with lights fixed to their caps . . . Children climbed over the thirty-inch wall, as did dogs, cats . . . If there was anything found in a midden that could be put to any immediate use, it was christened a 'lucky midden'.[23]

[The night-time scavengers] used to wear things like a
miner's light so that they could go down into the back in the
dark, and they had a strap they used to wrap round it and
round their heads as well to carry it [the bin] up the stairs
and dump it.

As a child you would be frightened of the midden men.
You didn't see the midden men but you knew they came at
night and they emptied your midden and they had lights on
their hats and they would trudge through your close and
these men looked terrible . . . midden men frightened you
when you were wee. Aye, they were all dirty and covered in
muck and they had the bins on their back and the dirt. And
people would throw a dead cat, and a budgie if it had died,
and a goldfish . . . it was all the muck and all the filth.[24]

Every tenement child 'raked the bins'. In his autobiography *The Real Gorbals Story*, Colin MacFarlane, born in
the 1950s, admits to 'midgie raking: going through the
middens in the back courts, to find ginger bottles or
"luckies" – discarded chattels that we could either make
money from or play with . . . There were rumours that in
posh places like Kelvinside the lucky might find priceless
pieces of jewellery or art.' It landed MacFarlane in hospital
for six months with a midden-related disease.

George Rountree, brought up in Govan in the 1930s,
would hide inside the close midden in games of hide-and-
seek: 'We would keep quiet and then somebody would
make a wee noise and they'd come up and peer in the
midden, and of course by that time we had prepared all the
ashes in old newspapers and when they came up to the wall
we bombarded them with ashes . . . I can remember happy

days in the middens bombarding somebody with ashes.'

One day his friend John Connell 'decided to climb over [into a midden] and was lucky enough to find a full packet containing ten cigarettes, which I shared with my chum . . . I became violently sick . . . [and] was kept in for the rest of the evening and severely warned about smoking.'

Infestation by bugs was also endemic to tenement living:

House-beetles would crawl out of the walls at night and go foraging, much to everybody's disgust. I well remember my father's routine most nights of covering the linoleumed floor of the kitchen with newspapers spread out before he went to bed. Once the light was turned off and silence reigned you could hear the rustle of the beetles (they were like black cockroaches) crawling on the newsprint. He'd give them a moment or two to assemble, then he'd leap out of bed and slaughter them with the back of a shovel. There'd be just as many the following night . . .[25]

You had the green van where it came up tae the house. That was your Health [Sanitary Department] . . . And the green van, when ye had bugs, and all the kids wet the beds, and the neighbours complained. And then the green van came up, took everything and fumigated it. The house and everything, ye know! And in the close, 'Whisper, whisper!'[26]

In the nineteenth century, waves of typhus and cholera tore through the poorest communities, raising the death rate of children in particular to unprecedented levels. Dr J. B. Russell, Glasgow's medical officer of health in the early part of the city's industrial history, recorded seeing—

> Their little bodies laid on a table or a dresser so as to be somewhat out of the way of their brothers and sisters who play and sleep and eat in their ghastly company. From beginning to rapid-ending the lives of these children are short. One in every five of those who are born there never see the end of their first year.

A century later, Betty Knox, born in Springburn in 1922, recalled smallpox, scarlet fever, and diphtheria as rife:

> Whole families o' kids got taken away, because the middens were all open middens. You'd be playing with a ball, and it maybe jumped into the midden, so you jumped in. You were black! And I think we were immunised. Many, many children round about where we lived died with diphtheria. And many more had scarlet fever.[27]

But statistics show that whooping cough and measles accounted for more deaths in Glasgow than either of these diseases, as Jean Faley wrote in *Up Oor Close*:

> The mortality figures for children under ten for 1910–14 expressed per million are: scarlet fever 721, diphtheria and croup 993, whooping cough 2,535, and measles 2,558. In pre-war years scarlet fever and diphtheria had to be reported to the Sanitary Department which made attempts to disinfect houses, and curtail their spread.[28]

In Anderston, the root cause of overcrowding got some Big Brother treatment from local inspectors:

> You'd a plaque on the door that said that this house would
> be allowed, say, seven people in the house, and apparently
> there were inspectors that went round, and if you'd more
> children than that you sent some outside when the man
> came to the door.[29]

The folly of such a strategy, guaranteed to widen the them-and-us divide, combined with the dictates of the Catholic Church and a failure to develop what Marion Smith calls 'family limitation' caused untold misery. The first Marie Stopes clinic, where a cervical cap was distributed, opened in London in 1921, and in 1925 Mary Barbour pioneered Glasgow's first family planning centre, the Women's Welfare and Advisory Clinic. But it took many years before apprehension was overcome and family planning became a success, and the Pill, which made contraception infinitely more reliable, easier and more accessible, was not made available on the National Health Service until 1961. Marion Smith reflects:

> Imagine what [the National Health Service] would have
> meant to my mother. And the benefit of being able to space
> your family. Family limitation. She wouldn't have had to have
> nine children. In the circumstances, there was no way of
> avoiding it. You just had to take the children as they all
> came. And never once in hospital! Several times she was
> very close to death because she had severe haemorrhages,
> and there was no blood transfusions as there is today, which

would have picked her up. And she had to lie in the bed there and we were all having our meals and our life going on all round about her.[30]

Childbirth was always undertaken at home and could be a hazardous business. A midwife was present, but rarely a doctor, and not until the 1930s did women begin to attend antenatal clinics. For a home birth, however, help was always on hand from neighbours in the close.

Generally, the cost of seeing a doctor made for inventive self-medication. Mothers took charge even in a case of measles or mumps. Castor oil was one all-purpose panacea, with a drop of orange to help it down. Liquid paraffin and cod liver oil were also in the homespun medicine drawer, and a soap and sugar poultice was used for cuts and abrasions. Marion again:

My mother had the old-fashioned sort of remedies. She made up each winter her own emulsion and it tasted far nicer than the ordinary one. It had cod liver oil in it, but it was made with condensed milk, which made it sort of sweet. And I always remember Ipecacuanha wine, it was in expectorant when you had a cough, and syrup of squills too. And if we had a wee sort of kidney infection of a chill on the kidneys it was sweet spirits of nitre.

And there was a stuff called Thermogene. It was a sort of pinky- or orange-coloured cotton wool. They sold it in a roll, and it was impregnated with something that was good for your chest, you know. They pit this on the wee ones. Back an' front with a slit for the head to go through. Put it on like a wee waistcoat thing back and front. And you wore that

next to your skin, 'cause the heat drew out whatever it was
from whatever impregnated the wadding. You had to wear it
all winter.

   You could get off of the chemist camphorated crystals
and put it in a locket. You wore it round your neck and it
had wee holes in it and the camphorated stuff came out and
it helped your chest too. But camphorated oil, my mother
did rub us with it if you had a very bad cold.[31]

Irene Hamilton was born in 1947, the year before the
inception of the National Health Service, but old habits die
hard:

When you'd a sore throat, my granny never believed in
buying medicine, didn't want to make chemists rich, so if
you'd a sore throat she'd put salt on the shovel and heat it
and tip it into a nylon stocking and put it round your neck.
And mustard poultices. The other great thing was cod liver
oil – my mother used to put it in everything, in your orange
juice in the morning, in tea. If you had a septic finger or
something she used to grate soap and put a spoonful of
sugar in it with a bit of boiling water and make it into a
paste, and put that on it.[32]

Marion Smith, born forty years earlier than Irene, recalled
that her mother almost died because she refused to see a
doctor. It wasn't just about money; there was a fear:

My mother took an abscess in her breast, and that was an
awful bad thing. She was in agony, and one of her brothers
came – he had been in the Sanitary [Department], and in the

RAMC in the army – and he said, 'You'll need to get the
doctor, Nan.' She had suffered so much with it, she sat and
looked at a little sharp vegetable knife she had. She said, 'I
thought if I could just maybe push this in . . .' It could have
killed her, if her brother hadn't told her to get the doctor.

Betty Knox recalled how the tenement women often had
no option but to minister to their children:

Aye, there were a lot of doctors. But then you didn't dare
get a doctor to come to your house, 'cause very few folk
could afford to have a house call. They couldn't afford to pay
a doctor to come unless, as I say, it was an urgent thing. But
then any minor childhood thing your mother doctored you
and that was it. But there was nothing to help you if your
mother hadn't the money. Forget it – you weren't getting
any.[33]

In the 1930s doctors charged 1s./3d. for a consultation,
and 2s./- for a home visit. Less than a decade later, prices
had risen, but there was a safety net – 'the green lady' or
charitable societies:

You paid your half crown for the doctor – that was the
standard charge – but it had to be pretty serious before
you'd go and see him . . . You'd the green lady in those days,
the health visitor.[34]

If you called the doctor it cost you two-and-six [2s./6d.] for
his visit, then you had to buy the medicine. But most people
were in societies and they paid the bills. Our family was in

the Ancient Shepherds who met in the Masonic Hall in
Vulcan Street.[35]

This lack of cash would seem extraordinary were it to
happen today to people putting in the hours and creating
the profits for the country that the workers were in
Glasgow during 150 years from 1800. Yet—

At every street corner from morning till night groups of
unemployed men of all ages spend their time hanging about.
Most of these world-famous firms paid starvation wages and
woe betide any of their workers who happened to mention
unions.[36]

Wives of shipbuilders in the Anderston area, Mrs Whelan,
Mrs Roper and Mrs Capaldi, and Miss McKerrell, recalled:

Our main problem during the First World War was poverty. I
remember one time the only food we had in the house was
one single egg.

Forty years later, it seemed to be no better, as Bashir Maan,
arriving from Pakistan as a student in the 1950s, recalls:

I came to Gorbals, Glasgow in March 1953. I was very
disappointed to see the Glaswegians dressed shabbily, the
buildings mostly dirty and black, people living in poverty and
grossly overcrowded conditions, a public bar at every corner
in the streets and on Fridays crowds of women and children
congregated outside the bars waiting for their husbands to
come out and give them wages, if there were any left, so

that they can buy food for their children. During the Raj we were made to believe that this is the land of milk and honey, beautiful and rich. Hence my disappointment was grave.[37]

Irene Hamilton made the point that there were levels of poverty:

I remember my mother telling me about the school I was at – it was a Protestant school – and her father only worked now and again. They were pretty poor, so they used to go there at about half past seven in the morning and get a bowl of porridge. Charity, you know? . . . There were always certain kids you were discouraged from playing with, certain families, but it was always the ones you wanted to play with. Some of them were running about in their bare feet, and there were ones you weren't to hang your coat next to theirs at school because they'd lice. There was a social scale even amongst the poor, we had our standards.

But in fact poverty seems to have been far more common to all a few decades earlier. Irene was born in Anderston in 1947. Crawford Dick, however, was born in the Gorbals in 1933, when 'nobody had any money':

The strange thing is looking back on it we must have been poor but we don't have any feelings of being poor, I suppose everything was sort of relative but, eh . . . nobody had any money . . .[38]

Nevertheless, birthdays and Christmas were times when the pinch was more obvious. Then there was a clear distinction between the 'haves' and have-nots', as Thomas Scott Wilson, who was born in the same street as Crawford Dick, in 1928 records:

> I remember going out one day and we were all out there with our presents and one of the boys, he came from Devon Street [on the west side of the Gorbals], he said, 'Santa Claus didn't come to me', and you know, when you think back, obviously, why not? – poverty. But it sort of shook us and we had no explanation for it so it just had to be – that's the way it was. It lives with you when you hear that and yet it must have been common too.[39]

Irene Hamilton's husband John's earliest memories of Christmas were in the 1940s:

> Christmas was the only time of the year I got chicken, chicken was a luxury. And the toys you got were very basic, after the war, and even the toys we got were pretty poor quality. I got a wee Air Force suit, with a hat and an armband and a bugle, and I thought that was marvellous. My dad worked overtime and got me a horse, but I gave it away for a basin with no bottom in it. I was only about five or six. A paint box was a great present, with four colouring books with it. It cost about a shilling.
>
> I still remember the candy apples, red ones, you got at the shows. And you'd wash the shovel at Christmas, and put salt on it to clean it, then put chestnuts in it and roast them on the fire. And we'd toast bread on the fire – my mother had a fork for it – and the other thing was we used to put tatties in the fire, and they charred, they were black on the

outside but when you got the skin off they were beautiful inside.[40]

But for others, like Mary Preece, Thomas Orr and Amelia Newton, brought up in the Great Depression of the late 1920s and '30s, 'there was no money, no money'.

[Birthdays] weren't celebrated at all actually. I can't remember any present being exchanged for birthdays or anything like that. It was just a matter of, 'Happy Birthday' and nothing more than that.[41]

Well, you couldnae say it was celebrations. It was just your birthday came and your birthday went. We just got a wee bit extra loving on that day. You know, we felt it. We would get something. But it wasnae very much. But we thought the world of it just the same.[42]

In the 1920s and '30s, during deepest economic depression, secondhand shops and pawn shops were everywhere:

You'd go in [to the pawn shop] with your man's good suit on the Monday and get the money for it, then when he got his wages on the Friday you'd go back and get it out again, so's he'd be well dressed for the weekend.[43]

There were pawn shops, maybe one in every street nearly. The only thing that you could say about the pawn shop was that you werenae borrowing from moneylenders and that kind of thing, where you paid interest. You werenae obliged to anybody for the money.[44]

It was then, too, that 'the Parish' played a crucial role in clothing poor children, but it was a terrible stigma 'to go on the Parish', and the clothes were very rough, heavy, like a uniform. Teachers were informed when a child went on the Parish and were supposed to check that they were wearing the clothes:

> 'So-and-so's got one pair knickers, one dress, one pair
> boots', and you were s'posed to keep an eye open to see
> them being worn. If not . . . 'Where's that beautiful dress you
> got from the school-board?' I had to ask. Sometimes it
> wasnae at the pawn . . . 'My ma biled it and now it'll no go
> on me.'[45]

The Gorbals was also the centre for Jewish migrants to the city, as we will see, and because so many of them were tailors, their children mostly wore hand-made clothes. 'That caused a bit of jealousy among the non-Jewish,' recalled Ellis Cohen, born in Eglinton Street in 1928, before moving to South Portland Street, still in the Gorbals Laurieston area. Poverty was as much a problem in the Jewish community, however, and, as ever self-sufficient, they set up their own efficient welfare board.

> We had a Jewish Welfare Board. If a family needed clothes,
> the Jewish Welfare Board gave them clothes. It was a whole
> community. You made a contribution to the Board. It was a
> disgrace to be on the Board. It wasn't a nice thing.

Even in times of greatest want, the tenement women, Jewish and non-Jewish, saw to it that there was food on the table. Home cooking, baking in particular, had to be good in times of great poverty, as these women, both born in the Gorbals in the early part of the twentieth century, recorded for the Stirling Women's Oral History Project:

Oh, my mother could bake, she was a rare baker of potato scones. And scones of all sorts. We had home baking, and plenty of soup, broth a speciality. Broth, potato soup, and she used to make dumplings, clootie dumplings – great big ones, you know, and you boiled them. I used to pour the water in – keep them boiling and put it on the top of a plate, after it came out of the cloth, turned it and put it in front of an open grate on a wee kind of fender affair at the front of the fire. You sat at the front of the fire and all, you know – the red embers for the dumpling to dry – and when she wasnae looking you used to go by it and give it a big skelp! Oh, but she made fig dumplings with sultanas, apples and cloves – a clove or two in the apple dumpling. She made lovely dumplings, she was a good baker, home baker.[46]

I can remember lots of soup, lots of porridge . . . Eh, stovies. Very, very few fancies, it was all plain fare, very good. And we were always there at meal times, at table, to eat it. Chicken soup was my favourite meal. I was awfully fond of chicken soup, but we didn't get a lot of butcher meat; it was expensive. We got sausages and the odd stew. My mother was a very good cook. She knew how to economise. I suppose having five hungry girls coming out and in all the time, I think it would make anyone economical, wouldn't it?[47]

Jean Kendal, brought up in the 1940s in Finnieston (close to Anderston), recalls that her granny's soup was the mainstay and its making a family event:

Friday was the night when my granny made the soup for the weekend. She was famous for her soup! Her soup pan was the biggest I've ever seen, and into it would go great big meaty bones, that would simmer away for hours to make the rich stock. What went in afterwards depended on the kind of bones. If they were from mutton or beef, the soup would have lots of barley. Split peas or lentils would go into ham stock. Chicken bones needed rice.

Often I got the job of cleaning the grains or pulses. They had to be vigorously stirred in many changes of water. The first rinse produced a grey cloudy supernatant liquid with scummy bubbles floating on the top. With each successive rinse the water became clearer until that bit of the job was done. During this process, the contents of the bowl had to be picked over and any little black specks, small stones or bad ones individually removed. There were horror stories about black ones causing a condition called 'St Vitus' Dance' that made people move about in an alarming way. (Years later I learned about ergot of rye and the persecution of 'witches'.)

Meanwhile, my granny would be doing the dangerous bit, chopping the vegetables into neat cubes. The work surface in her kitchen was like a butcher's block, made of wood scrubbed snow white, and uneven from much use.

Once assembled, the soup would fragrantly steam away, tantalising the nostrils of family and visitors alike, but not to be partaken of until Saturday.[48]

Traditionally, Sundays were also a day for a special treat, as others recall:

> I remember my father always had Finnan haddock, that was his, that was a Glasgow favourite dish for a Sunday morning, ham and haddie, and it was bacon, must have been fried I suppose and a big Finnan haddie put in the frying pan and the lid put on for a certain time then lifted out and it was delicious with bacon. I think we got the smell of it.[49]

> Sundays we were sent to Finks' Dairy for sour milk ['soor' milk or buttermilk]. We were given a glass of this with a teaspoon of cream of tartar. This made it fizz. We usually had a 'one-eyed sandwich' for breakfast. This was a slice of bread with a small piece cut out of the middle. Into this was dropped an egg and then it was fried in hot dripping.[50]

> A luxury we used to get on a Sunday was the sour milk. There used to be a man come round the streets with a big cart and he sold the sour milk. It must have been a penny a pint or something like that. And we used to go down with a big, big jug to get it filled. You used to see the butter all floating on the top of it like.[51]

Desperate to boost the family economy, children, young Crawford Dick among them, took a job, illegally, before leaving school:

> I well remember at Albert Road I started delivering milk when I was about eleven, you know, breaking the law. That was during the war of course. And I was getting up as my

father was going out the house, and picking up from Ross's
Dairy's this great trolley of milk and I remember the people I
delivered the milk to which is quite something. They lived
round at Queens Park overlooking the park but at that time
we had Dame Sybil Thorndike, Sir Lewis Casson and Jack
Radcliffe . . . There was a little square at the far end of
Queens Park and Sir Patrick Dollan lived there. He was [a]
past [lord] provost of Glasgow.[52]

Paddy Dollan, as he was known, was indeed an important
public figure of the time. He lived in a wally close, became
one of the leaders of the Independent Labour Party (ILP),
which grew out of the earlier Scottish Labour Party and was
established in 1893. Dollan was a champion of decent
housing for the poor of Glasgow, although he once said
that it was a woman who lay behind the initiative:

It was my mother who prompted me to agitate for better
housing. I remember her saying that it was a queer
Christianity which compelled a mining couple and ten
children to live in a single apartment while clergymen
occupied the best mansion in the village.

Crawford Dick had an unfortunate accident delivering
milk to the Dollans one day, and discovered firsthand what
the new socialism meant:

I remember dropping a bottle of milk on Lady Dollan's
doorstep. It shattered of course. I mean normally, if you
dropped a bottle of milk, if you were delivering to a prefab
the woman would come out and help you clear it up but not

Lady Dollan. She brought out a bucket and sponge and said,
'There you are, get wired in.'[53]

We will meet Lady Dollan again. Besides doing milk
rounds, children signed up to delivering papers before
school and selling firewood – anything that would enhance
the family income. All money earned would go straight to
the matriarch, the mother, who kept everyone afloat.

In 1929, Wall Street crashed and sent tremors throughout
the world. Unemployment rose from 2 million to 12 million
between 1920 and 1933 in America, and by 1931 nearly 6
million were out of work in Germany, a situation that eased
in Adolf Hitler. In Glasgow unemployment reached thirty
per cent and numbers seeking 'relief' soared:

Looking back now . . . speaking as someone who is seventy-
two years of age . . . I wonder how they got through it
because before I was born my mother was raising a family
on one pound and fifty pence a week [30s./- in old money] –
for six of them. That was all the help we got. It was the days
of the means test, but if my father took a casual job
someone could inform on him – these things happened.[54]

By 'Buroo day', a Thursday, the day the dole was collected,
they had probably not eaten for two days, so the money
went on food and the rent they had to pay to the
Corporation. George Fairley was born in 1935 in Jamieson
Street, Govanhill:

In the winter nights . . . my brother was in the Home Guard,
and there were other coats . . . so, I remember when I had to

go to bed my father would come through and he would lift coats out the hall and he had these big army great coats, big coats with big brass buckles, and he would throw them over you and make sure you were really warm . . . and we would get a pig [stoneware hot water bottle] in bed.[55]

Frances Walker's mother made it her business to ensure there was heat in the house, even when there was no money to buy coal.

In the middle of winter my mother used to get up very early, about four a.m., and she would get the old pram out and push it to the gas station where she would stand for ages so she would be the first to be allowed to buy the dross. She would bring it home, mix it with flour and salt and other things I can't remember, then pour in some water and mix it into balls and cook it in the oven. This made her own briquettes. God, I loved my mum. She would stand up to her knees in raw sewage to clear blocked toilets on our stairhead so that we didn't have to wade through it. She was a real mother to us.[56]

Getting out of the tenements and away from the industrial sprawl was, until after the Second World War, only possible for the few. And what would it afford a man to do so anyway?

In the famous play by Robert McLeish, *The Gorbals Story*, performed more than 600 times between 1946 and 1949 and turned into a feature film in 1950, there's a Highland migrant to Glasgow, a baker called Hector, who sees people looking into his eyes and wondering what the free sort of life in the Highlands is that he has left behind. When they hear his brogue, people smile:

> After twenty years in Glasgow I still see them smile when they hear the lilt of the Island in a man's tongue – you can see them sendin' searching looks into your face an' them all ready to laugh because you're a Highland man . . . [but] it's only when a man comes to live in a place like this with people packed on top of one another like herrings that they realise that a Highland man is just like themselves . . . [In the Highlands] you have to fight the sea if you want to go with the drifters and you've got to fight the land if you want to make things grow. That's what puts the lilt in a man's tongue, that he can live and get the better of all things that would hold a man down . . . Aye, and it's the same here too, Peggy – nothing can keep a man down for ever, no matter how hard or powerful it is . . . Back home in Mull, I've seen people with sore hearts at a bad catch or a bad harvest, but never so they would despair. No, they would bend their backs and work harder.
>
> *Peggy*: The less they get the harder they have to work. That sounds awful familiar – just like Glesca.[57]

In 'Glesca', in the twenties and the thirties, most of those who wanted out had no opportunity to flit. There was no way out. The first schemes of 'desirable residences' were built in the mid-twenties, but fell foul of housing allocation policy. According to Seán Damer, they went to 'respectable, professional or white-collar workers, nearly all of them Protestant . . . Catholics were conspicuous by their absence from Mosspark.'[58]

Mosspark (built in 1924, south of Govan), along with Knightswood and Riddrie (to the west and east of the city respectively), were among the most coveted housing schemes created in accordance with the 1919 Housing Act.

Maria Fyfe, the daughter of a tram driver, was born in 1938, in a tenement in Bedford Street in the Gorbals, 'a room and kitchen with a lavatory on the staircase we shared with neighbours. We had moved from the Gorbals to Govanhill by the time I was four (to Govanhill Street).' Govanhill is only a little further out from the centre than the Gorbals, but 'we were stepping up in the world,' she told me. 'There were bright electric lights in the house – no more sputtering gas lamps – AND our own inside toilet. Then – I must have been about six [1944] – we moved to a council house in Knightswood for a short time, west of the city, and I thought it was absolutely wonderful. Then, in 1947, we got the house that we stayed in, in Braidcraft Road in Pollok.'

Pollok, south of Mosspark, opens onto Pollok Country Park and Pollok golf course today. Following the Second World War, Pollok was one of the areas earmarked for those tenement dwellers judged respectable enough to look after the new housing. Some clearly did not fit in to the new countrified setting: When asked by a fellow workmate what was the name of the street he was living in, a Pollok man said, 'Do you mean what lair am I in?'

Others were grateful to get out, however, and the Fyfes were among them, as Maria recalls:

Tenants were allotted houses not only according to need, but assessment by the local factor's office. Cleanliness, care of the property you were currently inhabiting as well as its fitments, rent, and tenancy records were all checked. You only got a good house if you were considered not to require supervision. Identity cards were checked. References were sought. If graded for 'rehousing' – the lowest category – the tenant underwent regular supervision by the Health and Welfare Department until considered to have made sufficient improvement.

We were allocated one of the brand new houses in Pollok, built to a high standard of workmanship by the Corporation's own direct labour . . . in a terrace of six similarly pebble-dashed, up-and-downstairs houses, with a large front window looking out onto a patch of mud that would soon be transformed into our own garden. The house was still smelling of fresh paint. We excitedly trooped in to view.

At that time the post-war Labour government had been two years in power, Clement Attlee was the prime minister, and if the Labour Party was united on one thing it was the absolute necessity of getting slum clearance and bomb damage tackled, and houses built that met modern standards . . . In 1946 an astonishing 172,320 out of 281,000 homes in the city were deemed unacceptable on standards of density. In Scotland as a whole, more than 400,000 homes were without toilets. In the cities, three out of every five had no bathroom. Homelessness was common, 170,000 young couples who had married during the war had no home of their own, and had to live, overcrowded, with relatives . . .

. . . We needed aid from the United States . . . Between the end of the war and March 1951 the number of public and private sector houses completed was 865,000.

Without exception the tenants where we lived set to work, learning gardening from scratch. They planted privet hedges from cuttings, and grew flowers and vegetables from seed. We walked around on a summer's night, observing what other people had been doing in their own patches. We grew our own strawberries, carrots, lettuces and potatoes, and for the first time in my life I saw lupins, snapdragons, sweet peas, marigolds and primroses. In our own garden! A rambling rose grew up our back wall, and I could cut as many as I liked for display indoors.

You see, I think an awful lot of nonsense gets talked about – sentimentality about – missing the old tenements. My parents were delighted to get out of a tenement and they never looked back. My mother was in seventh heaven at getting a house with a back and front door and a proper bathroom, she was just happy about that.

Maria cannot countenance that 'anyone in their right mind would want to stay in a very grotty tenement flat with only a small indoor lavatory and no bath. Having to go to the public baths to get a bath, you know?'

I put it to her, 'So nothing, you would say, was lost with the disappearance of tenement society, nothing that you would like to have now, which isn't around now?

'In my own experience . . . Well,' says Maria, 'I left the tenements when I was very small anyway. When we got the house in Pollok I was delighted to have a garden, to have trees and flowers all around.'

What then of Scots folk singer Adam McNaughtan who, like others, has written nostalgically for the days of the tenements?

Oh, where is the Glasgow where I used to stay
The white wally closes, done up wi' pipeclay
Where you knew every neighbour frae first floor to third
And tae keep yer door locked was considered absurd . . .

Jean Faley, who rose from tenement society to become Professor of Sociology at the University of Wisconsin, sides with McNaughtan, or at least understands his point of view.

The tenement house. To some, a forbidding, blackened building, dilapidated and vandalized beyond repair. But other memories linger too, happy memories. A glowing fire, a welcoming bowl of soup, the smell of clootie dumpling. The sound of a melodeon or mandolin and voices raised in song. Giggles from brothers and sisters snuggled together in the recessed bed; and Mother rapping through the wall, 'Go to sleep!' Sleepy sighs and the chime of a clock.

But a family of seven or eight or more in two rooms? No hot water, shared toilets? . . . For Glaswegians over fifty (or even forty) their . . . nostalgia may be pleasurable, but it is often, as the Greek root of the word suggests, a painful longing to return to a place where they feel they belong. There is a strong sense of loss, which is not unmixed with anger, arising as it does from the destruction of a way of life without people being able to choose which elements of it they would have liked to preserve. It is natural to dwell on things which were valued and have been lost, to return in the mind and conversation to once loved places and times. Nostalgic feelings are an escape from the present, but on them can be built a critique of the present, an attempt to understand why changes have taken place, an exploration of

the possibility of salvaging cherished values, an argument for
greater control over the way things are . . .[59]

Faley bewails the loss of 'a way of life', which sounds
like the loss experienced by the weavers in the eighteenth
and early nineteenth centuries, when they lost their
rural communities to mechanisation and the industrial
sprawl.

Alex Ferguson writes that workers in the big industries
in Glasgow carried the sense of belonging, which we have
seen especially strong in the shipyard, into their lives
outside, into the tenements:

> In a community that relies heavily on a single industry, there
> is an intensity of shared experience that draws people
> together and tends to make them appreciate the need to
> support one another.[60]

Ferguson puts his own success as manager of Manchester
United – 'in handling men, and especially in creating a
culture of loyalty and commitment in teams I have
managed' – down to his upbringing 'among the working
men of Clydeside'.

Should there be any difficulty in identifying the culture
of the 'working men of Clydeside' and their wives and
families, a visit to the People's Palace on Glasgow Green
will dispel it. The Green, between the Gorbals and
Bridgeton, is itself a palimpsest of working-class history. It
has seen pitched battles between rival street gangs, political
mass demonstrations of Red Clydesiders, and long ago, on
winter afternoons, the dying lights of fires flickering low in

the gloaming, lit by armies of women heating water in baikies, to tub their washing. Where better to explore—

> A palace of pleasure and imagination, around which the
> people may place their affections and which may give them
> a home on which their memory may rest.[61]

The Palace was completed in 1898 as a cultural centre for the people of the East End, when this was one of the most overcrowded parts of the city. Here were reading and recreation rooms, a museum and art gallery, with concerts held in the elegant, glass-circumscribed Winter Gardens. Today, it is just as magnificent, and carries a year-round exhibition of every aspect of life in Glasgow during the Industrial Revolution.

There is no doubt that the working people of Glasgow share a common identity. In the Industrial Revolution, this identity drew strength not only from the spirit of the men within the huge, dominating industries, but also from the spirit of tenement society, which had precious little to do with 'the working men of Clydeside'. Tenement society was the woman's domain.

CHAPTER FOUR

The Women of the Tenements

_____

There is, and has been throughout the documentation of Glasgow's industrial history, a preoccupation with the working men of Clydeside. Characteristically, Alex Ferguson salutes the _men_ of Clydeside and makes no mention of the role of the Clydeside women. Yet, while the men were busy massaging their macho fantasies in the shipyards, and later relentlessly broadcasting them in books and films, there was in reality many a henpecked husband living in fear of her indoors.

The women did a magnificent job of feeding and clothing their families in the face of abject poverty. But they did far more than this. And while history tends to consign their contribution to the 'Miscellaneous' file, and the popular picture is of the marauding alpha male who spends his wages on a Friday night in the pub and comes together in a violent collision with his wife that night, the tradition of bringing the wage packet home 'unbroken' in fact persisted in many households. A man finished his week's work and then laid his pay packet on the kitchen table for his wife. She worked out the week's running costs . . . and handed her husband his pocket money. *She* was in charge. The tenement hoose was her domain, and because what these women managed to do – both within and beyond this domain – was never understood or taken on board, the feminists of the 1970s mistakenly cast them in the role of victim rather than heroine.

Men knew to keep well out of the way of anything within the wife's domain. For example, Graham Hoey, born in 1922, had a clothes shop (Hoey's) in Springburn and recalls men embarrassed to be seen shopping:

> We'd an enormous trade in men's caps. The back door on Gourlay Street was a fascinating place to be because it entered straight into the men's department and the technique, if you were a man working in Springburn and wanted a new cap, was you came and opened the door and still keeping your hand on the handle of the door, you said, 'A bunnet,' and somebody gave you one and you put it on your head and said, 'Aye, that's fine,' and gave your one-and-eleven [1s./11d.] or whatever it was and got out the door as quickly as possible! They were terrified.
>
> It was totally embarrassing. Nothing was ever bought by a workman except that. The wife bought a semmit and drawers, wife bought socks for him, wife bought everything

for him. He didn't like to be seen, so it was in the door, as I
say, and we couldn't have the caps at the far end of the
department, they had to be up at the door, so that they
could just grab them, put them on their head and out again.
It was quite an extraordinary state of affairs when you think
about it now![1]

Shopping was a 'wumminly' thing, as was cooking and
cleaning. Angry feminists in the 1970s read this as gender
typecasting or worse, victimisation of women by men, but it
wasn't. It was tradition. The women didn't want the men to
do the shopping, and the men didn't want the women to
work.

As Alexander McArthur and H. Kingsley Long wrote in
their much maligned novel of life in the Gorbals in the
twenties and thirties, *No Mean City* (published 1935), the
'common ambition' of tenement-dwelling young men is
'that one day they would get "a good, clean home" with a
pretty young wife to look after it'. Henceforth, the pretty
young wife would not do paid work, she would not seek
employment outside the house. This was as true in Maria
Fyfe's family as in many others:

No, my mother never worked a day's paid work after the day
she got married. That was the tradition among many
working class women.

I thought that that might be because women had so many
children, but no, it was tradition even if you had one child
only. This might seem a bit stultifying to some women in
today's society, but not so in tenement society, which was so

close and yet open to neighbours and all kinds of goings-on, to which I will come.

In 1950 there were around half a million Glaswegians in employment (out of a total population of some 1.1 million). Of these there were almost exactly twice as many men (some 343,000) recorded as working for a wage as women (some 170,000) . . . Gender also determined working lives – with Glaswegian men's lives dominated by a life-time of paid labour fulfilling their preordained role as 'breadwinners', whilst women toiled as wage slaves in paid labour up to getting married or having their first child, then their lives became dominated by the unpaid drudgery of the home.[2]

There was drudgery both for the men in the workplace and the women in the home. No doubt about that. But equally, just as there was a hidden ethos of camaraderie in the way men worked in the shipyards, so there was a special character to the life of the tenement women, a certain spirit which infused the community and became the thing that even today people weep for and miss.

In 1915, a year into the First World War, landlords and factors opportunistically put up tenement rents, hoping to cash in on the influx of munitions workers into the city. Up to 20,000 Glasgow households were affected.

Now, as far as the tenement women were concerned the factors fell within their domain. They were the ones who had to pay the rent. Most men don't even know how much the rent was for a house, so the women were the ones who had to do something about it. Notices appeared in tenement windows declaring the 'RENT STRIKE

INCREASES. WE ARE NOT REMOVING'. One of the demonstrators' placards read: 'While my father is a prisoner in Germany, the landlord is attacking our home.'[3]

In several tenement closes, first in Govan and later on the north bank of the Clyde in Partick, women pledged themselves not to pay the increases and warned that they intended to resist any attempt made to evict anyone for refusing to pay them.

Each close elected a committee of two women and organised outside meetings. Over 500 women handed in their names as pickets. In 1984, almost seventy-five years later, in a film called *Red Skirts on Clydeside*, Jenny Woodly and Christine Bellamy for Sheffield Film Co-op assembled women who were either related to people who took part in the strike or had an expert knowledge of it, including Jessie Findlay, a political activist who gave a most moving and faithful account of how the women made the strike a moment that defined once and for all who was in charge of tenement society:

> Now, as far as the rent strike was concerned, the women played a very important part in this, and Partick and Govan were the hotbeds at that time. When there was an eviction of anyone, doesnae matter who they were, the women got busy. At that time of course the back courts of tenements were congenial to having an outdoor meeting, because all they needed was for the speaker to get on the top of the midden, or the refuse heap, and speak, and the women in the houses just opened their window and hung out the window and listened to what was being said.
>
> Now, they were organised in different groups and when

it came to an eviction, the women came out with bells or football rattles and whenever they started ringing the bell and winding these rattles, [the pickets] gathered. They all had certain areas to gather in and they gathered. And of course they were then told who was likely to be evicted . . .

At that time, the Sheriff officer could only put anyone out between the hours of ten in the morning and four in the afternoon, so the women could go away until ten in the morning. [One day] they all gathered at this particular house . . . a Mrs Noble, and she refused to pay her rent of course and she was going to be the test case. [The factor] was going to put her out. She'd only a room and a kitchen, she had three boys and to begin with she suffered greatly because of that. However, they all went down and they stood in the close at the stairs, and whenever he came, this Sheriff officer – they had small bags of soot and piece meal made up – they tied them up tight and they threw them at him.[4]

Then, apparently with the assistance of two soldiers, who were on leave and happened to be standing in the close at the time, the women threw him into the midden.

They took him and just threw him into the midden! And that was the end of the Sheriff officer.[5]

Among those who led the tenement women against the factors, were Helen Crawfurd, Agnes Dollan and Mary Barbour. Crawfurd was the wife of a Presbyterian minister and a formidable suffragette, who went to prison for her pains to get women the vote. She used her maiden name,

Jack, when on active service, and was one of the founder members of the British Communist Party. Dollan was more of a backroom girl, but no less committed. Married to Paddy Dollan (then a journalist) of the ILP, she represented an important link between the tenement women and a number of male ILP activists.

Then there was Mary Barbour, who, in 1915, organised the tenant committees on whose strategy the women drove out the sheriff's officers and resisted evictions. Later, she became Glasgow Town Council's first Labour woman councillor, representing Govan Fairfield ward. Barbour was also a GP and opened, as I have mentioned, Glasgow's first family planning centre. She campaigned ceaselessly on issues affecting women, mothers, and children and, later, organised seaside outings for the children of the Glasgow poor.

The connection to these three impressive women, with their socialist, suffragette and peace-movement affiliations – there was simultaneously a terrific rumpus over Britain's needless war with Germany – is highly significant. It gives women in Glasgow a political dimension that has all but been ignored in the social history of Clydeside, adds lustre to our perception of the women themselves, and gives a whole new perspective on life in the Glasgow tenements, as I will show.

The rent strike was a tremendous achievement. It was a great victory for what Helen Crawfurd described as a 'women's fight'. The tenement women won. Faced with such solidarity and effective community action, the government conceded defeat, passing the Rent Restriction Act (1915) which froze rent levels and introduced State intervention in the private housing rental market for the first time. But the victory was shamefully buried, some say because the Clydesider men wanted the limelight. For instance, Willie Gallacher, one of the leaders of the Clyde Workers' Committee during the First World War, dismissed the rent strike in a few sentences in his report on the Clyde.

Woodly and Bellamy found and interviewed Mary Barbour's two granddaughters, Mary and Jessie, who pointed to the independence of the tenement women behind the strike, quite at odds with the traditional view of their subservience to their macho men folk. Said Mary Barbour:

> It must have taken some doing. I mean . . . when they go home and tell their husbands, their husbands will say, 'Oh, you're not doing that.' . . . But they all did it, they all defied their husbands . . . and it really was very, very good.[6]

Significantly, the women were backed by the Co-operative Women's Guilds. These guilds were set up in Glasgow from the 1890s onwards. According to former curator of the People's Palace, now Director of the Smith Art Gallery in Stirling, Elspeth King,[7] Kinning Park Co-operative Society (south of the Clyde, west of the Gorbals, and another community, like Springburn, Govan and the Gorbals, rich in reminiscence) is credited with creating the first Women's Guild. King, who was another telling voice in *Red Skirts on Clydeside* and wrote about the Co-op in *The Hidden History of Glasgow's Women* (1993).

The Co-operative Society was a kind of touchstone in tenement society. Those that can remember the chain of stores in the fifties tend to think only of the quarterly 'divi', the dividend or share of the profits that accrued to everyone who shopped there and was a member. Receipts were given with every purchase no matter how small, and these were logged against the member's number. Every family knew their Co-op number as well as they did their own street number. At the end of the quarter, purchases were added and the dividend calculated. The money was either added to the Share Book, if the member was in a position to save, or spent on necessities like school clothes and shoes. In 1952 the average rate of dividend paid out was one shilling and sevenpence [1s./7d.] in the pound . . . The divi was a significant economic fillip, always providing you could afford to shop there in the first place. As Ina Wotherspoon put it:

> I don't think half the people would have survived without the Co-operative, you know. I think eventually people must have cleared their debt as the family grew up, but the Co-operative was a constant lifeline.[8]

But the Co-operative Society meant much more than the 'divi' to the tenement women, as Agnes McDonald and William McGinlay observe:

> The Co-operative had their own butcher's shop, their own chemist's, their own furniture store, their own draper's store, their own optician's, and every wee part of Springburn there'd be another grocer's, another dairy belonging to the Co-op. On Petershill Road there was a Co-operative fish shop and a clothes shop.[9]

They had homes for their customers. If you'd been ill and produced your doctor's line that you'd been really, really ill, you could have a week or a fortnight maybe at Largs or Galashiels, and they'd another one I think at Dunoon. They got that and all they did was pay their own fare. It was a beautiful hotel that one at Largs, oh yes. It was like a first-class hotel! Oh, they got their meals and the people say that the meals were marvellous; oh yes, it was very good.[10]

More even than this, at its inception the Co-op was a political ideal. There was a genuine expectation that Co-operative principles could create a better world. And this principle was the one by which the women of the tenements went about their daily business, as Elspeth King explains:

The Church was the spiritual order and the Co-op the temporal. Evenings were spent in Co-op halls, singing in Co-op choirs, acting in Co-op drama groups, being involved in any number of educational activities run under the Co-op umbrella. For many working-class women in Glasgow, the Co-op offered a framework to life and a support system. It offered the opportunity to become involved in community and political life and it taught the basics of democracy . . . Shieldhall, Hutchesontown and Tradeston had large manufacturing plants. Those in Springburn who were not employed in the railway works were employed by Springburn Co-operative Society . . .

The Co-operative movement disseminated principles which are now curiously out of fashion. The movement spread the belief that if co-operation were pursued in preference to competition, and that if people worked on the principle of mutual aid, the resulting society would be better.[11]

Tenement life was in many ways the model in the making of the new socialist state, to which, as we shall see, some extremely militant Glaswegian activists were committed, men like John Maclean, James Maxton and William Gallacher, the so-called Red Clydesiders from whom the suffragettes, the ILP, the anti-war lobby, and the rent strike leaders all drew inspiration.

For the tenement women, radical politics were of no great or lasting interest, however. They were *living* the 'co-operative' socialist ideal:

The community spirit of the tenement, the neighbourliness, was the thing . . .[12]

There were family loyalties, tenement loyalties – loyalties within the close and among perhaps two or three closes, and street loyalties.

I can remember working-class families in the 1950s who were lifelines for poorer families in need, offering food and kindness and any help they could. The Glasgow camaraderie then was very strong indeed.[13]

The nature of a woman's work in the tenements was of necessity collaborative, a model of *co-operation*, and it is to the loss of this principle of community and co-operation to which people respond with nostalgia today. No sentimentality, no blind yearning for poverty and filth, just good sense, a desire to recover the co-operative principle on which tenement life turned, which flies in the face of the competitiveness and selfishness that drives so many of us today.

The women organised life in the tenements in such a way that the spirit of community thrived; and it was a matter of good organisation. As Seán Damer observed, 'The tenement stair was self-evidently a natural setting for the social organisation of the women.'

> Mothers took turns at cleaning the stairs, scrubbing the cement steps and then decorating the edges with marvellous patterns in pipe-clay.[14]

Crawford Dick recalled:

> Most of these little closes were virtual villages in themselves. The senior citizen, the longest tenant, was basically in charge and everybody had their day when they cleaned the stair or the close mouth or whatever, and the whiting went on the edge of the steps. There was a very strict sort of discipline in the court living, and even the use of the back courts. If you were the last tenant moving into that close you were told which was your day for the washing green and the washing house and that was controlled until you moved up a social status within the close mouth itself.[15]

> They had a wash house in the back court and everyone got a turn, everyone in that close got a turn of the wash house. You got to take your turn. Some would take a whole morning, and somebody else would get in after them.[16]

There was a strict rota for its use – as there was for washing
the common stair.[17]

As Gorbalite Rita Moffat points out, 'One of the biggest
crimes for a women was to lose, or be late for the handing
over of the wash house key.' It was the worst thing to let
anyone down, so much so that losing the wash house key
became another butt for music hall and pantomime jokes.
It was a matter of co-operation for the common good.

These women were human, of course. Within the community there were elements of competitiveness and one-
upmanship. There was a social ladder in tenement society:

Well we started in just a single apartment when I was just a
wee thing, in a tenement close, and then we moved three
closes down to a room and a kitchen. The toilet was on the
stair. Then we moved across the landing to another hoose
that had two beds and a kitchen and one in the room – that
kind of thing . . .[18]

Inevitably, some families who had two rooms looked down
on those who had one. Also, respectability was, as ever in
society, a motivation, particularly in the tenement women's
preoccupation with 'keeping things decent'. Whitening
the steps with pipe-clay was not the half of it:

The front door-brasses in each flat always gleamed, as they
generally took a great pride in 'first impressions'. Doors
would be varnished and my mother was a dab-hand at
'combing' wood-grain effects on the surface.[19]

Rita Moffat recalls there was a competitive element, too:

> You were very much judged as a woman on how early your
> washing went out in the morning – six a.m. wasn't unusual
> in the summer as there was always a battle for the washing
> lines and poles. It was always a way too of displaying your
> prized clothes and bed linen. Weans and baby clothes were
> always a competition. I remember two women who battled
> it out every dry day to show off what dresses their respective
> daughters wore. One was handy with a sewing machine, so
> she always had two lines full of brightly coloured dresses.
> Sheets wi' holes, and the not so nice stuff, were kept for the
> indoor clothes pulley.[20]

Pride, an emotion echoed in the husbands' work ethic, was
mixed up with one-upmanship, but the one-upmanship
could never go so far as to override the essentially
co-operative nature of the laundry work. Or tenement society
would break down. Use of the laundry was, by its very
nature, collaborative, and there was a very real effort to lift
everything out of the dustbin culture into which life could
so easily have sunk.

> The material poverty of tenement life brought its own brand
> of co-operation among the women who were trapped
> there . . . living in a tenement in cramped conditions and in
> close proximity to neighbours with whom you shared the
> wash house and stairhead toilets, enforced the need to
> co-operate.[21]

In any case, keeping things spotlessly clean wasn't just about wanting to be thought more respectable than your neighbour, it was justified on the altar of necessity – to keep infection at bay. 'My mother used to wash my face with a loofah! Chickenpox, scarlet fever etc. were killers in those days – not to mention the big killer that TB was,' recalls Rita Moffat, who can list 'at least a dozen people whose relatives died with it'.

Everything that was done was an elegant balance of necessity and love for family and the community in which the socialist principle of co-operation first appeared. It was another 'wumminly' thing.

The women comforted their neighbours, the wives of too often drunken, violent husbands. They took their neighbours into their own homes and tended them and their children. The tenement children belonged not only to a family, but to the whole close community, playing all together every day in the back courts and streets, binding the 'close' families together, with their mothers often as not leaning out of the tenement windows and throwing down a 'piece' (sandwich) to them. Even in the 1950s and early '60s, Gurdev Pall, who was born in Logan Street, Oatlands, at the back of Govan Ironworks, belonged like this to her close and neighbouring closes:

> There would be half a dozen of us there [in the back court], and that would be us muckin' about . . . [and] if you were kind of hungry you would shout up, 'Ma, can you make me a jelly piece?' And it was jam and butter spread over it or sometimes just sugar and it was spread and it was the thick loaf . . . what was it . . . Mother's Pride . . . it's called the pan

loaf, the pan loaf, yeah. And even though with my mum's
limited English she knew that if the kids shouted up and she
happened to be in at the time, the back window would go
up and the bread, wrapping and that would be thrown out
the window.[22]

The street was our playground and safe enough. Mothers
had no need to be anxious to let us out to play
unaccompanied, as they do today.[23]

**Playing in the back courts and streets was the stuff of earliest
memory for all tenement children, as Maria Fyfe recalls:**

I had a wooden peerie [spinning top], and took ages to learn
how to flick the thong so that it would spin properly and hit
the ground and keep moving, instead of falling over pathetically.
All the children created simple designs on their peeries with
coloured chalks, so that our artistic efforts could be shown
to good effect when the peerie spun round and round . . .
  In the summer there was so much going on in the
street . . . Girls sat on the pavement with their backs against
the grey sandstone tenement walls, crocheting blankets for
their dolls' prams with wool unravelled from old cardigans.
Or somebody would bring out a length of old washing rope
and we would play skipping games while we chanted some
doggerel:

House to let, apply within
Lady put out for drinking gin
Gin, you know, is a very bad thing,
So Jeannie goes out and Mary comes in.

Another favourite ditty went:

> There she goes, there she goes,
> Like an elephant on her toes,
> Look at her feet, she thinks she's neat,
> Holes in her stockings and dirty feet.

> Mothers sat on kitchen chairs. Knitting or making fireside
> rugs out of small scraps of cloth. Boys ran after the lorries
> hurtling down the street, grabbing a hold of the tail end for
> a hurl and jumping off when they slowed for the corner.

Girls, and sometimes boys, could also be found playing shops in the muddy earth of the back courts. Second generation Italian-Glaswegian Tony Jaconelli (his father came from Italy when he was eight) remembers how it was in 1930s and '40s Shettleston:

> Playing shops with imaginary goods, sometimes made from
> clay which appeared miraculously because our court was of
> earth . . . I cannot recall whether the 'shop' came first or the
> discovery of some clay prompted it. Transactions were paid
> for with pieces of broken crockery and pieces of the china
> with gold gilt on them were considered to be 'sovies', or
> sovereigns.[24]

Jean Kendal feels certain that shops had been played for a century or more before it became her and her friends' favourite game:

It would start with somebody saying, 'Come on, we'll play at a wee shop.' We never set out to rival Galbraith's or Lipton's, or even the Co-op. Our wee shop was modelled on the little corner shops – a 'Jenny a' thing', where you could buy food and a wide range of household goods – like Humphrey's along the road.

We set up our shop in a corner of the back court, using upturned cardboard boxes as our counter. My granny lived in a block of flats, three sides of a rectangle . . . Most of our stock we mustered from the area that formed the fourth side of the rectangle. Once, a tenement building stood there. I believe it had been bombed in the war. Although the rubble had been largely removed, a bit of digging unearthed small 'treasures'. Nuts and bolts and other ironmongery were plentiful. Once we found a tiny fluted baking tin that we used to make our compressed-earth pies . . .

[For] our currency system, we used broken crockery that we found on the bombsite . . . China was worth more than earthenware: patterned shards were of a higher denomination than plain: any piece with gold was very special; we called that a sovereign. Most intriguing was a piece of blue and white crockery we called delft . . . Delftfield pottery was last produced in 1824. From where did our knowledge come? I believe we were passing on folk memories, that 'oor wee shop' had been played in some form or another by many generations of children . . .[25]

The Delftfield Pottery was, in fact, set up in 1748 by brothers Laurence and Robert Dinwiddie, who were prosperous tobacco merchants; the site chosen was on the north bank of the River Clyde near the Broomielaw Quay in Anderston.

Street and back court games for boys included marbles (jorries), cowboys and Indians, 'fitba' of course – it was every boy's dream to play for Rangers or Celtic – and hide-and-seek (either release or kick-the-can).

> We played kick-the-can, and 'release' – you'd have two teams of maybe eight or ten, and one team would be what we called 'het'. And the other team would run away, they went and tried to hide, and then the team that was 'het' would chase them, and if you caught someone you'd put him against a wall, called the den, and you'd maybe to guard him, and they'd run off and catch someone else, and then someone could run through and if you could get in and shout 'release' then everyone in the den would be set free. It took maybe an hour to catch all the team, but you could release them and it could go on all day.[26]

> Kick-the-can was played with an empty tin as the den. So long as the keeper [of the can] had a foot on it his charges were secure and could not be freed. If you showed yourself then you would probably be 'spied'. To free those held captive you had to wait until the keeper left the can unattended and kick it as far away as possible, allowing everybody to find a hiding place before the one who was het could retrieve the can.[27]

Tony Jaconelli remembered another version called Alevio, 'which might have derived its name from the French, *allez vous?*, it had one variation and that was that any free player could release those caught by running through the den calling, "Alevio!"'

These games could last for very long spells and got very complicated. No one was ever sure who all the other players were. The participants changed constantly as players left, for whatever reason, or new players joined in.

Street football was of course endemic to the tenement villages, though the Glasgow police, implementing a rather poor PR strategy, made a habit of intervening. Nevertheless, games could continue in the tenements for hours. Here, John Pollock recalls the way things were in a corner of tenements just north of Cowcaddens:

At Seamore Street and the corner of Napiershall Street there was a lamppost, and at the corner of Seamore Street and St Clair Street there was a right angle and another lamppost. These were the goals. We used to play at night until we saw the pubs closing, that meant it was time we were home you know, in the light summer nights.

The goalie's job was also to look out for the police, because at that time they chased us, you know. The police would catch you and take your name, but we were never charged because my father was a policeman anyway, you know? The thing is you see, the ground floor windows, people lived on the ground floor and there were no gardens, just a pavement and you could break a window playing with a ball, and of course people objected to that. When the police came, we used to run through the close into the back court and there was railings [on the dykes], and you knew when your railings were slightly wider and you could sneak through, and if they chased you they couldn't catch you and sometimes you just had to run and leave the ball,

you know? They loved catching you for playing football in
the street.[28]

More sacred even than football, because it was something
of a rite of passage, was 'dreeping' in the back courts: 'It
became . . . sort of, when you got older you had to jump
higher and higher dykes or bigger distances in-between,'
said Charles McLaughlin.

'Was there a challenge?'

'Yes, you had to prove your manhood.'

'Were there any accidents at all?'

'Quite often you had broken legs or broken arms as
people fell off.'[29]

Accidents did happen, as Colin MacFarlane writes in
The Real Gorbals Story:

> Some of the walls had sharp iron railings and we all knew it
> was dangerous . . . there were rumours that the nearby
> Caledonian Road graveyard was full of children who had
> been skewered while playing . . .[30]

But the accidents didn't seem to deter anyone, even girls,
as Maria Fyfe recalls:

> Govanhill was where I acquired the heritage of every
> Glaswegian tenement child. I, too, ran along the top of the
> high, back court brick wall – for some reason called a dyke –
> and dreeped fearfully to the ground . . .

When it was too wet to play outside, young Marie McDonald
McLaughlin Lawrie would organise 'sterr parties'—

Stair parties. We'd get dressed up and borrow some make-up. And our mums would give us treats for the party, like a packet of biscuits or a bag of sweets to be divided up between us.

The stair well [in the close] was like a huge echo chamber, with the most wonderful acoustics. We'd sing songs that floated up the stairs into every 'hoose', where mothers could listen and be reassured their children were safe and happy.[31]

Everyone sang. A typical evening in, pre-television, involved a sing-song, but of course it helped if you had a voice like Marie, later to find fame as Lulu. Her father was an offal dresser in the Glasgow Meat Market and occasional shipyard worker. The Lawries lived in Soho Street, then Garfield Street, in Glasgow's East End, although Marie was born in 1948 in Lennoxtown, far to the north of the inner city. Her father told her she had a voice 'like a coalman', but anyone who has read Lulu's autobiography knows that it was rough-hewn at the coalface of life in Glasgow, and can imagine a hard, very human expression of all that made her echoing up the cold staircase of the tenement where she lived.

Another clear and widely held memory of tenement life centred around the annual communal bonfire.

I was talking to my friend there, Charlie Chambers, he lives in Rutherglen, about a time I used to find exciting when I was young. At the end of October, November – Halloween cum Guy Fawkes, as we called it, 'Bonfire Night' – we used to have a bonfire. We would spend about two or three weeks before that going all round the district trying to get wood for the bonfire and while you were storing the wood people would be stealing your wood for their bonfire and we would be in other places stealing their wood. This seemed to go on.[32]

Then, of course, there was Hogmanay when the new year would be seen in on the Clyde by shipyard hooters and ships' horns and clamour everywhere, much more significant than Christmas, and an occasion that took you inside a whole series of tenement homes.

The principal thing ye had tae get was a bottle of whisky for first-footing. You had to save up for it: it wasn't easy to afford. You saved for it. So ye had a wee half bottle. So before ye went tae your eventual party, ye went tae friends. And ye went in there with yer bottle. And ye had to be dark-haired. If ye weren't dark-haired ye had to carry a piece of coal. If ye were light-haired, if they hadnae been first-footed before they probably wouldnae let ye in. They'd tell ye to go back, 'Yer bad luck!'

But if ye went in there, the first thing they did was offer you a drink, a shot of whisky like. So, you drank the whisky and they wished you all the best. Then, immediately after, you gave them a shot of your bottle. On the table they had the shortbread and the currant cake, the black bun, and they'd offer ye a piece of that. Ye stayed and spoke tae them for a wee while like, and then ye left and ye had tae go see another one . . .

Now most places there wasn't a big carpet, ye just took away the wee carpets, and ye were all squashed in and dancing like the Gay Gordons, or the quickstep, foxtrot, waltzes. Just in a wee room, all right together . . . The table was put in the other room and it [the room] was completely bare. So it was big enough to do the dancing and the games. Oh you would have thirty or forty people in a wee room playing a reel. It was really good.[33]

Then there were the summertime back court concerts, as Norman Ross and Annie Docherty recall:

Some of these were performed by local children who each did their party piece, and sometimes parents could be encouraged to perform also. We also had wandering performers who went from back court to back court. One of these was Charlie Chaplin, and a second was The Major who apparently had been one during the war and acted this part well, singing posh songs. Another was a coloured guy, who called himself Darkie Marshall. He played the bones and spoons (or clappers as we called them). I hope the politically correct mob don't come after me, but we never used the name as an insult and it was never accepted as one. His son (guess his name), went to school with us and was part of our gang, and his colour apart from his name was never mentioned.[34]

I remember the back court concerts well. I was usually one of the performers and I remember the boys sitting up on the dykes booing us, but we were not deterred.

Characters were the Clean Tottie and Jonie Campsie. Jonie had a plate in his head from the First World War and he would march up and down the street like a soldier with a gang of us kids following him.

As for 'Darkie Marshall', we all knew and loved him. He used to come into our house and play the clappers, along with Joe Donnelly who played the fiddle. We called him Darkie to his face. To us it was just his name and that was all. There was never any thought of colour.[35]

Everyone wanted to learn to dance, and most took their first steps on the pavement or back court in the 'clabber jiggings', as McArthur and Long describe faithfully in *No Mean City*:

Dancing was then, in 1921, and still is, the most popular sport in Glasgow's slum land. And some fine dancers have been bred in the tenements . . . Outside the Rose Street pub there were only two couples dancing, a young man and his girl and two other girls waltzing together. A ragged, bleary-eyed fellow, lamentably undrunk, was playing his mouth organ like an artist . . .

'Wull we split that couple?' said Bobbie to his friend.

Johnnie laughed and did not answer. When the girls whirled within reach, he stepped forward neatly and took the bigger of the two round the waist. Bobbie caught the other and waltzed away with her so that the step was never broken.

At the conclusion of that dance someone gave the mouth-organ player a penny. He changed from *The Merry Widow* to a one-step. Johnnie danced that and then gave his partner the go-by, but Bobbie and the smaller girl went on dancing until the 'orchestra' stopped playing. A considerable crowd had gathered, whistling the tunes and clapping their hands to the beat of the music. Bobbie and his partner were good. The Gorbals pavement critics approved of them.

'We'll be seeing you at the jiggings yet, Bobbie Hurley,' came a voice from the crowd.

'Ay, and Lily wi' him, likely,' shrilled a woman.

The young couple broke awa from one another somewhat sheepishly, and Bobbie rejoined his friend.

'It's a fact,' said Johnnie dispassionately. 'I've seen worse dancers than you and Lily McKay at the jiggings. Ah'm gaun up to the hoose for ma tea.'[36]

Jiggings are organised dances at dancehalls, Clabber jiggings are spontaneous pavement or back court events, popular right into the fifties, as Seán Damer recalls:

You'd put up a washing line and hing old blankets over it, sort of like a stage. We all brought our chairs out. Some would hing oot the windae, and everybody would give us a song or a dance or something. Sometimes there would be a squeeze box or a banjo or a penny-whistle, or a moothie. It was great.[37]

You *had* to be able to dance, and the women who produced and reproduced the co-operative culture of the tenements, saw to it that everyone did.

Meanwhile, community life in the close ebbed and flowed year in, year out, thanks to the women.

Neighbours were neighbours in those days, people in the same street would look out for each other.[38]

Your neighbours used to come . . . if they wanted a wee bit butter they came in and took a wee bit butter, and if you

needed sugar they gave you sugar. It was great, it was
fantastic! It was more like the one big, big family.[39]

You borrowed and lent with your neighbour, and nipped in
for a cup of sugar, partly because you were poor and
needed the sugar, partly because you valued your neighbour's company and wanted to sit down, have a cup of tea
and a blether. And so doors were left open and mutual
trust arose as a value in working-class tenement society.

Ye could leave yer doors open. I've seen every door being left
open on the landing. Every door, for three stairs up, every
door left open. Oh, no fear of burglars or anything at all. But
oh, as I keep sayin' tae ye, Springburn at that time really was
an entirely different place to what it is today.[40]

There was a great homely feeling. If you lived in that block of
red sandstone tenements across there, you never locked your
door. I'm not saying that neighbours trailed in and out your
house all day. But ye never locked your door. And if ye had
children, they didn't play oot in the street. They played in the
back court. And they came up and the door would be open,
ye know, it would just be open. It would never be locked.[41]

Showing you how reliable people were in these days. Being
trustworthy, people who had a letter box would tie the key
onto a bit of string, put the string onto the outside door
handle and then drop the key into the letter box, so it hung
inside the door. So you used to see bits of string sticking out
of letter boxes. This was people's keys!

There was very few house-breakings going on. Generally

people who were working class never stole from each other . . .
Nobody thought of sneaking in the way they do today.[42]

Doors were left open in celebration of this, not simply because there was nothing worth stealing. Anything could be nicked and sold for a few vital pence in Paddy's Market or the Barras, and in any case the inhabitants of these tenements were not uniformly poor, as I have said. One or two were even rich, but could be just as trusting of poor neighbours.

Tommy Gilmour, foremost boxing promoter in Scotland today, was born on the south side of Glasgow in Oatlands, in April 1952.

The area itself was poor, but we were very wealthy because we had betting shops, although my mother came from the notoriously poor tenement known as the Dwellings, in Bridgeton.

Two generations of Gilmours were rooted in Glasgow's East End. Tommy's father wanted to be a fighter, but his career was cut short by cataracts. He became instead a manager-trainer, 'Scotland's Mr Big in boxing', a 'Mr Fix it'. The Gilmour story begins with Grandfather Jim, who boxed for the Olympic team in 1920 and was at one time champion of Great Britain and Denmark, 'the latter crown won when he beat the Danish champion, which was the way in those days.'

Jim Gilmour had two gymnasiums: Barrack Street and the Scottish National in Olympia Street, Bridgeton Cross. Like the celebrated Kid Lewis, who would ride in an open car down Whitechapel in London's East End flinging handfuls of silver, Jim Gilmour would distribute half crowns to the poor in Bridgeton on his way from his home in Tullis Street to the Olympia. 'That was the way in those days for the wealthier ones,' says Tommy. Jim was a show-man and a gambler and had frontline pitches at major Scottish racecourses.

The point is that the Gilmours had money, a lot of it, but mutual trust was as much a value on which life turned as it was for the poor of the area. When Tommy's father (also called Tommy) married, he set up home with his wife Lizzie in Rutherglen Road, where eventually they were 'probably the wealthiest family in the whole area':

> We had this Ford Zephyr, we had a fridge, we also had a television and on the Queen's coronation the whole close came in to watch it in our house because we were the only people who had television. We had the television, the fridge and the car. We stayed up the close, we never locked the door. Such was the trust in the neighbours.

Lizzie Gilmour will have seen to that. Co-operation, give-and-take, mutual trust made life possible in tenement society. This willing participation is the opposite of what Jimmy Reid referred to as the rat race, which is all about competition and 'entails the loss of your dignity and human spirit'.

For these women the human spirit was central to the whole thing. They were proactive in the family's economic survival, and in the survival of friends and neighbours in the closes round about.

Seán Damer points out that it was 'the women who sold goods which fell off the back of a passing cart. It was the women who got the intelligence of a new consignment of fruit and veg at the local shops, and told their neighbours. It was the women who crowded the warrant sales [enforced sales of debtors' possessions by Sheriff officers], bought up all the goods for a song, threatening and warning off dealers and outsiders, and giving the goods back to the victims.'[43]

Crucial to survival was the menage the women organised among themselves in the closes, like the 'tontine' in Liverpool and the 'club' system in London's East End. It was a way for a network of local women to buy into a fund and save money. There was pride in what you could achieve among yourselves, even without much money, and ways of saving and making a little extra were often collaborative community procedures.

> Any odd remnants my mother would pick up and made [something out of them]. Oh, she used to have piles and piles of wool, a big table full of wool that she knitted, for neighbours and that. The wee shop that she used to go and get her patterns in. The woman says, 'Oh you knit, Mrs Milby.' She says, 'Yes.' 'Oh,' she says, 'I have a daughter in Canada with two children,' she says. 'I wonder would you knit something for them?' My mother says, 'Certainly.' Of course she paid her for it. And that is what she was doing it for, payment. That was always an extra shilling or two.[44]

Once the business of the back court wash house was transferred to the more public 'steamie' – precursor to the launderette except that what you got was a boiler, a sink, and an iron – there was a unique opportunity to express the community spirit. As Colin MacFarlane tells us in *The Real Gorbals Story*:

> Posh ladies, of course, never went to such places; it was a strictly working-class domain . . . That patter was usually up to the best standards of any music-hall routine, with gossip and scandal flying everywhere.
>
> 'Hey, did yer hear aboot her up the road wi' aw the carry-oan?'
>
> 'No, white happened? Is she still up tae her auld tricks, is she?'
>
> 'Aye, well, ye know that fella she left her man fur? Well, he's ended up in jail again . . .'[45]

It was also the women of Glasgow who created and first operated the famous city markets – Paddy's Market between Bridgegate [the Briggait] and Saltmarket, and the Barras, east of Glasgow Cross, bounded by the Gallowgate and Ross, Bain and Stevenson Streets. However, because it was above-line trade, this womanly province was soon invaded by men. Wrote Elspeth King:

> Both of these markets had their origin in the nineteenth-century rag and secondhand clothing trade . . . A woman with no trade, no income and no means of support could always sell rags. The rag-wives were at the bottom of a vast economic trade, which started with the gathering of the material. There were huge rag stores all over Glasgow (the bane of the Fire Brigade because of the dangers of

spontaneous combustion), from which the goods were exported to Ireland, or sent to the mills to be turned into paper or rag-flock for bedding.[46]

Writing of a covered market in Greendyke Street, just south of the Barras and east of Paddy's Market, in 1917, Peter Fyfe, the Chief Sanitary Inspector for Glasgow, marvelled at the body of women who ran it.

One of the mysteries of the underworld of the city. Busy human 'ants' may be observed now and again scurrying out of closes with huge bundles on their backs, and, if followed, may be seen picking out the usable from the unusable, the woollen from the cotton, and generally classifying their wares for sale.

Likening the tenement women to ants is apt, because ants are organised, collaborative, and go about their business largely unnoticed. Continued Peter Fyfe:

Some of these 'collectors', like those in the higher walks of life, occasionally seek to make a 'corner' in such material. To secure a 'big stock' and wait for 'the rise' is the game of some rag pickers as well as the market manipulators. One of them filled her two-apartment house four to five feet deep with rags and cast-off clothing, till Mr Waddell and his Fire Brigade found her in flames one night, quenched her rags and her miserly ardour with cold water, and covered the back court with the accumulation of years.

Maggie McIver was 'The Barras Queen'. Born Margaret Russell, she married James McIver in 1898.

> They put their savings into a small fruit shop. They got a few barrows, then started to rent barrows to other traders in the years following the First World War, then by the 1920s they owned the land and rented out the barrows – at one point over three hundred barrows for rent. The Barrowland ('Barras' locally) was underway. Got a roof covering it in 1928. Officially recognised and opened by local Labour MP Tom Maxton in 1931. By 1958, when Maggie McIver died, she was a millionaire.[47]

Ellis Cohen ran a stall there for two years and saved up enough to stock a little shop.

> You got a permanently built stall and you rented it. You came down and there was a queue. The woman who owned the market place and her son, said, 'What do you want? Do you want a single stall, a double stall, one with a light?' So-much got you a light, five bob [5s./-] got you a stall. And before the day was out, when you'd had a chance to get a few bob in, three or four in the afternoon, they'd come round for the money.
>
> My hands had great hacks on the back it was so cold working at the market. Glasgow had a dressmaking industry. Now I could go to a dressmaking factory and they could sell me the trimmings from dresses, right? My mother had a sewing machine and sewed them up two together into a nice little scarf. Another thing, people with stalls at the market would come along on a Saturday morning and offer

you something sale or return. And a chap came along one morning with a whole assortment of brassieres, which he knew nothing about, couldn't tell you anything about the sizes. Nevertheless, he said I could sell them for a tanner [6d.] or a bob, or what have you. A young boy used to work with me and one of our regular lines was tartan tennis balls, and he used to shout, 'Get your tartan balls here,' and he had two balls in a brassiere.

In the Barras, the guys selling mainly ladies' dresses were guys with big, big lorries and their patter was good. But many a time a patter salesman would sell a lot of things. He'd sell blankets and he'd say, 'One, two, three, four blankets, two sheets, pillows, blah, blah, blah, thirty quid. I'm not asking you thirty. Fifteen? I wouldn't even ask you fifteen,' and then you'd get the whole thing down to about a fiver and you thought you were getting something for nothing. It was all cheap stuff. But for a fiver it was worth it.

In her book *Barrowlands: A Glasgow Experience*, Nuala Naughton tells stallholder Frank Bennett's favourite story involving a punter who took a liking to an old stag's head on Frank's stall:

'How much?'
    'Twenty quid,' says Frank.
    'But it's only got one eye,' says the punter, to which Frank retorts, 'Aye, well if it had two eyes, Ah'd be wanting thirty.'[48]

The apocryphal Barras story is of an illiterate guy refused a job as toilet attendant, because he could hardly sign his name—

So, he was thrown back on his own resources. He became a midgie-raker, that is, one who goes round all the back court middens to see what he can 'rake up' from all the rubbish. It's amazing what people will throw out. In no time he had gathered enough to fill an old pram, and he wheeled it down to the Barras, where he took up a place on the fringe and sold his pram-load of odds and ends in a morning. He returned the next week with another load, and so on until he had to hire a cart to take his rubbish, now called 'antiques', to the market. He eventually made enough to become a licensed trader. The McIvers didn't worry how shaky his signature was.

He went on to used cars, and then to car hire, and eventually to plant hire with the aid of Enterprise grants and ended up a millionaire owning a trading estate on the Edinburgh Road. Even though he still had a difficulty signing his cheques, he was by no means stupid, merely unalphabetic or dyslexic. He was never able to write more than his name. When an associate asked him what he might have made had he been able to write, he replied, quite truthfully, 'A lavatory attendant'.[49]

Many of the stall holders were real comedians who were expert at jollying the crowd along. Amongst them was a man called Vickery who always drew large crowds and who was sure to have the crowds laughing at all the things he said. His repartee was first class, and he would come back at the crowd just like a flash and like all mock auctioneers, he was an opportunist. He used to maintain that the reason his goods were so cheap was because they were stolen. Just after the war when goods and materials were still rationed he obtained a supply of women's knickers. He gave his usual spiel about how the knickers were made from the finest American nylon and would stretch a mile before they would tear an inch, and even though it was breaking his heart he would give them away for two bob [2s./-] a pair. There was a big rush to buy and one woman was quick to notice a fault in her pair so she shouted out, 'I've been done!'. Vickery shouted, quick as a flash, 'There you are, another satisfied customer. Lucky knickers, half a crown a pair.'[50]

The tenement women were dealing with day-to-day life, but the principle of co-operation and community, which invested their routine, customs and existence, was simultaneously being expounded and encouraged by women who were more politically committed. For example, charities for the poor were being set up, notably the Guild of Aid in the Gorbals, under the aegis of renowned social worker Marald Grant from 1926, as Marald records in Elspeth King's *The Hidden History of Glasgow's Women*:

When I came in 1926 the poverty was at its height. In some of the houses I visited they hadn't even water . . . or just a wee sink in the window and this one tap . . . They had no gas even. They had a little coal fire, and I got swees and pots for them. Eventually, I got gas cookers installed in the hall. These houses were just appalling. In a number of houses there were eighteen children. There was at least three in Coburg Street with eighteen . . . I started a nursery, and it was a shilling a week that they paid, and we were open at eight in the morning so that the children could be looked after when their mothers were at work. The fathers couldn't get work.[51]

The Guild also offered domestic education, holidays for the poor, free medical attention for the young, an adoption agency for illegitimate babies, even dancing classes:

> There was a Miss White; she was sixteen or seventeen, and a dancing teacher. She took a hundred of our children for dancing lessons every year . . . A lot of them were in their bare feet at that time, and I had to find socks and shoes. The mothers would sew their children in for the winter . . . they wouldn't have thought of taking off their clothes to wash them. When they had their pantomime, we filled the Kingston Hall for two nights with the mothers and parents . . . I had men come who had jobs in the Corporation, and they formed a wee orchestra for me. And voluntary workers came down, and they started making dresses for the children. They had to come early to be dressed, and we discovered they were all sewn into their clothes. We had to get scissors and clip them out, and then we had to sew them back in at the end of the show.[52]

Women also became involved with the Clarion movement, which centred on a newspaper of the same name and had an educational purpose and espoused a kind of *al fresco* healthy socialism (scouts, cycling, rambling . . .), a new way of life. It had many ordinary tenement women members.

The same women were also members of any number of socialist choirs. Sadie Fulton, interviewed in the film *Red Skirts on Clydeside*, was asked, 'Can you explain what it meant to be brought up as a socialist?'

My father, as far back as I can remember, was a socialist, and I had been in the Socialist Sunday School to begin with, what they originally called the Proletariat School . . . so that all through my upbringing I heard discussions and arguments in the house. Reading material and that, you would never get away in our house with reading comics; it was politely taken out of your hand and a proper book put into it. So, it was just basic socialist training, which stays with ye all your days, your whole outlook reflects on it . . . My Dad died in 1929 and I had to switch my Sunday school then.

So they had socialist choirs in those days?

Oh yes, socialist choirs. We had about five, didn't we? There was the William Morris, there was a Paisley Socialist Choir, then the Co-operative choirs, and did you mention the Socialist Choristers? We went down to a festival, a socialist festival for ten days. They were all in the Socialist Sunday School movement, they were all brought up in the Socialist Sunday School and I have been a member of the party all my life, it was just how we were brought up.

Women who belonged to such organisations were also largely responsible for setting up and running the socialist Sunday schools. Mary and Jessie Barbour were asked, 'Was your granny [i.e. Mary Barbour, who organised the rent strike committees] in the Socialist Sunday School movement?' They replied alternately:

Yes, yes. Mary was named in the Socialist Sunday School.
    Christened, christened.

We call it named. In the Socialist Sunday School you were named.

Instead of being christened in a church. I was christened in the Socialist Sunday School.

The way that the Sunday School movement was run, it was a case that the children themselves were encouraged to run their own organisation. In charge of the different Sunday schools there was one superintendent, who was a member of the adult movement, of the adults in the Sunday school, and they gave guidance to the children. The children took the minutes, they dealt with correspondence, they organised who they wanted as speakers and when the speakers came then of course they were prepared with the questions that they wanted to ask . . .

Now, a variety of subjects were taught, or spoken about, and in particular I think, ones that demonstrated the principles of the movement and also what [the movement] was trying to put over to the children . . . in the manufacturing side of the country, the likes of miners, bakers, textile workers and so on.

One of the important speakers, well more than one, a number of important speakers that came to the Sunday school movement included John Maclean, Jimmy Maxton, Helen Crawfurd, and David Kirkwood, and a few more.

John Maclean and James Maxton were among the rebels who from 1910 proposed a fundamental change in the politics of Glasgow, and whose energies lay behind the whole socialist movement of the time, in a higher sense epitomised by tenement life. David Kirkwood worked in the Parkhead Forge in the East End of Glasgow before becoming leader of the ILP. As a Labour MP he was a vociferous opponent of the 'means test', which so often added insult and indignity to privation in the depths of economic depression during the 1930s.

Radically expressed, Maclean and Maxton's Red Clydeside policy was that the Clyde, particularly just after the First World War in 1919, was as ripe for a workers' revolution as Russia had been two years earlier. Glasgow was 'Britain's storm centre', said the communist Allen Hutt in 1937.

The tenement women, meanwhile, remained uninvolved with radical revolution. Matriarchal, unselfconscious, they lived the reality of socialist politics. They demonstrated that the socialist principle of co-operation rather than competition did not need bloody revolution to achieve. The fact that the Red Clydesiders buried the story of these women may say a great deal about why ultimately the men's way failed.

CHAPTER FIVE

Street Magic

The Gorbals was a mixed community, diverse characters in a colourful street drama, played out in the canyons formed by dark tenement fortresses. Thomas Scott Wilson was born there in 1928. He lived at 26 Mackinlay Street on the west side, in the same neighbourhood, as it happened, as Darkie Marshall, the man we have already met who performed on the clappers (the bones and spoons) in the back court concerts:

> We had some Roman Catholics . . . Bernard Mullen and his
> sister, I think her name was Tessa or Tessie. We had the
> Jewish family up above us . . . eh . . . the Maxwells, and we
> had the kind of Brethren type above us, the Hendersons. The

Highland people went to the Gaelic church over Partick way
and the rest of the people, those who did go to church,
went to either the one at the foot of the street or the one at
the top of the street. We went to the one at the foot of the
street [Devon Street].

There were no Muslims or Hindus or anything. There was
no coloured people at all in Mackinlay Street in those days
[1930s] but . . . there used to be a man who . . . I think he
was . . . secondhand clothes or something like that, but he
was black and white . . . you know . . . mixed race, and he
was always known as 'Darkie Marshall'. You couldn't call him
that nowadays, but that was the way he was seen.

Monty Berkeley was born sixteen years earlier than Wilson,
of a Russian Jewish family, and lived first in Tollcross, east
of Bridgeton, before moving to the Gorbals:

Gorbals had a whole series of streets that were virtual dens
of iniquity, really . . . You had a great deal of alcoholism,
drunkenness, bad lighting on the stairs. They were spiral
metal staircases going up the various flights, and you'd have
as many as four tenants on a landing in flats with only one
room and kitchen. The worst area was Thistle Street, Hospital
Street, Govan Street . . . In the twenties and thirties there
were whole areas that were Jewish in the Gorbals and this
coincided with these streets.[1]

The story of the Jewish ghetto in the Gorbals is unique in
the context of Glasgow. The Jews didn't have a ghetto in
quite the sense that Monty suggests – there were no streets
or even tenements that were exclusively Jewish, nor did the

Jews dominate the scene in the way that they did in London's Whitechapel before the Second World War. But they did maintain a certain ghetto-like autonomy.

Ellis Cohen lived in South Portland Street, close to the territory both Thomas and Monty mention:

> Across the road from me was a big Jewish synagogue and a Jewish club and in those days every Jew lived in the Gorbals, and the exciting part is we were poor, we came from Russia, we could hardly talk English, and we couldn't get a job. So, we all become self-employed. My grandparents came from Poland, emigrated round about 1896. My father's family were all born here. My father had a fruit shop.

In the third quarter of the nineteenth century, a steady flow of Jewish refugees had settled north of the Clyde, founding the first purpose-built synagogue in Scotland, in Garnethill in 1879, but the vast majority of those who followed and sought refuge in Glasgow made their home in the Gorbals, a slum-ridden district already playing host to large numbers of Irish Catholics. So many Jewish people joined them in the 1890s and early decades of the twentieth century that, soon, more than half the pupils at the Gorbals Primary School were children of Jewish parents.

The immigration was precipitated by oppression and massacre in Eastern Europe. So-called Ashkenazi Jews came to Britain from Russia, Poland and Lithuania, fleeing from the pogroms – the systematic destruction of Jewish families, their property and interests. The Tsarist cavalry, the Cossacks, would ride through villages pillaging and destroying homes. Many who found their way to Glasgow had bought tickets to America, only to find that the tickets they'd bought were good only as far as Britain. The influx continued up to the First World War, and began again in the 1930s, after Hitler became German Chancellor.

As elsewhere in Britain, for example the city of Leeds in Yorkshire, and in East London's Whitechapel, the incomers proved adept at forming themselves into self-sufficient communities. Being thrust into the Gorbals ghetto intensified the natural spirit of Jewish togetherness, identified not only by their religion, but by a street-language; a concoction of German and English and Hebrew (their answer to the Glasgow patter).

Recalled Ellis Cohen:

> The other incredible thing about the Jewish people, we were illiterate like everybody else, but we invented Yiddish! And you were German, you were Polish, it didn't matter who you were, you spoke Yiddish . . . they could all communicate. They could all speak Yiddish.
>
> Everyone in the ghetto spoke Yiddish, and many non-Jews understood it. Your 'btm' was your 'tochus', and a non-Jewish boy would say to you, 'I'll kick you in yer blinkin' tochus, if you give me any more.' They'd pick up on the naughty words and just use them.

Earlier, however, there was an even more secret language, as literary historian David Daiches recorded in 1956:

> Recently I received a letter from the son of the man who was stationmaster at one of the small railway stations where the earliest trebblers [Yiddish pronunciation of 'travellers', i.e.

Jewish travelling salesmen] would alight; he told me how, at
the very beginning of this century, these Jewish immigrants,
not yet knowing any English, would converse with his father,
they talking in Yiddish and he in broad Scots, with perfectly
adequate mutual intelligibility. Scots-Yiddish as a working
language must have been developing rapidly in the years
immediately preceding the First World War. It must have
been one of the most short-lived languages in the world. I
should guess that 1912 to 1914 was the period of its
flourishing. The younger generation, who grew up in the
1920s and 1930s, of course did not speak it, though they
knew Yiddish; and while there is an occasional old man in
Edinburgh who speaks it today, one has to seek it out in
order to find it, and in another decade it will be gone for
ever. 'Aye man, ich hob' getrebbelt mit de five o'clock train,'
one trebbler would say to another. 'Vot time's yer barmitzvie,
laddie?' I was once asked. 'Ye'll hae a drap o' bamfen
(whisky). It's Dzon Beck. Ye ken: "Nem a schmeck fun Dzon
Beck."' ('Take a peg of John Begg', the advertising slogan of
John Begg whisky.)[2]

The fabric of the Gorbals' Jewish community was a network
of religious, cultural, social, charitable and educational
institutions. There were nine synagogues, the Talmud
Torah religious school, the Board of Guardians with its
welfare centre, a Hebrew Burial Society, the *Jewish Echo*
newspaper and a kosher hotel in Abbotsford Place. They
even had their own theatre company, the Glasgow Jewish
Institute Players, formed in 1936. Philip Berman, born in
1914, remembers:

It was a sort of ghetto. They were happy, they lived the best way they could. And then, they were helped. There was the [Jewish] Board of Guardians. They were helped if they needed anything . . . Everyone got what they could . . . it was just like a village, everyone helped one another . . .

Above all, the Jews were family focused. Community meant everything to this rootless race, and, next to their religion, family was the source of the sense of belonging they craved. In this they were in tune with wider tenement society.

Soon, there were Jewish bakers, butchers, grocers, tailors, furriers, wholesalers and other businesses, and people would come from all over Glasgow, especially on a Sunday, to buy rare European fare from their delis and bakeries. Philip Berman remembered Sunday as the day the Gorbals declared its Jewishness to all Glasgow:

There were no Jewish shops in Glasgow, except in the Gorbals. If you wanted to buy Jewish food you went to the Gorbals. On a Sunday, Gorbals Cross was packed with Jewish people – meeting there and talking there.

It was a ritual . . . to meet and have a blether. We would do our shopping in the Jewish shops and go to the café to have a coffee. We called it the Cross – there was Gorbals Street and Ballater Street. The Jewish shops were all kosher. Flaxman was quite a good one, a delicatessen – cheeses, all kinds of herring, things like that . . . There was August on the left hand side there [and] one in Rutherglen Road called Miller . . . Fogel's and Callender's were the two bakers; Callender's in Hospital Street, was the best, they used to make cholent – potatoes and beans and a nice piece of fatty meat; they used to cook it all night in the oven. And Glekin on the other side, and Ettinger's and Linderman and Leon. There were about a dozen bakers. Butchers too, of course. The herring was out of a barrel, salt herring. They'd sell you one or two, and you used to take it home and cut it up with vinegar. It was lovely. They used to sell butter-cake – the milk-cake, biscuits, home baking, a lot of foreign stuff, maybe from Holland, continental baking. They used to sell sour cream – we called it Shmetana – olives, pickles, mustard pickles, pickled cucumbers – also out of a barrel.[3]

The lively presence of crowds of young Jewish men is well remembered by those who lived in the Gorbals during the years before the Second World War, as Eddie Perrett records:

On Sundays, Gorbals Cross was always a busy place . . . All the young Jewish lads would gather round dressed in their best. The Jews having the reputation of being the best tailors in the trade could make a show . . .[4]

Even though at school Ellis Cohen's classroom was composed almost entirely of Jewish children, he had both Jewish and non-Jewish friends as a boy, and the non-Jewish boys enjoyed dipping into the foreign culture.

Saturday was the Sabbath. On Sunday every shop was open. The place was full of butchers. This chap, Lucas, had worked in America and his was full of American Jewish dishes. There were all these pies and big thick salt beef sandwiches. He would sell the salt beef and a shop at the corner would sell

Jewish bread, slice it up for you, and you put a big piece of
salt beef in it.

On a Friday night we kids used to get drunk. We'd go to
the synagogue, to the service. At the end of the service – we
use wine just as a blessing of the soil shall we say, not as
blood or that – the children were allowed to go out after the
guy had said his thing, and they poured into wee silver cups
a drop of wine for every child. And we knew another
synagogue that was just starting and we'd dive into that . . .

What we did have [to ourselves] was the Talma Torah,
where we went to learn Hebrew – five o'clock to seven
o'clock, five nights a week, after school, because all our
books were printed in Hebrew. Everybody learned to read
and write Hebrew. It was a way of life.

Hebrew was the foundation of the Jewish culture. 'In the
beginning was the word . . .', the infallible word of God.
They alone understand it in the original, and this was the
fundamental inspiration of their community, as Ellis
Cohen recalls:

It was a whole community. For example, the Jewish Welfare
Board. If a family needed clothes, the Board gave them
clothes. You made a contribution to the Board. During
Passover, when you eat special food for about eight days,
the Welfare Board would send out a circular to needy
families, you just tick what you want and it goes to one of
the Jewish delicatessens, and they deliver it, and no one
would know it was Welfare. So, everything was done very
tactfully . . . They never belittled them, but it was belittling.

Nevertheless, some western habits did find their way into the Jewish culture, not always for the best, as Philip Berman recalled:

> My father's uncle used to get his wages on a Friday night and his wife never saw him until Saturday. It was all men in the clubs, gambling. It was quite common . . . they sat all night playing cards – only cards (there was no roulette) – poker, blackjack, different card games . . .
>
> This man, Black, had a bookmaker's. It wasn't a place you would just walk in off the street. It was an office. It wasn't advertised . . . ninety-nine per cent had an account with him. You just phoned up to make a bet. You only went in to pay money or collect money.
>
> You would give your nom de plume. You wouldn't give your real name . . . You might give number nineteen. Somebody might use your name, but if you had a nom de plume, nobody knows who you are. Except the bookie. I used to say, 'Filly' – my name's Philip.

The Gorbals Jews started up not only retail, but also all kinds of manufacturing businesses, notably in the tailoring and furniture industries. Philip's father was a furniture manufacturer:

> My grandfather was one of the first cabinet makers in Glasgow. And all the ones after that worked for my grandfather . . . His business was in Gorbals Street (in those days it was called Main Street). The factory was on three or four floors, a big business.

The Gorbals Jews were entrepreneurs and would-be capitalists, and yet, on account of their poverty and experience in Eastern Europe at the hands of the Tsarist troops, there was a left-wing political edge to their outlook and ambition, which was, fortuitously, in tune with the politics of the non-Jewish dock and shipyard workers and their tenement families, as Monty Berkeley and Alec Bernstein recall.

> The Communist Party had more Jews in it than the ILP (Independent Labour Party).[5]

> When I was in my teens and my twenties there were quite a number of Jews who were very left wing. Some of them joined the Young Communist League or the Communist Party . . . In the Workers' Circle, for example, you had the Jewish Institute. The Workers' Circle is very left wing and where they weren't members of the Communist Party, they were definitely sympathetic to it . . .
> I went into the Workers' Circle and in no time I was holding lectures about Spain and so forth . . .[6]

In July 1936, the fascist General Franco participated in a coup d'état against the elected, left-wing Popular Front government in Spain. The coup failed and evolved into the Spanish Civil War. Left-wing sympathisers took actively against him, many Glasgow Jews among them.

> Most Jews were identified with the Workers' Circle and with trade unions and with political activity, [which] erupted more when we had the experience and information of what was happening in Nazi Germany . . .[7]

Some became quite radical in their support of the Communist Party:

> Jack B____ was a tailor and a member of the Communist Party. I don't think he spoke at street corners, but Jack was what we call in Yiddish a meshugana. He wasn't rational!

Political conviction could be so strong among the Jews that it even persuaded some to turn against their fellows. In the rag trade, Jewish bosses were not immune from censure by their own kin for noisy, claustrophobic conditions and poor pay, as Monty Berkeley recalls:

> The first picket I did with the Young Communist League was organised by the Tailor and Garment Workers Union somewhere off Stockwell Street [just across Victoria Bridge from the Gorbals] – the tailoring shop strike of young women . . . because of conditions and bad pay. The conditions were atrocious. The employers unscrupulous. Many of the young girls who worked there were Jewish. I was about sixteen, nineteen.

Yet, for all this colourful, communal living in the Gorbals, there was never any doubt that the Jews would get out at the first opportunity. At bottom, they were not a Clydeside community but a Judaistic one: autonomous, epiphytic, and by their very nature mobile.

Unattached to any country, they skedaddled as soon as they had established themselves: to Shawlands and Battlefield, and to areas on Glasgow's fringes, just as the Jews moved from Whitechapel to outer circle places in

London, such as Clapton, Kilburn, and Golders Green, as soon as they could afford to.

> Just after World War II, the scene had changed. Many of the Jewish families had left the district. Being industrious people, many had got on in life and moved out, firstly to Queens Park, Langside and Newlands, then to Giffnock, Broon Estate and Newton Mearns. The Cross now was much quieter on Sundays.[8]

There would never be any of the sentiment expressed by the non-Jewish Gorbals residents for the old days, for the lost community, because the Jews took their community with them. Extended families, neighbours, friends, the shops that supported them, and the welfare back-up: whole sections of society moved out as one. The Jews are not a nation; they know no homeland, other than within. They travelled with their cultural centre – Judaism – intact, and for them moving up and out was instinctual, as this comment of Hannah Frank Levy, a child of the Gorbals, shows:

> Children going without shoes, barefoot, and women wearing shawls. I remember saying that I didn't want to be an old woman and wear a shawl.[9]

What the Jews did take with them from the Gorbals experience was a sense of what it was like to be a Glaswegian at (some say) the city's richest cultural moment, the time of the shipyards.

One Jewish old-timer did stay, Ellis Cohen. Although he

also has a flat and bank account in Spain, he still lives in a tenement apartment in Govanhill's Allison Street today. He says that the Gorbals experience did affect the Jews:

> In the Jewish Institute nobody would dream of taking a ham sandwich, whereas [for Jews] in the Workers' Circle it was quite common . . . which would shock some of our people.

For children in the interwar years, the Jews and their colourful culture were just one intriguing aspect of the kaleidoscope of life. For many, looking back seventy, eighty years, what gave the scene its magic were the Clydesdales, the large, heavy horses which drew the carts to market, and on which John and Irene Hamilton would hitch a ride to Lipton's store.[10]

Thomas Lipton was born and bred in the Gorbals, and though his first grocery store opened in Anderston, just north of the Clyde, his Gorbalite childhood informed the retail nous that built his business into a chain of stores throughout Britain. The Hamiltons recall Lipton's generosity:

> We used to go with the carters, and sit up there on top of the horse and carts, and they'd take you in, and all you could smell was these smoked hams, it was fantastic! They used to give you something to take home. Every year up 'til about the 1930s, on Thomas Lipton's birthday I think it was, everybody used to go up and get a free box of chocolates.

Even into the 1950s there were few cars evident in the streets; only one or two people had them in the tenement villages – the doctor perhaps, and one or two others; some people remember a priest on a bike, which proved just as fascinating. Horses remained the main form of business transport, as Thomas Scott Wilson recalled:

> A pony and trap used to come with two barrels of tripe. [My brother] Jack and I loathed tripe but we were sent out with a plate to get a pound of tripe and he (the trader) picked it up with tongs and sliced it off . . . it was awful . . . Occasionally the rag-and-bone men would come round . . . blow a bugle, and ice-cream men with a wee barrow . . . they used to park down at the school during the summer when the school was in motion [term time] and that was the only transport I can remember. Another feature of Mackinlay Street in my very young days was . . . they used to bring sheep in to go to the market and they must have come up from Eaglesham or the Mearns way, but they turned in to Turriff Street, down Mackinlay Street, down Abbotsford Place, along the riverside, and up to Melbourne Street . . . you know, where the meat market was in those days. But we saw horses coming down . . . eh . . . sheep coming down there . . . Mackinlay Street . . . quite big flocks.[11]

Bread and coal were delivered from horse-drawn vehicles. May Hutcheson recalls the scene on coal day in the 1920s as if it were yesterday:

> The coal came in lorries, horse-drawn lorries, and you see we lived three storeys up, so this coal man would bring a sack of coal up. He would shout from the bottom, 'Coal, Mrs McCain!' He would shout right from the bottom, so that you

would have the door and the lid of the coal bunker in the kitchen open. You had to have this lid up, he had no time to spare, he just swung the coal bag over into the bunker and you can imagine the dust.

In *Gorbals: The Way We Were* Ellen McAllister recalled the tragic side of horse transport, when a horse fell:

The carter would get lots of men willing to help. They would put lots of sacking around the horse. I think this was to help it get a grip on the road and to keep it warm. Ropes were then put around the animal and men would pull on these ropes to help it to its feet but sometimes it would slip and sparks would fly from the hooves as it tried to regain balance. This was a bit terrifying to watch and I would get very emotional. I felt so sorry for the poor horse as it showed the whites of its eyes in fear. When the horse was safe, everyone would give a sigh of relief and a loud cheer would be let out.[12]

Again, almost everyone remembered sitting on the edge of the pavement watching the buskers, 'singers, bands playing jazz, tap-dancers, even fire-eaters and organ-grinders with small monkeys'. And they recalled the clog-dancer, too. Thomas Scott Wilson:

This was an old coloured chap, wheeled a pram and had a portable gramophone and he carried the board and he was always dressed in . . . I think it was a red jacket and blue trousers and some kind of hat. He wore clogs and he would set up in the street, put the board down on the street, wind up the gramophone and start to give us a dance. He was a regular.

And then, only once do I remember two men came with accordions and they played jazz music and I had never heard jazz music . . . There was a chap used to come around with a dulcimer, he always went down into the back courts and from what I remember he was excellent, but every time I saw *The Third Man*, with Harry Lime with the dulcimer, it just took me back to this chap coming around Mackinlay Street.

We had various singers who sang out in the street and the one I can remember best was an old tramp type, he was always dirty and dishevelled and he only had the one song, eh . . . and I'll sing it—

When it's springtime in the Model
The Model in Carrick Street
And the birds begin to yodel
And the ludgers cannae sleep
They get up and they read the papers
And wash their dirty feet
When it's springtime in the Model
The Model in Carrick Street.[13]

Carrick Street is off the Broomielaw, near where Tazza Macleod remembers greeting another magical figure of the past, the 'all-powerful lamplighter'. He used to come up Buccleuch Street to Dalhousie Street, where her grandmother lived:

He would carry a slim lighting stick in his hand and with this tall magic wand stick he would flick it up the lamplight quickly and it would suddenly glow and burn light to the area. Hail, rain or snow he would be there. The lamplight was a tall, outstretched, ornate iron lamp standard in the shape of a 'T' . . .

This would be the signal that play had stopped for the evening and we would all go home, reluctantly. Occasionally he would stop and speak with us, very briefly, but usually he was a man with a mission and off he would go very quickly. Onward, to the next lamplight.

It was never the same when it went electric.

Occasionally we would throw a rope on to the outstretched arm of the lamplight and make it into a swing or maypole thing. God help you if you were caught doing this. Mum would say that if the lamplight was broken we would all be gassed to death. This threat never stopped us doing this.[14]

Peggy Taylor's abiding memory was of the rag women, who used to come visiting up closes regularly:

You kept all the old togs below the bed, maybe in an old bath. Now when the rag woman came up and you gave her the clothes, she had to give you something. You see, a lot of them were gypsies. They had to give you something or it would bring bad luck or break a friendship. Sometimes it was a cup and saucer or a ha'penny. Sometimes it was only a kiss and a cuddle. And mind you, sometimes they hadn't washed in a long time! But you took the kiss anyway, and sometimes you had her in and gave her a cup of tea.[15]

Come the late-1950s, all these colourful people had disappeared, and it was as if they had never been there: 'I missed seeing these swarthy colourful people and our playtime games with them,' said Tazza. But even at the time, of course, there were more things for children to do than gaze and wonder at the drama of life in the street. School, for one.

May Hutcheson started at Scotland Street School, to the west of the Gorbals in Kinning Park, in 1925. I found her wandering around the classrooms; she had arrived an hour early for a school reunion.

The building has been turned into a museum, which is no surprise because it was designed by Glasgow's most famous artist-architect, Charles Rennie Mackintosh (1868–1928), leader of the famous group known as 'The Four', who came out of the Glasgow School of Art.

Mackintosh, Herbert McNair and two sisters, Margaret and Frances Macdonald, worked in every medium and transformed design in Britain in every area of life, from cutlery to buildings including this one, influencing other designers throughout the world ever since. Mackintosh's style is sort of art nouveau, an expression I believe he despised. For certain, his work vibrated with a new freedom and had no roots in his academic studies. Scotland Street School is all about purity of light and space – vast rooms, high ceilings, roomy staircases, and the whole thing bathed within in natural light. I was shown by museum staff how he had even installed an air conditioning system, way before its time. It could be operated by teachers using levers in the ceiling, set well out of pupils' reach. It was indeed 'nouveau' for its time, but the beauty of it is that the school's design also draws on Scotland's ancient past. There are massive modern banks of horizontal windows, each pane of which is said to cost £250 to replace today, and a plain recessed façade, but the north front of the school has the appearance of a Scottish castle, with two great towers dominating.

It is such an amazing design that I open my conversation with May, a quiet, composed lady, who would, I dare say, have been happier losing herself eighty-three years down memory lane on her own, by saying that, 'Mackintosh really knew what he was doing didn't he? There is light everywhere.'

May replies, 'We did a topic on Charles Rennie Mackintosh once and it was extremely successful, the children just loved hearing about him and knowing that their school was something he'd designed.'

We had met in a reconstructed classroom, with rows of double desks rising in terraces to the back of the room, bright light crashing in through tilting windows on one wall, a map of the British Empire on another, and a dunce's hat on a stool in the corner.

'This is the type of desk that we were at, as we progressed,' May confirms. 'To begin with I think they would have been more individual.' I ask her whether the desks were raised like this, but she cannot say for sure. What she remembers more clearly is what happened in her class:

> I was a twin and my sister [Nan] was always top of the class. There was one teacher who was very kind to me, because the top of the class were always sent [to deliver] messages – you know, if the teacher needed to contact somebody. And this man gave me a shot too, because I think he thought I might be jealous of my sister, or something.

May remembers his name, 'It was a Mr Skelly.' Such kindness can ensure immortality, it seems.

May tells me that if you were at the bottom of the class you had to sit closest to the teacher. The idea was to work your way to the back. She was always sat at the front. 'I think that I had this attitude that I didn't need to worry because my sister was top of the class. Because later on I was very good at school, I got double languages at senior school.'

School Certificate?

'Yes, yes, exactly. Our parents had to promise that we would stay at school until we were fifteen, that was a year longer than you had to. And so, yes, I got French and then the second year I got French and German. So it wasn't that I was stupid. I just didn't try at school.'

May shared her seat at the bottom of the class with 'a very poor wee girl with nits in her hair, which my mother didn't know':

> So, when it was our birthday, this girl was invited to come with her older sister to tea at our house. This older sister was a very cheeky girl . . . I think my mother got quite a shock when these two children came on our birthday and one was absolutely irrepressible. I don't think my mother listened to Nan and me much, I don't think she had time, you know. I really don't. I think she was so busy. We were subdued children, you know? And this girl was so cheeky and horrible . . .

May and her twin sister, Nan, lived with their parents in Shields Road, which runs southwards off Scotland Street. I ask her what sort of tenement house it was.

'My mother thought it was a slum she was living in, that's how she would describe it. We had two bedrooms, a kitchen, uh huh oh, and we had an inside toilet!' I expressed amazement. On that basis, surely, it wasn't a slum at all.

'Well, I suppose in a way. There were three [sets of] stairs up and this sort of *well* all the way down – the dungeon we called it.'

I assumed that she and Nan walked to school from Shields Road.

'We would walk to school, yes, and my mother didn't believe in eating between meals. So, other children, most of them, well maybe not most of them, but a good number of them, their mothers came up at break time, about eleven in the morning and gave them ['jeelie' pieces] through the bars in the playground.'

'But you didn't get any?' I say.

'No, no! My mother was very strict.'

'And did any of the others share their pieces with you?'

'Oh no! All of us would go home for lunch, and come back in the afternoon. Our mother didn't work. We would have our main meal [at] lunch time and at night we would have bread and cheese and a banana, something like that. You know that sort of thing, an uncooked meal at night, mostly. And immediately we had had your tea, we went out to play.' May laughs for the first time: 'We had a lovely broad street which had a very, very smooth covering, great for hopscotch and ball games. And we were playing shops and things like that in the back court, yes. It wasn't grassed, it was just sort of mud, that was where the slum bit came in.

'We progressed through the school, you know as we got older, and one day we marched up the stairs in classes and there was somebody playing the piano, we lined up in the hallway and then we marched up and I loved that . . .'

May and I were now walking into the cookery classroom, the kitchen furniture as it was in her day, with a twenty-foot dresser along one wall – designed by Mackintosh – and three big tables with rolling pins and so on, plus a complete kitchen range.

'Is that what you would have had in the kitchen at home?'

'Oh yes, absolutely, yes. Well, the kettle sat there in the middle over the fire. These were hot plates and the two ovens either side. The ash pan at the bottom which had to be emptied.

'My parents were very political, very political. We were very much involved with the socialist movement, with the *culture* of things. There was a choir and the open air walking, rambling as we called it.'

'And when you were walking with your father,' I ask. 'Would he tell you stories about earlier days?'

'No, he was a very quiet man. My mother was very dominant, she was far too strong really for my father.'

I say that yes, I had come to believe that was often the case.

'Oh yes, yes,' says May. 'I find it difficult to accept this story about women being subjugated and so on. My mother was the boss, there was no question.'

'It's funny isn't it,' I say, 'that one is given the notion the whole time of what a relentlessly masculine place Glasgow was in the old days, and yet I get the feeling sometimes that in the home at least, the wife did rule the roost.'

May's response to this is interesting: 'Yes, well, I know

my father didn't drink. He was teetotal, he had signed this pledge . . . His parents came from Skye . . .'

'Skye, yes, a beautiful place,' I say. 'So, his father would have been a crofter?'

'He had been a crofter, but of course the croft couldn't be divided between all the family, so my father came to Glasgow and he . . . on my birth certificate it said he was working in a soap factory in Glasgow.'

May Hutcheson had rolled out my whole story of Glasgow in one go – the Highlander father moving from country to town, the dominant tenement mother, the socialist dream (or regime, depending on your view) on which tenement life drew. There was an alternative, a sad life which many lived and to which we will come. May knew that. It was the reason she said, 'My father didn't drink.'

Others reveal a violent school experience. For Crawford Dick, Gorbals-born in 1928, strangely it was his art teacher who was to blame:

> I really wanted to do art in my Higher and for some reason this art teacher did not like me. We were issued at the start of term with a new envelope for our work and for some reason . . . I must have had a mental aberration . . . I drew a pair of lips on this envelope of mine. Big red lips, and I was taken out into the corridor and I was given six of these from the art teacher. This was a thrashing. I mean this guy wanted to kill me. I mean this was psychopathic. There was a deathly silence when I went back into the room. Now they would get jailed for doing that and I would probably be looked on as some sort of aspiring art freak [for drawing the lips].[16]

John McLaughlin discovered that female teachers could be just as vindictive:

> Miss Byrne the big spinster with her hair swept back in a bun. She was very strict, she was very strict. I remember her, she was very, very strict. I remember a guy in a class at school called Tommy McKay, he came from Polmadie, and he came in . . . I think he was ten minutes late one cold winter's morning and McKay, 'Why are you late?' He said, 'Oh Miss, it was a cold morning and I was heating my hands at the fire before I came out.' 'Oh I see, just hold them out and I'll heat them again,' she said. And he got two of the strap and that was the kind of discipline at school.[17]

For George Fairley, who attended Holy Cross School in Govanhill, Mr Reynolds was the perpetrator:

> I can see him . . . he had a checked grey suit, he had a face like a bull, should never have been a teacher, had big thick glasses and he always told things that happened to him as a boy . . . put to bed naked and whipped . . . 'That's what you should be getting – you know.' He was a real bully . . . He would go on about some particular subject and one day it was spelling. So he gave us a composition, he read it out and we done it then. He went around us and he said, 'Right, every word you get wrong I'm going to give you the belt.' Now, he never marked my book and he gave me fifteen of the belt. That must have been a matter of trust. I put my hand up fifteen times and fifteen times I got belted, so that told you two things – one that I was honest and two that I was stupid.

Another time he got me and he really shook me and he gave me such a shaking – it wasn't for talking in class or being disobedient, it was to do with arithmetic. I remember he kind of got me by the lapels of my jacket and I was just a child and he shook me and shook me and shook me and I was crying then I got sent back to my seat but it was lunchtime and rather than go home I came out of Holy Cross and down Daisy Street, but instead of turning right to go home I went left and walked all around Victoria Road and went into my mother's late – I had wiped my tears on my jersey – never told my mother.[18]

Once a year everyone, all but the very poorest, would leave Glasgow and go on holiday. This was a tradition from the late-nineteenth century until the 1950s. The occasion, oddly, for it must have detracted from the success of the event, coincided with the Glasgow Fair fortnight in July, which has been a feature on Glasgow Green for centuries.

This mass exeat was a pilgrimage by excursion steamer down the River Clyde to towns such as Rothesay on the Isle of Bute, Dunoon, and Largs.

How could people afford it? First, competition between the paddle steamers and the rail companies kept rail and boat fares among the lowest in Europe.

I can remember my father and mother and all of us going into Glasgow, to the Broomielaw, and for about one-and-sixpence [1s./6d.] per head, maybe sixpence for the children, we could sail from the Broomielaw to Dunoon. We had several holidays in Rothesay and in Dunoon when we were all young.[19]

People contributed to a holiday fund all year, so that they could go.

> You paid a shilling a week and at the end of the year you
> had two pound, ten shillings [£2 10s./-] or two pound fifty
> [£2.50p] as it is now and that took you your holidays. We
> used to go down to Ayr a lot then. We went down there
> and spent our holidays there.[20]

Tazza Macleod's family chose to go to the Co-op camps at Rothesay.

> Even when it rained it was still good fun. I can still remember
> the excitement of getting ready to go on our holidays. Going
> round all the aunties for our holiday money. The big trunk
> full of our best clothes and the Marks and Spencer's sandals.
> I think we took a taxi to the station. Setting off in the big
> puffing train with the corridor to our seats. Dad was in
> charge of operating the window with the big leather strap
> thingo. Then the long wait until we saw the sea. It was so
> magical.
>   Then waiting to go onto the ship at Wemyss Bay and
> then we were off on our adventure to the camps. Our
> overseas adventure island.
>   When we got to Rothesay there was a special bus for us
> campers to get on. By that time we were high with
> excitement. Our parents must have been exhausted with us.
> Then to see the camp with all the chalets and the most
> wondrous dining room that never failed to deliver meals at
> the set times of the day. Woe betide you if you were late for
> your turn, called 'the sitting'. I also loved being called up to

wait in line to be served your meal from the hatch.

If a family was late, the procedure was to bang your spoon on a plate. What a racket and big shame, but I loved it. It was fun until it happened to us then I never did it again. Another place where our mum went frequently was the launderette. Very posh, not like the steamies in Glasgow, lovely washing machines and dryers. A place to gather, meet people and blether.

There were organised games for the kids that involved all the families at the camp or we could walk or take the bus to the beach. It was such a good holiday. I especially liked the film nights, like going to the pictures without paying I thought. Also exploring the fields and countryside for hours outside the camp and seeing the farm animals close up.

I can't remember how many holidays we had there but anyway it was good fun for the kids. All good things did come to an end when our mum broke the bad news that we were never going back to the camps because it got too expensive. I could never understand that.

Butlins was never like this.[21]

Memories on holiday are special anyway, but one incident stood out most especially for another young girl waiting for her father's arrival on holiday in Rothesay. It was so primal that it remained with her for almost the entire century:

Our father made sure we got holidays even when we were wee. We went one year to Rothesay and one year to Dunoon, and my mother would take a house. I remember one year, I must have been just over five, because I was five when my brother was born and he was the baby . . . We were down at Rothesay and the baby had taken a cold and my father was coming down on holiday. We had been down for a fortnight [already], and my father was coming down and my mother didn't know what to do because she couldn't take the baby out, so she sent me. I remember I was told not to speak to any man, but to speak to a lady to ask her, would she help me across the road to get over to the pier. I remember doing that, and I saw my Daddy all right. He came off the boat and I went up to him and I stood there – I had an umbrella I remember that – and I says, 'Here I am, Daddy!' And he looks around about – he was looking for my mother with a pram with the baby – and he sees it was me. However, I took him up home, showed him where to go, I always remember that, one of the things I remember.[22]

For entertainment closer to home, 'it was theatre and pictures [cinema], theatre mostly, my mother and my sisters we all went there, you know plays.'[23] Here, on the one hand, was a great, possibly unique, tradition of workers' theatre: the St George's Co-operative Players and the Clarion Players rose with the socialist ferment, as did the Scottish Labour College Players, which the communist John Maclean founded. The Glasgow Unity Theatre (sister of the just as famous Unity in London, to which we will return), the Glasgow Workers' Theatre Group and the Clydebank, Govan, Govanhill, Kelvinside and Shettleston ILP Players complete the picture, all part of a tradition to which the much later 7:84 Theatre Company, founded by John McGrath and, among others, Bill Paterson (the wee bairn of the Molendinar), also belongs.

Much of the material these groups performed – including some great plays, such as Robert McLeish's *The Gorbals Story* (1946) and Ena Lamont Stewart's *Men Should Weep* (1947), which found fame farther afield – dealt with tenement society, Glasgow in the Depression, and wider but related issues, such as the Clearances in the Scottish Highlands. The Clearances – the eviction of Highlanders from their land in the eighteenth century – were not unlike the pogroms of Eastern Europe, though somewhat less violent.

That intelligent fringe theatre was so popular may surprise some, but the serious, artistic, intelligent side of the Glasgow working class is sometimes forgotten amidst the more visible poverty, humour and caricature.

> My father [a docker] was a book worm, he just read books.
> He was a Burns man, he could read Burns from end to
> end . . . He knew Burns all through, like he was a
> Burnsite . . . On the twenty-fifth of January they had him
> reciting poems and that kind of thing. He was interested in
> Burns and that was it. My mother and I used to go to my
> sister's [in Allendale] and when we came in at night, put the
> key in the door, you always heard voices. You heard a voice.
> And we thought my father had company in, but he didnae
> have, he was reciting Burns – out loud! So he was! That was
> what he was doing.[24]

This is far from an isolated instance. As Colin MacFarlane points out, men and boys used to stand for hours in the shower after swimming in the public baths, 'indulging in conversation'.

The topics ranged from politics to football to almost anything under the sun. Many of the men were self-educated and had spent hours reading books from the Gorbals Library on subjects like history, politics, philosophy and economics.[25]

Indeed, a move away from the city centre took the working man away from his books, as this girl recalls.

My father was a great reader. And he used to go when he was very much younger to the Mitchell Library in Glasgow, where he got lots of good books, and sometimes he went in from Milngavie [whence they moved] by train for his books.[26]

MacFarlane recalled a newspaper vendor called Peter operating on the corner of Crown Street and Old Rutherglen Road in the Gorbals, centre of what he calls 'the University of Life':

The older Gorbals men – the 'bunnet brigade', as we called them – stood [there] every night . . . There were hundreds of topics, night after night, ranging from football to politics, economics to history, religion to crime, to what was the best tip for the next day at Ayr or Aintree . . . They all looked the same with their tartan bunnets on. It was a Gorbals tradition . . .

But then, even so, no one in Glasgow was ever far away from humour either:

I remember the Metropole, it used to be in the Saltmarket. That was where I first saw Chic Murray. His daft patter, you know? 'I was walking down the street – I know I was walking cause one leg was going past the other.'

It was sixpence and ninepence [6d. and 9d.] for the stalls and the balcony, and it always seemed really steep on the balcony, ready to tip over when my mother used to take us, me and my mother and my sister.

When we first saw Jack Milroy, and the [Jimmy] Logan family . . . their patter was Glesgae. You were hearing it every day in the street, it was just normal but hilarious at the same time, and you could relate to it.

From there we migrated to the Empire. It was a graveyard for English comedians – they all collapsed there. Max Bygraves was about the only star that made it in the Empire, all the rest got killed. You hear Des O'Connor mention it still occasionally, and Frankie Lane got roasted in the Empire – and he was a big star. Perry Como I think got away with it, 'cause he'd a big female following.[27]

Impersonator Stanley Baxter defines Glaswegian as the lingua franca of Scottish comedy, and writer Ian Pattison agrees:

What I do think about Glasgow is that it has a very vibrant language all of its own and things that aren't themselves intrinsically funny when said in a Glasgow way can be funny on the basis of the wordplay alone.[28]

Glaswegian comedy is analytical, insightful, but warm, with a Dionysian disrespect for the establishment, and serves to delineate the special character of its people. Billy

Connolly's Billy Connolly, Ian Pattison's Rab C. Nesbit (played by Gregor Fisher), Stanley Baxter's professor in *Parliamo Glasgow* are all analytical of the Glasgow psyche. And they are part of a rich tradition.

Without TV there were fewer opportunities for outsiders to hear the Cockney or Scouse or Glaswegian accents, which threatened to limit the appeal of many comedians. In the 1930s, Glasgow's own, great Tommy Lorne was counted a risk to perform elsewhere, even a few miles away in Edinburgh. The only reason they gave him a chance was that his act was very visual and it was thought it didn't matter that Edinburgh audiences would not be able to understand what he said.

Stanley Baxter's *Parliamo Glasgow*[29] sketches on radio and television pick up on the colloquial element, the patter, by parodying a BBC language programme *Parliamo Italiano!* ('Let's Speak Italian!'). Baxter, in character as a well-spoken English professor, translates from the Glaswegian into English in a series of situations chosen to caricature the Glaswegian character. For example, he experiences Hogmanay, pays a tribute to Robert Burns, and goes shopping, whereupon he discovers a link between the patter and Japanese. A young mother of a girl called Hannah hails a shop lass, Anna, with, 'HAWANNA!'—

Next she made her wants known with 'AWANNABANANAFURMAHANNAH'. From across the counter came the reply in the authentic argot of Tokyo – 'YIJISWAANTRAWANBANANAHANNA?' The banana was handed over and the housewife indicated she wished to purchase a pan loaf... 'ANAWANNAPANANNA'.

At one stage the professor decides to participate in the annual Glasgow Fair holiday and prepares to take a train and boat to Rothesay. Requesting directions from 'a sturdy young native' to Central Station, he nearly ends up instead in the Royal Infirmary—

> 'AWORRAL,' he sighed, 'AWORRALKNOACKYURHEIDAFF.'
>
> Fortunately a small patriarchal gentleman perceived our linguistic impasse and came to my assistance. 'CENTRUL STATION,' he intoned. Then, to my amazement, he commenced to conjugate one of the lesser known Latin verbs – 'GERRABUS . . . NORISBUS . . . ANURRABUS . . . O, HEERABUS.' I complimented him on his erudition and hired a taxicab to convey me to the Central Station.

Baxter is of course a brilliant mimic and, being a Glaswegian, he doesn't limit his performance to script or book. In the 1970s I worked for a sharp, West Coast American businessman called Ralph Fields, who was chairman of a company called Howard and Wyndham. He told me that he once sat opposite Stanley Baxter in a train travelling north out of London Euston. They struck up a conversation and for the entire trip Baxter imitated Fields. At first, Fields was doubled up with laughter, but so completely did Baxter excavate his psyche that in the end the effect of the mirror he held up to this normally super-confident, suave businessman was distinctly unnerving.

These may be relatively modern comedians but they belong to a 'one-of-us' tradition which holds a special appeal to the dominant class, the working class, whose patter was learned and constantly refined in every avenue of working-class life:

> A completely different form of communication from that used by the middle classes . . . It was like having your own language within a language.[30]

Comedians such as Rikki Fulton and Jack Milroy (Francie and Josie) and Chic Murray, and catch phrases like 'Hellora, china!', were hugely important ingredients in the self-identifying cultural cache of downtown Glasgow.

> Chic Murray's patter was surreal. He looked like the older men on the streets of the Gorbals, with his tartan bunnet and sardonic expression. When he was on TV we couldn't stop laughing. He'd say things like: 'My girlfriend's a redhead – no hair just a red head . . .' 'She's been married so often she bought a drip-dry wedding dress . . .' 'I went to the butcher's to buy a leg of lamb and asked, "Is it Scotch?" The butcher said, "Are you going to talk to it or eat it?" I then asked him if he had any wild duck. "No," he replied, "but I could aggravate it for you."'[31]

But the point about Glasgow is that audiences and comics breathe the same air, they all regard themselves as inspirational effects of the one persona that is Glasgow. Comedienne Elaine C. Smith provides some wholly credible statistics:

> In the last census that we had in Glasgow, seventy-four per cent thought they could be funnier than Billy Connolly,

seventeen per cent that they were funnier than Billy
Connolly, nine per cent that they were Billy Connolly . . .
That for me sums up the Glasgow ego for you.[32]

Cinemas of course drew even more crowds than the
theatres. Sam Gilmore recalls that when he was a child in
the 1940s, 'there were cinemas everywhere'.

This was before television. In Glasgow, cinemas and
dancehalls were everywhere. Within a hundred yards of your
house there'd be at least two or three cinemas. And the news
was Pathe news. Movietone news. And every time Churchill
appeared on the screen everyone in the cinema stood up and
booed. I thought it was obligatory! To boo Churchill.

Winston Churchill was unpopular with Irish Catholics
because he represented the Union Jack, banner of the
Orangemen, their Protestant foes, but there was a keener
political edge in Glasgow than anywhere, as we will see, and
Churchill's politics ran in opposition to the socialist and
communist elements that dominated working-class and
union politics in the city at the time.

A survey in the centre of Glasgow in the twenties and
thirties by Scots-Italian Joe Pieri shows that in an area of
just a few hundred metres square, there were picture
houses galore. By contrast, there is now only one (multi-
plex) cinema in town, along with a small arthouse cinema,
with all the others in huge complexes outside the city.

My father paid me two pounds a week in wages, which was
really pocket money, since I had no living expenses, and on

my weekly day off I could jingle a few half crowns in my pocket and could treat myself to a good seat in the pictures. We were surrounded by picture houses. Directly across the road was the Savoy cinema, just round the corner in Sauchiehall Street was [where] the Gaumont cinema had its entrance, and directly across the road from it stood La Scala. A few yards further west the Regal was to be found, and still further west at Charing Cross was the Kings, with the Norwood, one of the legendary entrepreneur Pickard's cinemas, close by. Round the corner in Renfield Street there was the Regent and the newly opened, state-of-the-art Paramount Cinema, whose neon-lit frontage, with the first neon illuminations to be seen in Glasgow, drew large crowds to see this marvel of modernity. I remember the opening film, a Bing Crosby musical, *We're Not Dressing*, with Carole Lombard as his co-star.[33]

Right into the 1960s Glasgow was also considered the dance city of Europe, but it was an obsession even a century earlier, as this excerpt from the 11 March 1872 edition of the *Daily Mail* shows:

Glasgow literally swarms with cheap low dancing places where the youth of both sexes among the lower ranks of society meet regularly once or twice a week to dance, drink and enjoy themselves.

The first purpose-built dance hall is reckoned to have been the Assembly Rooms in Ingram Street, a building in the heart of old Glasgow, close to Glasgow Cross, which was built in 1796. By the 1920s there were eleven ballrooms

and seventy dance halls in the city, more than anywhere
else in Britain.

> On a Saturday night you got *The Times*. You'd all the dance
> halls on one page. Where'll we go tonight? Maybe go to
> Dixon's Halls or maybe to Govan Halls . . . Take your pick.
> The Tower – all these places. In that era, if you didn't dance,
> you were a wallflower.[34]

Among Ellen McAllister's favourite dance halls in the 1930s
were the smaller local venues, often with a particular dance
speciality: Diamond's (Gorbals Street), Orange Halls
(Cathedral Street), Workers' Circle (nicknamed Red
Circle), and Morris Green's Dancing (again in the
Gorbals):

> At this time Glasgow was the Dancing City and we were all
> really keen to learn . . . My girlfriend and I went to
> Diamond's in the Gorbals. This hall was next to the [Royal]
> Princess's Theatre (now the Citizens') and next door to that
> was the Palace picture hall. The dance floor was presided
> over by 'Old' Joe Diamond who always wore a black velvet
> jacket. He was very strict: boys at one side of the hall and
> girls at the other and woe betide anyone who stepped out
> of line. He taught us the basic steps of the quickstep and the
> waltz. We then went to the Orange Halls in Cathedral Street
> where a man called Dobson taught the tango and slow
> foxtrot.[35]

At Morris Green's in Steel Street, Ellen learned Irish Select
dancing:

The hall was next to a rubber tyre works. It had originally been a cock-fighting pit before this blood sport had been banned. Later it had been used as a boxing club and now a dance hall. The floor was circular . . . the music was played by a man with a fiddle.

At the Workers'/Red Circle in the early 1930s, a new dance came to town:

The Workers' Circle [was] at 150 Gorbals Street, just above the Gorbals swimming baths . . . It was open on Sunday night and run by the Young Jewish Men. It was there I saw the first demonstration of the jitterbug, a dance style that originated in America and was the forerunner of Rock 'n' Roll. I think this hall had been a house at one time and to get to the cloakroom we had to climb up a ladder and hand our coats to a man in the attic. There was some fun getting back down the ladder when other boys and girls were trying to climb up.

The jitterbug swept Britain as Adolf Hitler became Chancellor of Germany, withdrew from the League of Nations and vowed to rearm his country, though world war was the last thing on the mind of most dancers. It evolved from the Lindy Hop, which itself evolved from the 1920s' Charleston, jazz and tap steps, and it was danced to big band music.

Betty Knox was similarly swept up in it all:

Och they came in their thousands. Glasgow was the city of ballroom dancers in those days, who were really interested in ballroom dancing, some of the finest ballrooms in the world were in Glasgow.[36]

The Barrowland ('Barras') dance hall opened in 1934 for the market traders' Christmas party. Situated above the market, it could accommodate 2,000 people and became Ellen McAllister's all-time favourite:

> The Barrowland I liked best of all, with wee Billy McGregor and his Gaybirds. This was a cheery, fun band and fairly packed in the crowds. During the war, the coloured GIs would go into Bugs Alley and demonstrate their jitterbug and, later, Rock 'n' Roll. These boys could really move. It was a sad day when wee Billy was ousted from the Barrowland. Billy was the Barrowland. With him gone, it was the end of the ballroom era as we knew it.

The original hall burned down in 1958, the same year the founder of the Barras, Maggie McIver, died, but it was rebuilt and opened in 1960 and the Barrowland on Gallowgate remains a venue for bands touring in Glasgow today.

> The Plaza was a very elite hall and also had a more expensive entrance fee. We used to say a girl could get in with a fur coat and nae drawers, but no way a boy could get in without a tie!
>
> In the late twenties, the Plaza employed dance hostesses and also gigolos. Patrons were charged about sixpence to dance with these boys and girls who received commission on their wages.[37]

Dancing was a skill to be proud of, and there was a pecking order, but it was also of course an opportunity to meet girls, as Tony Jaconelli recalls:

When I became a teenager Saturday nights became a bit of a ritual. When I started chasing after the girls. The Barrowland, the Locarno, any other ballroom we could get into – the Dennistoun Palais once, but only once. It was very clannish, snobbish. Boys tended to stand on one side, girls on the other, and you'd walk across the floor and you said, 'Are you dancing?' She said 'no', you'd ask the girl next along and next and so on, and eventually a girl would say 'okay' – and you'd hope she wasn't a dog. But there was no way you were walking back off that floor.

The Locarno was good, you used to get Joe Wallace, some of the bigger bands. There was a resident band, and they'd a revolving stage – that's how they used to change over at half time. The resident band would play then the big band would come on and cheer everybody up. In these days you danced with your partners, you had your actual hands-on stuff – didn't just stand on other sides of the hall and go 'hiya!'. You'd waltz, tango, quickstep – Scottish, though mind you you'd never get a girl up for the Scottish. No way – women only. They wanted to do them with their friends, no guys. That was taboo.

The Barrowland was good. It was kind of L-shaped, and there was a bit called 'bugs alley', that was where jivers used to go. I couldn't go though, 'cause I'd three left feet you see.

Dancing was really another pilgrimage for us.

In them days, if you went over and asked a girl to dance and she smelled drink on your breath, it was the boot. Drink was definitely a taboo. There was a wee tea and coffee shop up in the corner. It was cheap to get in – half a crown.[38]

Many met their future spouses on the dance floor, but dance skill was the point.

To break into the big-time social scene in Glasgow in the thirties one had to be a 'rerr' dancer. There were literally hundreds of dance halls in Glasgow, from the classy Plaza and Albert to the not-so-classy Hibs, Tower and Tripe (the tripe was an empty shop in the Tradeston area, with the band stuck up on a shelf in a corner).

How then did one reach the exalted position of being a 'rerr' dancer?

I was lucky. My pal had five brothers, four of whom were keen ballroom dancers. Every other night they practised dancing up and down the close with my pal and me as their partners.[39]

It is difficult to appreciate today just how seriously everyone took the art of dance, even the hardest of men.

A gang leader of the time was James Dalziel of the Parlour Boys whose HQ was the Bedford Parlour Dance Hall in Celtic Street. Amazing at it seems now, this fellow, known as Razzle Dazzle, considered it too effeminate to dance with girls and chose his partners from burly gangsters. He died in a bloody brawl with San Tan members [a gang from the Calton] in the dance hall, stabbed in the throat.[40]

Gang violence was always a possibility and not only in the seedier halls, on account of the fact that here all Glasgow gathered and it was a high visibility, catwalk opportunity for street-corner gang leaders to strut their stuff in front of mere mortals – the similarly impoverished but more respectable tenement dwellers from in and beyond the area:

'Don't look round,' Andrew murmured. 'It never does to draw attention to yourself when half a battalion o' the Bruce Street Boys decide to grace us wi' their presence.'

'The Bruce Street Boys?' Taking her cue from him, Jean kept her voice low.

His was grim. 'Aye. Down from the Temple and looking for a fight. Which they're undoubtedly gonnae get. There's a fair few o' Partick's own local warriors in here the night. You and me,' he went on, taking her hand and already beginning to pull her across the dance floor, 'will now gravitate towards the exit. Unobtrusively. But swiftly.'

She might have laughed at the dramatic emphasis he had given that last word, if her attention hadn't been caught at that precise moment by the flash of cold steel.

Jean gasped, and followed the razor's trajectory up from its owner's waistcoat pocket to somewhere not very far away from her face . . . [She] felt Andrew's fist in the small of her back, edging her towards the glass doors that led out into the foyer. Unfortunately the man with the razor was standing right in front of them. Jean found herself unable to take her eyes off him. Or the vicious weapon he wielded.

'Nae offence, pal. She doesnae know the score.'

The tall young man looked at Andrew. He was smartly dressed, his dark suit and matching waistcoat a dramatic contrast to hair the same colour as boiling toffee. 'I don't fight wi' lassies.' His smile was as wide as it was unexpected, as charming as it was chilling. 'Or non-combatants.' He stood aside to let them pass. 'On your way, youse two.'

'Your cloakroom ticket.' The words were rattled out like rifle shots.

'What?' Jean asked, out of breath after being hustled at speed across the foyer. From the expressions on the faces of the lads who now filled it, none of them had come here to dance. Yet there was a kind of ghastly choreography in the way so many of them moved as one, pushing back the jacket fronts of their suits to expose the ivory-coloured razor handles sticking up from their waistcoat pockets.[41]

The ingénue Jean, the deathly potential of the razor, sharpened legitimately on the leather strap that hung beside every barber's shop chair, before being applied with dexterity to a client's face or nape of neck – the razor was as much a thing of wonder to a young boy at the barber's in the 1950s as the much-thumbed copies of the sex magazine *Health and Efficiency*, forerunner of Hefner and Guccione. Beyond that chair, its potential for disfigurement was diabolical. In a way, these razor kings were all demon barbers. One swish and you were scarred for life. Favourite target was the ear, a protuberance asking to be separated from its host, and sadly so close to the jugular that murder was often an unfortunate mistake.

Anyone brought up in the fifties and sixties and not totally hidden from the world is likely to have experienced the sudden, supercharged thrill of violence in, say, a youth club dance hall. Elsewhere in Britain it was generally a clash between or among chain-wielding, leather-clad rockers, or the smarter teddy boys with their flick knives, or later the finer-featured, pill-popping mods. I mentioned this to Sam Gilmore, a sometime resident of gang-strewn Calton in Glasgow's East End. He scoffed: there was no comparison to a Glasgow gang-feud.

Ach no. They were tame. They were viewed as a bunch of phoneys, paper tigers.

Such a feud between local gangs took shape at the Gorbals Masonic Hall one night when a boy from Plantation, a dockers' area north-west of the Gorbals, by Prince's Dock, set upon a local Gorbalite from the Queen's Head, who had been dancing with Betty, a Plantation girl. The scuffle ended with the attacker collapsed on the floor, and Betty screaming for 'Gus! Gus MacLean!'

MacLean had been 'awa' oot to get a wee drink' while all the trouble was brewing. He had come back just at the psychological moment to hear Betty's scream. And now the worst, or best, fighter in the Plantation was charging into battle with flashing weapons.

Johnnie had not begun to carry razors in his waistcoat pockets at that time that he and Mary went to the memorable dance at the Masonic Hall . . . One man, unarmed, stands little chance against a razor fighter, but Johnnie Stark was fighting mad and bayonets would not have given him pause. He ran three or four steps and then leaped clear off the floor at big Gus. They fell together with a crash that shook the floor, but Johnnie was on top. Quick as a cat, he regained his feet and kicked, and kicked again with iron-shod boot, against a defenceless head. Gus lay still.

Every bottle brought into that hall was smashed during the fight, which ended only with the arrival of the police – three or four of them swinging drawn batons. Dancers, fighters, men and women, everybody able to run, made a wild rush for the exits, and most of them, including Johnnie and Mary, got away.

Thus were reputations won and lost in the dance halls, on the streets, or in the pubs – among the tenements of the Gorbals, in the Calton, in Bridgeton, and elsewhere. The police rarely got to the bottom of a 'rammy', because there was an unwritten law never to divulge the name of an assailant. It was second nature.

The Masonic was open for dancing again on the following night . . . [and] Johnnie stood upon the threshold with his thumbs in the armholes of his waistcoat, forcing the jacket wide open. The handles of two brand new 'weapons' projected from the upper pockets.[42]

CHAPTER SIX

Class War

The face of Glasgow may change, but not its character. Character is something given to a city by its people, rather than its buildings. The Glaswegian has been described as an individualist, a stubborn and perverse fellow, tough but warm-hearted, a blunt, down-to-earth person with a commendable dislike of fuss, sham and humbug, and a habit of seeing the funny side of everything, including himself.

The opera singer Norman White, arriving in Glasgow in the, wettest-ever, summer of 1967, commented that 'the gloom of the weather was washed away by the warmth of the Glaswegians'.

> Like other strangers I wondered who Jimmy was till I
> discovered it was me. And I learned that Glasgow was the
> only city in the world where first thing in the morning you
> could throw open the curtains and then the windows and
> listen to the birds coughing.[1]

But that violent streak, which we saw in the last chapter emerging on the dance floor, is an element too. Where does it come from?

The aspiration of many Clydeside young was to follow the authentic ideology of working-class life, but I knew the great icon of working-class Tyneside, Catherine Cookson, for fifteen years before she died and she used to say to me, 'What is the working class? I can tell you of five different classes in our street.'

Maria Fyfe, born in the Gorbals, was surely working-class Glasgow, but her parents, both of whom left school at fourteen, had expectations of her. I put it to her that in spite of her birth she was not authentic working class, because her dad was a tram driver who read books, and her mum wanted up and out of tenement society.

'In a sense you were part of a new class,' I said to Maria, 'leaving that working-class tenement life with expectations.'

'The upper working class!' she exclaimed with a hint of sarcasm.

'You can call it that,' I said. 'Or lower middle class perhaps. I mean Margaret Thatcher was also part of that, if you think about it . . . daughter of a grocer, great expectations, etc.'

We were sitting in a pub. For a split second time stood still. The garrulous Glaswegians at the next table froze, their pints of lager poised between table and chin. Maria Fyfe was a well-known socialist Member of Parliament from 1987, in direct ideological opposition to Margaret Thatcher when she was in power. Fortunately, she also has better manners than I, and a tolerant smile crept over her.

'Oh God! I know what you are saying, but her father was better off being a grocer. Within the working class, and this is not new, it has always existed, there are *gradations*. In Glasgow there were things like, "What kind of close does your tenement have? Is it just painted or is it tiled?" If it was tiled, it was called a wally close. And part of the same street would be considered better than another, just on small grounds; like, "Do they have wee bits of garden in front of them or not?" Anything could make a difference.'

'So, there was expectation to rise the whole time, for everyone?'

'I think working-class people who work hard at their job, and are responsible parents and look after their family well are more dismissive and critical of those who don't than other classes. They don't romanticise the working class.'

As I saw it, Maria belonged to 'that class of the working class' which wanted to better itself, to leave something that characterised 'working class' behind. 'It's partly the Scottish educational system, I think,' she said. 'People tended to value education. I wouldn't say it was common now. A lot of working-class parents were keen for their children to acquire an education, and they felt pride in their family's achievements, pride in their ability to make sure that happened.'

Maria's parents sent her to Notre Dame, 'the most desirable Catholic girls' school in Glasgow', a day school with competitive entry in smart Dowanhill, in the West End, not far from where Glasgow University now is.

'They were keen that I should get one of the best educations possible. They were ambitious for the family. They couldn't afford to send my brothers . . . and then I came along when they were older, and the fees weren't that huge anyway. I was the only girl on the bus going into the West End. I travelled from Pollok to Dowanhill and I was the only girl, as far as I knew, to go to Dowanhill. Most children went to the nearest secondary school.'

Interestingly, Maria did not shine at school, as she tells in her recently written memoirs. She did not come to politics from intellectual conviction. In true socialist style, her career arose out of her own experience of the exploitation of women in the workplace, and she had grown up wanting to be like her grandfather Daniel O'Neill, a tireless campaigner for the Irish Catholics in Glasgow:

He was blacklisted for rousing fellow workers to join a trade union when he worked in an ironworks in the East End . . . the striking workers brought production to a halt. Then there was the time Mr Healy, a wealthy man who owned a chain of ham and egg shops, a speciality common in those days, offered the local branch of the Ancient Order of Hibernians a five pound prize – a great deal of money in those days – for some competition or other. Granddad stood up at a packed meeting in their hall that night, and expressed his concerns forcibly. 'We cannot accept this money,' he declared, 'until Mr Healy pays decent wages to his shop staff.' The ensuing row broke up the organisation.

So, even though she rose socially, Maria did take something of her birth culture with her, as surely as did Billy Connolly. Nevertheless, there was something proud and a bit brutal missing from the original working-class mould in Maria's case, call it, if you like (and she did), 'a lack of deference'.

For families like Maria's, the working-class *street* culture simply did not impinge, the drinking in the pub with work-mates, the watching of football – a physical contact sport which epitomised competitive manhood. The authentic working class shared a common upbringing on the streets, and the men progressed to the pub and the dancing, to football and a flutter. Maria's father was a lifelong Celtic supporter, but he would never have gone to a football match, or drunk in the pub, or placed money on a horse. And I wasn't surprised when I asked her about the gang violence, that she said, 'People didn't really used to talk about it.'

> My brothers were of the same generation as Jimmy Boyle, Glasgow's most notorious (and now famously reformed) criminal, when he was growing up in the Gorbals. No one in my family ever accepted that being born there was any excuse for becoming a 'hard man'. When my mother and father read his biography, they shook their heads and said that wasn't the life they and their neighbours lived . . . Boyle's mother would give her sons a row when they stole something from a local shop, but – crucially – didn't make them return the item. What kind of a way was that to teach children honesty?

When Maria was born in 1938, the fearful figure of Johnnie Stark, 'Razor King', was casting its shadow over Glasgow, and everyone was talking about it. Three years earlier, the world had been shocked by publication of the infamous novel *No Mean City*, which followed widespread accounts in newspapers of a violent criminal underworld flourishing on the city's streets:

Razor slashing: — Sir, It is depressing nowadays to take up one's paper and read the daily catalogue of assaults and murders with knives, razors and other lethal weapons. Indeed, razor slashing and stabbing are becoming so common that they appear to be accepted as part of our modern youth's recreation . . . (Letter to Editor, *Glasgow Evening Times*, 14 March 1930)

John R____*, 22, leader of the Billy Boys Gang, and known as the Razor King, was sent to prison for eighteen months at the High Court in Glasgow yesterday for having assaulted William R____ and seriously injured him. (*Daily Herald*, 16 August 1934)

The spear of a swordfish and a wicked-looking Gurkha knife were among the number of weapons taken possession of by the police following an alleged gang fight in Kerr Street, Bridgeton, yesterday afternoon. The 'battlefield' was strewn with weapons after the fight . . . a piece of copper tubing . . . a brass headed poker . . . a cudgel two feet long with a knob of wood as thick as the head of a drumstick . . . a wooden baton . . . an axe weighing 1½ pounds . . . a steel file two feet long . . . a bayonet-like knife . . . and an iron rod three feet long with a hook at each end. Many of these articles, it is stated, were thrown away by the alleged gangsters in their

From the 18th century, spinners and weavers were herded together in factories in the city, losing their centuries-old craft skills to more efficient machines.

Above: The High Street, 1868, once a track linking high and low Glasgow.

Right: Glasgow Cross, a time-slip of a place where even today you can detect vibes of the mediaeval hubbub.

Below: Glasgow's guiltiest secret, the notorious 'pens' or 'back loans' hidden behind the on-street tenements.

Above: 'The thrill of sailing down the Clyde, staring in awe at the skeletons of great ships yet to be launched.' Fairfield shipyard, 1891, where Alex Ferguson's father worked.

The riveter – 'The boy throws the hot rivet to the holder-on who picks it up, sparking hot, and rams it through the hole with a back-hammer. The riveter drives it in.' Once a rivet was banged in so hard it flew across the Clyde and killed a sheep on the far bank.

Below: The *Queen Elizabeth* at John Brown's shipyard, prior to its launch in 1938.

Above: A ship launched on the Clyde, the best advertisement for Empire you would ever see.

Workers leave the *Queen Elizabeth* during the lunch hour.

Right: The culture of the shipyard. Robert McLeish, third worker from left, wrote the classic play *The Gorbals Story*, a massive success from 1946, and a feature film in 1950.

Left: Seamless rows of tenements, in Hospital Street, Gorbals, 1936.

Right: One big family. 'There would be half a dozen of us there [in the back court] muckin' about … If you were hungry you would shout up, "Ma, can you make me a jeelie piece?"'

Below: Five boys from Govan. 'The strange thing is looking back on it we must have been poor but we don't have any feelings of being poor.'

SCOTTISH FOOTBALL MUSEUM, HAMPDEN PARK

A record crowd at the 1937 Scottish Cup Final. Hampden Park's capacity used to be 183,724, and the 'Hampden roar' was heard miles away.

Right: Jim Gilmour boxed for the 1920 Olympics and was patriarch of an East End boxing family pre-eminent still in Glasgow today.

Maggie McIver started The Barrowland ('Barras' locally) after the First World War. By the time she died in 1958 she was a millionaire.

TOMMY GILMOUR

Above and top right:
May Hutcheson and twin sister, Nan, and the Mackintosh designed school they attended in 1925. 'My parents were very political. We were very much involved with the culture of things.'

Inset: Ellis Cohen, Gorbals born in 1928, far left with his brothers and parents. 'We were poor, we came from Russia, we could hardly talk English, and we couldn't get a job.'

Right: The Blitz, March 1941: fireman John Stewart carrying a child from the ruins of one of the 12,000 houses in Clydebank, only seven of which suffered no damage at all.

Right: Second generation Italian-Glaswegian Tony Jaconelli, vilified in the war: 'I learned to survive because I was a "wee Tally bastard" for a time.'

Far right: Tommy Stewart, fifty years a shipyard blacksmith, and his welder comrade Billy Connolly (*below*). 'We'd go in in the morning and laugh until we came out.'

Inset: Maria Fyfe with her parents: born in a Gorbals tenement and destined for great things.

Yard Meeting Votes Yes

Pollok, 1950: one of the areas earmarked for the new housing to replace the tenements. Jean Faley wrote: 'There is a strong sense of loss, which is not unmixed with anger, arising as it does from the destruction of a way of life.'

The Red Road flats, tallest in Europe, riddled with the 'magic mineral' (asbestos). The builders were nicknamed 'white mice' because they were covered in the stuff; many died.

The Gorbals became the main area of settlement for Asians in Scotland after the war. Shewa Kaur Singh was seventeen when she came from India to marry, knowing no-one, nor anything about Glasgow.

flight from the police. (*Glasgow Evening Times*, 17 June
1931)

No Mean City, written by Gorbals-born baker Alexander
McArthur and London journalist H. Kingsley Long, was
hailed by contemporary critics for what a Glasgow *Herald*
reviewer called an 'unfalteringly realistic' depiction of
savage gangland warfare, and it has contributed to Glasgow's
image as a violent city ever since.

Some have denied its authenticity – the novel was
banned from city libraries as soon as it was published, and
as recently as the1990s, politician Pat Lally opposed plans to
honour the book's author, dismissing the tale, set in his
native Gorbals, as 'a distorted work of fiction'.

What did Maria believe?

There were indeed razor gangs . . . but the vast majority had
nothing to do with them, and fully supported the authorities'
efforts to stamp them out . . .

One Saturday night, when [my father] was still in his first
job as a conductor, the tram was heading for Garngad after
the pubs closed at half past nine and he saw a man stepping
forward to board, swaying a little as he went. Two police
constables, seeing an easy 'drunk and disorderly' arrest,
made to lift him, but Dad said, 'OK, officer, I know this man.
He's never given any trouble.' Dad didn't know him, he just
felt the police were being unfair. The man sat down, saying,
'Thanks Jock,' and Dad thought no more about it.

Some weeks later, going through Garngad on a Sunday
afternoon, he was on the top deck collecting fares when
four young men started taking the mickey [refusing to

pay] . . . Dad went through to the front of the tram and called down to the driver, 'Hey, John. Stop the car. Some people upstairs areny payin' their fares.'

A man's voice rose from amongst the upstairs passengers, 'Whit's the matter?'

'Some guys areny payin' their fares,' my dad replied . . .

The man turned round, saying, 'Who'll no?' It was the fellow he had rescued from a night in the cells. The four young men got into an immediate state of agitation. All dipped their hands in their pockets at once.

'Aw right, Joe, only kiddin'. Nae harm meant.'

'Who's that?' Dad asked one of the passengers, and got the reply, 'Take a look at his breast pocket when ye're passin'. If ye annoy him, he takes aff yer ears. That's Joe the Bull.'

He had three razors neatly lined up behind his hankie in his pocket.

Maria Fyfe was sheltered from this vicious world. Her family didn't venture into the gangs' territory – the pubs, the streets at night, the betting shops, the football stadia. Partly, too, the razor-gang culture didn't impinge on her life because the gangsters weren't interested in her or her people, as Tony Jaconelli, who lived in Shettleston to the east of the Calton in the 1930s, recalls:

I used to walk up and down in the days of the razor gangs, but they fought amongst themselves, they didn't bother anyone else. Me and my pal used to walk on Shettleston Road at night time, and we knew all the guys on the corners of the streets, but they never bothered us because they knew we weren't part of a gang – but if one of the gang members walked past, of course that was a different story. I remember gang fights. The Bowery used to fight with the Kenmore, which was Kenmore Street, and they used to fight with the Tollcross guys. Our lot run at them, and they stop and turn round, then their lot run at us and they run away. It was a frightening time, but there was a sense of humour in it. I heard about a guy who slashed a guy on George Square – 'Can yer ma sew? Get her tae stitch that.' – they kind of made a joke of it, probably just to flush it to the back of their minds. We used to go the F&F's dancing in Partick, that's miles away, and naebody bothered us. Not a soul, even out of our part of town.

Unlike Maria's family, the Gilmours were right in the eye of East End street culture: 'At every street corner it was football and boxing. We Glaswegians were famous for boxing, football and shipyards.' This was the collective 'we' that Tommy Gilmour was giving me. It referred to a different class of the working-class from the one to which Maria Fyfe's family belonged. There are, however, some similarities between the two families. Both are Catholic Irish, and the Gilmours had expectations too.

Tommy's father once bought his mother a bungalow in a smart part of town, but she wouldn't move from Rutherglen Road. The East End was where the family's roots went down. Similarly, though both Tommy and his father began working outside boxing – Tommy as an engineer, his father as a machinist in the Acme (aluminium) works – both worked up their own position in boxing at the same time. There were expectations, but not ultimately beyond what everyone knew the Gilmours did.

Tommy's childhood experience of his grandfather's gym, the Olympia – sweat mingled with cigarette smoke and embrocation, macho exhortation, camaraderie, and the honest, primitive tensions that characterise the boxing scene – was etched on his psyche.

One of Jim's rivals in the early days – Judah Solomon in Florence Street – had had the Gorbals icon, Benny Lynch, in his stable. He and trainer-manager Sammy Wilson had watched Lynch win the Scottish title from Jim Campbell in 1934, and the following year demolish the Englishman Jackie Brown, returning home as Scotland's first ever world champ to the cheers of hundreds of thousands of people lining the route from Central Station, where he disembarked, to his home in the Gorbals.

Hard-fighting, explosive characters like Lynch, who was taught to fight by a local priest, filled the bill as Gorbals hero, and sadly the boxer became so engrossed in the role that he died aged thirty-three from pneumonia, caused by years of alcohol abuse.

In his autobiography, *A Boxing Dynasty: The Tommy Gilmour Story*, written with Robert Jeffrey, Tommy Gilmour describes Bridgeton as 'a little working class place in the East of Glasgow, almost a village, a place where people were fiercely proud of their roots and their ability to carve out a life for their families in tough times. A vibrant, cheery place as well as sometimes a violent one.'[2]

Being more than three generations established here, I found Tommy has an engrained sense of his family's identity, for his roots run deep in local working-class culture.

My family come from an Irish background, coming over in the mid-nineteenth century, the potato famine . . . And my grandfather worked in the shipyards, boxed for Great Britain in the 1920 Olympics and turned professional late in his life. He was a lightweight, at that time nine stone seven lbs. If you see photos of him, he had the most magnificent physique imaginable. But he was a man's man, you know? A 1920's man's man. He smoked, he drank, there was a lot of back slapping; he thought nothing about rolling his sleeves up and having a wee roll in the cobbles, as we would say. I'm sure that if my granny was sitting here she would say, 'After we were married it was a miserable bloody life,' because he was a grumpy old . . . He probably made money out of his businesses [which included illegal gambling], but he knew how to spend it. He would meet his old pals and they would go in and have a beer and so forth, and by the time he had got from there to there, he'd done his money.

But growing up, you know, I remember my granny best. It was like most families, it's no really anything to do wi' my grandfather. You could go into the room and see all his trophies, but it was Mary Gilmour, my grandmother, who held everything together. She for me was the most important person in the home, she was one of these . . . My grandmother had this great thing that she could get us all together and she could tell us stories and things and she would really have us enthralled, she was a great, wonderful story teller.

The 'man's man' and the matriarch – with Tommy Gilmour we get closer to the accepted notion of the working-class Glasgow I have described. Love and respect lie at the heart of it. 'My dad was very good to make sure that his mother was OK. By the time I was grown up, my grandfather worked for my dad; he'd a wee office in the Olympia on Brigton Cross, no much bigger than the booth we are sitting in now, and people coming in, and he sat up on his chair like a school teacher – he had a tall stool, which when we were kids we used to climb up on, I remember. As my grandfather was getting older, my dad was pretty wealthy and my grandfather's name was running the shows, and if the shows made money my grandfather got the profits and if the shows made a loss my dad would get the bills. He had great respect for the old man. He had great affection . . .'

Naturally, Tommy's father married a local girl, Elizabeth Bryson, known as Lizzie. She came from the Dwellings, a particularly impoverished tenement block in McKeith Street, lowest of the low:

> My mother Lizzie's family were very poor, for all that they only lived round the corner from Tullis Street [where the Gilmours lived]. Her father, Grandpa Bryson, had a wee job working for my dad running messages, he would get a couple of bob off my dad for doing it. He was one of these guys who, when people would say, 'What about the good old days?' he would say: 'These are the good old days. I've never had a better life. I get a few quid off my son-in-law and get a few quid off my daughter and I get a wee drink in between.'
>
> He, his son Matt and daughter Cathy (Lizzie's sister) went to America in the Depression, so they knew what is was to be poor. I mean, a lot of the traits and beliefs that I have

today, the way I run my business, are from my mother, the
early tuition I got from her. Her philosophy was that you had
to be really careful, very organised, careful with your money.
If you didnae have the money, don't spend it.

There was such a camaraderie surrounding people in
those days. For all the nightmare stories you hear, there was
probably a lot of good, because a lot of people would help
one another and everyone knew everyone. I mean a couple
of months ago I was walking through Brigton and somebody
called out, 'Thomas!' I didn't think there was anybody still
alive who called me Thomas. It was a name only my old
family used. It turned out these were the people who stayed
in the first stair landing, who go back to Rutherglen
Road . . .

Tommy Gilmour's family is classic East End working class.
Its only concession to appearances was a decision a
hundred years ago by old Jim to change the spelling of
their name from Gilmore (the original Catholic Irish
form) to Gilmour (the Protestant form), and that was
because the West of Scotland Protestants were buying more
tickets to the boxing. Otherwise they are authentic, the real
East End thing, stuff of legend, and I was hopeful of a
connection to the street gangs, particularly as I had read a
story in Robert Jeffreys' *Gangs of Glasgow*, which appeared
to connect them.

Jeffrey tells of a protection racket at Carntyne races
involving the Redskins, a gang from the South Side. In
court a bookmaker called Frank Gilmour described how
one of the Redskins had asked him to 'drop us a dollar' to
pay a lawyer, and when Gilmour paid up other members of

the gang thought they were on to a good thing and approached other bookmakers in force, beating up one Arthur Green, who had unwisely declined. After the hearing, Gilmour, who spilled the beans, was chased and threatened, and a gun was fired when he took refuge in a nearby close.[3]

I mentioned this not to Tommy, but to his cousin, Sam Gilmore, the side of the family that hadn't traded up to the Protestant spelling. Sam laughed and gave me a different tale.

> My father, Maurice – he thinks he got his name off a Jewish cobbler – was the second youngest of six brothers. He reckoned that in his time Frank was a millionaire. In the race track industry there was a very big Jewish influence, and these gangs went and demanded protection money off the different bookmakers. They were only small bookies, there were nae Ladbrokes or anything. Licensing was 'incidental' at the time.
>
> Now, they came to Frank. He told them where to go, jumped down off his box and set about three of them. They ran like scalded cats. So then [the Jewish bookmakers] employed Frank as their protector. And he went, as far as my father said, from strength to strength. And the Gilmours, they all moved into the bookmaking business. There were protection rackets going on, but they never overcame the Gilmours.

Tommy says that his grandfather picked up the gambling bug from playing lunchtime pitch-and-toss at the Fairfield shipyard in Govan. Thomas McSorley tells of pitch-and-toss schools operating beside the canal at Port Dundas. Tony Jaconelli often looked on at the one beside the brick works at the bottom of Earnside Street in Shettleston. All of them were illegal and there was generally a 'cop watch':

I can still hear the cries of, 'Heads a dollar!' You could bet as much of the five shilling as you could afford and the 'toller' would keep calling until the dollar (five shillings) was covered. Basically, the call meant that to win the tosser would have to throw a pair of heads on the two pennies he used. If he threw a pair of tails you won and he lost. If the result of the throw was one head and one tail it meant a re-toss.

To toss the coins the thrower had to put the two pennies, tails up, on to the index and middle finger – a two finger toss; or the three middle fingers – three finger toss of the throwing hand. He was not allowed to cover the coins with his thumb, usually called 'using the flam', as this was seen to put some sort of advantage on the throw. He also had to make sure that the coins went high enough into the air so that they got quite a few turns before landing within the tossing circle.

To start, the person electing to throw would put whatever he felt would suit him into the pot but usually five shillings (a dollar). Each time he threw heads, the amount of his bet was doubled. That happened for three throws and then, if successful, the toller would take his cut, hold on to double the original stake and give the rest to the tosser. The process was repeated in series of three tosses, only stopping when a pair of tails turned up. When the stakes were too small to allow a lot of people to get involved, there were side bets between those who couldn't get into the action.

Betting was part of the way of life, and not only for the men:

> My Granny Anderson was a sucker for a bet and I used to be her 'runner', putting on her bets with Pat Flood in the gable end opposite the bottle works in Old Shettleston Road. Her favourite punt was a Three Cross; three fourpenny doubles and a fourpenny treble, the princely sum of one shilling and fourpence being the stake. That's nearly seven pence in modern currency. When I had a couple of coppers I used to make her treble an each way, or place, bet. More times than not I got money back when Granny got nothing, her three horses coming in second or third in their respective races.
>
> Another little ploy I learned was to listen to Granny as she read from the morning papers. She would say something like, 'I fancy that one,' naming the horse. I would take note of it and listen for the rest. Later, when I went to put on her line with the bookie, I would check for the ones he hadn't written down. I would then put them on for myself, if I had the funds, and wait for the results. More often than not at least two of the horses Granny had fancied but didn't take came in first, and I got money back.
>
> There were at least four bookies in our area. Apart from Pat Flood there was one in the Bowery (Pettigrew Street), one in Kenmore Street and one at the bottom of Earnside Street, which is now part of the Greenfield housing estate. So if one or more of them got raided there was always another place to go.[4]

Tommy Gilmour told me that a lot of bookmakers started up a close – 'Take the bets off the people, jump over the

back court, and disappear oot the way. These things were
going on.'

We were never street bookmakers. We always took premises.
The betting shops were situated outside the big works, one
facing John Brown's, one opposite the Acme (aluminium)
works, and one just around the corner from the Olympia. The
Olympia, when you went up the stairs, you went left to go in
the gym and right to go in the betting shop. On the South
Side in Oxford Street, the first floor was for the betting, the
next floor was for the snooker, the next floor for the boxing
gym. For all it was illegal, everybody knew what it was. You
knew that every so often you were going to get raided. I
don't know how they did it, whether they done it on a rota.

I asked Tommy whether money was going to the police?

See, the police would come up and have a cup of tea and
maybe even a wee glass of whisky . . . You always knew
more or less when you were getting a raid. We would know
it was coming, the majority of the time. You would go down
to the punters and say, 'By the way, we're getting a raid this
afternoon and if you want to stay around there's ten bob in
it for you.' So it looked like you were running an operation.
It wouldn't have looked good for anyone if there was
nobody there, because everybody knew they were there. So
you would go round the guys who were skint and say,
'Here's half a quid for staying in.' And they'd say, 'Nae
problem.' So we'd get raided and they'd all get lifted and
they'd be taken in to the police office and then they would
appear in the court and we would pay their fines and they

got their ten bob. That's what it was until next time.

We'd also make sure there was only twenty pound in the till, not two hundred, because what would happen . . . the money would get confiscated. One time . . . perhaps we didn't know they were coming . . . there was a few quid in the till, and Uncle Bob [no relation, but a very close friend], who worked Monday to Friday in the carpet factory, used to work for us part-time at weekends, skipped over the back with the money in a bag, broke his leg and ended up with a permanent limp.

Bob was a great influence in my early childhood, along with my parents. It wasn't until he died that I found he was a Mason. His father came from the Highlands. He was the most honest straight person you could ever meet.

But were the gangs involved in either the boxing or the gambling scene?

At one time the King of the Billy Boys, Billy Fullerton, used to work for us as a ring whip, a helper. Boxing draws that type of element. But Billy was loyal to us.

Yet Tommy looked down his nose at the gang culture in his society.

Of course, you see some violence. There was a real hard guy on the South Side, and you'd see him fightin' Saturday night, just roll up his sleeves, put his glasses in his top pocket and have a square go. He didnae look for a brick or a bottle. But there was those who done that, but see the majority, no. They were reasonably decent people.

To get to the root of the gang culture and street violence, we need to take a tip or two from McArthur and Long's (in this matter) well-informed novel, *No Mean City*. The hero, Johnnie Stark, has a brutal upbringing. His father drinks, beats up his mother and eventually lays Johnnie out, before being imprisoned and dying of an alcohol-related disease. The suggestion is that his brutal upbringing led to his violent lifestyle.

Here, indeed, was violence bred, according to Mr H. Campbell, who wrote to the Glasgow *Herald* in July 1916 that, 'Juvenile crime . . . has to do with parental neglect and bad example.'

Nine times out of ten in Glasgow, dysfunction in a family is due to alcohol abuse. When Stone Age Egyptians brewed man's first alcoholic drink some twelve thousand years ago, little could they have known of the effect their invention would have on the inhabitants of modern Glasgow.

Scotland's largest city has long held its reputation for heavy boozing, and the image of the perpetually drunken Glaswegian has etched itself in the minds of millions across the world. Arriving in Glasgow by car one Friday morning at half past six, I was not surprised to see a sign – 'Don't drink and drive' – lighting up the motorway gantry into the city. As far back as the mid-nineteenth century, observers were shocked about the city's alcohol-sodden nature. A particularly outspoken leader in the *Scotsman* newspaper proclaimed, in 1850:

That Scotland is, pretty near at least, the most drunken nation on the face of the earth is a fact never quite capable of denial. It may seem strange . . . that Glasgow, where the

clergy swarm, should be notoriously the most guilty and
offensive city in Christendom.

Government attempts to reduce alcohol consumption
from the late nineteenth century onwards had some
limited success – by the 1930s, higher taxation had reduced
the level of spirit consumption to a quarter of the amount
drunk in the 1890s – but still alcohol had a firm hold on
the city and not only at Hogmanay, when you'd have the
party one night, the people downstairs or next door held
the party the next night, and so on for four days. In-
between times, you went to bed, you slept maybe for three
or four hours, then got up and the first thing you'd do,
you'd get a shot.

Drunkenness of course might relieve the problem of
frustration, want and dire exploitation, but when consciousness returned, it exacerbated it, and caused most of
the crime in the town. The men worked hard and they all
drank hard on a Friday night. Because they worked hard,
they felt they had the right to drink the money away when
they earned it. Almost all liked a drink; it was a fact of life
which everybody accepted.

There was also a macho attitude attached to Glasgow's
drinking culture. Great feats of alcoholic consumption were
viewed as praiseworthy and heroic. So notorious were the
drinking habits of a large proportion of Glasgow's working
men that wives would often strive to catch their drouthy
husbands with their wage packets before they spent the
money in the local. A Glasgow wife, born in 1940, claims:

Women had to meet their men at the factory gates to collect
their wages before they went to the pub. It depended on the
man, usually his wife got what was left of his wage after he
had been in the pub.[5]

This ties with the memory of one P. McG, who remembers
his grandfather coming home from the docks to give his
wife two pounds of his pay-packet then going out himself
with four pounds drinking money for the weekend, as
being 'just the way it went'.

Certainly there has never been a shortage of places to
find alcohol, with drinking forming such a large part of
many people's lives. When Hugh Savage was growing up in
Bridgeton in the 1920s, East End drinkers were spoiled for
choice. In *Born Up A Close: Memoirs of a Brigton Boy*, he
claims more pubs for Bridgeton and the Calton than any
other Glasgow village, one at every street corner.

The hard work, the exhaustion, the frustration, the
humiliation, the indignant rage at the working man's
inability (especially the discriminated against Catholic
working man) to get up over the breadline, turned many to
drink. It is difficult not to see the huge number of pubs in
the city as the final solution in the enslavement of the
worker, alcohol the effective lobotomy. But it wasn't as if
the pubs alone were sufficient.

Illicit drinking dens, called shebeens (the word comes
from Irish Gaelic séibín or síbín) were a prominent feature
of the Glasgow drinker's landscape. For most of the
twentieth century Glasgow pubs were forced by law to close
no later than 9:30 p.m. through the week, and to remain
shut all day on Sundays, but hardened drinkers could seek

out a local shebeen in which to keep their night going. Though some of these illegitimate hostelries, generally little more than a back room in a house, were undoubtedly clean and friendly establishments, many more are recalled as seedy pits of iniquity.

Another popular way to get round the strict time-limits on drinking was to take a trip on a Clyde paddle steamer, as the boats were exempt from a 1953 law prohibiting the sale of alcohol on Sundays. The term 'steaming', meaning drunk, apparently relates to the reputation of these steamers as being little more than floating pubs. A desperate drinker could also circumvent the restrictions by venturing outside of the city, due to a loophole allowing genuine travellers to drink on the Sabbath so long as they were undertaking a journey of more than five miles from home. In *River of Memory: Memoirs of a Scots-Italian*, former police officer and restaurateur Joe Pieri reminisces about the drink-infused daytrips that would result:

> These were the days of the 'bona fide traveller', when anyone wishing to partake of alcoholic beverages [on a Sunday] could take a tuppeny tram to drive out to Milngavie or some such outlying district. There a drink could be had at the local inn by signing a register saying you were a traveller at the time of purchase and you could then proceed to drink yourself blind.[6]

For many, illegal drinking dens are tied with memories of tragedy and violence, but also of entertainment. In his autobiography, *A Sense of Freedom*, gangland criminal turned author Jimmy Boyle remembers children actively looking forward to pub closing time on weekends, as it was virtually guaranteed that a fight would break out.

Meg Henderson's 'favourite entertainment' was watching the drunks who took detours weave their way, singing, through the back courts on their way home. The O'Briens, Meg's father's side of the family, used to heat pennies before throwing them to the drunks to catch 'for the sheer pleasure of never giving a sucker an even break'.[7]

Any night of the week, the streets were littered with men, blind drunk, staggering home. Colin MacFarlane and his young mates used to roll them for the usually meagre contents of their pockets, either when they were holding the jackets of two far-gone fighters, or when a man was so drunk he fell in the street unconscious to what was going on.

Tragically, because drink does not relieve humiliation, nor does it make a true hero of a man, and because the pub was a male preserve and drinking became bound up with the macho element of a man's character, it had a terrible effect on the community, and in particular on women. Pumped-up and indignant, a man would turn his resentment on his family, and the precious thing that had been won in the process of his exploitation at the hands of the industrialists, the thing that had survived from the old culture and been strengthened by his living in hardship – the deep sense of belonging that was the best-kept secret of the working class – was lost.

For years, women took domestic violence as part of the daily round, bottled it up and didn't complain. They had no alternative. The great problem for the battered wife was what to do about it. If she went to the police she needed witnesses, and husbands don't commonly batter their wives in public. So, it remained a hidden problem, even until the 1970s, when at last safe houses were set up for the victims.

This anonymous interview made for a television programme, but not transmitted, is a typical refrain:

'How bad were things with you before you came here?'

'Very bad, it coudnae get any worse.'

'In what sort of way?'

'No money, the kids starving and him every penny made he just drank it.'

'Did you ever ask him why he was doing this?'

'He'd just tell me he had tried Alcoholics Anonymous . . . This made him you know nervous, which turned into aggressive and violent, extremely violent.'

'Which he took out on you?'

'Yes.'

'You got thumped on the nose quite recently didn't you?

'Yes.'

'And you have decided now that's it.'

'Oh yes, that's it, finished.'

'What did it do to your wee girl?'

'Well, she's terribly highly strung, she talks and talks and talks because she's nervous . . . They took them away [two children] on Saturday.'

'But you are going to try and get them back?'

'Oh yes . . .'

'How long have you been married?'

'Ten years.'

'It's a long time to suffer abuse, isn't it. Why did you put up
with it for so long?'
'For the kids' sake. We had no place to go, and then it just
got to the stage when I looked at the kids and . . .'

Another much battered and beaten wife describes the
episode that brought her to Foresthall Home and Hospital,
a temporary refuge in Glasgow in 1974:

He drinks all the time, he takes my money . . . and he come
back through the door and I wouldn't open the door. So, he
come through the door and he caught me with the
screwdriver . . . They [neighbours] sent down for the police.
He kicked me and punched me, and chased and everything
and all that, y'know? I was pregnant, so I went to my
mother's. The girls [her daughters] came in at night, after
being with their girlfriends, and he didn't give them time to
speak, never give them tea nor nothing, just dropped them
on the floor and kicked them.

The then deputy director of social work in Glasgow, Robert
Mummey, shocked at the recently revealed high incidence
of the problem, admitted:

It is a very significant problem, it is difficult to put an
accurate measure on it because much of the wife battering I
would guess doesn't come to our department at all. But to
the extent that it does come to our department, I have no
area officer who would not be getting this kind of problem,
once a week let's say.[8]

If it was news to the social workers, it was not for tenement families, who had long sought assistance from their own, among them a policeman called Arthur Waugh.

> Arthur Waugh was a legend in the Gorbals and I learned a lot from him. Any time we saw a battered woman on the street, Arthur would establish where the husband was and, while I stood guard, he would pay him a visit. Summary justice was administered and many an evil husband would think twice the next time he thought of raising his hands to his wife.[9]

Such familial dysfunction was the background to *No Mean City* hero Johnnie Stark's pretensions to be the 'razor king' of the Gorbals, but it is not the whole story, for in McArthur and Long's novel Johnnie has a brother, Peter, who in spite of coming from the same background opts for a steady, sensible, respectable job (in a warehouse). He smokes and drinks little, saves every penny he can. Yet, and this is a significant point that McArthur is making, the sacrifice didn't make for much of a life. Once within the respectable, moral straitjacket of society, Peter finds he has to put off marrying until he and his girlfriend have saved enough, whereas Johnnie, who has no job but great standing in the neighbourhood, and who is never short of a few bob, is free and can marry when he wants. Johnnie confronts his brother with the folly of his way of life:

> 'You think you're helluva clever and I'm a mug. Well, there's more than one kind of mug. I've seen your kind before – plenty of them, likely fellas, goin' to toil every day, kissin' the

boss's backside when he throws them a good word; readin'
books and newspapers; winchin' brainy bit of stuffs wi' good
clothes over a duff figure; keepin' aff the booze, talkin' and
walkin' and dressin' and mebbe spewin' like a bliddy
bourgeois, and dead sure, every one of them, that they're
goin' to get on in the world.

'Ah'm no blamin' you; Ah'm sorry for you. What happens
to them aw? They get married and they have kids. An' the
wages doesnae grow with the family. An' they take to drink
a little later instead of sooner. An' the shop shuts or the yard
shuts down or there's a bliddy strike. An' there they go, back
to the dung heap, haudin' up the street corners, drawin'
their money from the parish, an' keeping' awa oot of the
hoose all day, awa frae the auld wife's tongue and the kids
that go crawlin' and messin' aroon the floor.'

Johnnie paused for breath. He had spoken with a queer
gathering passion not directed so much at his brother as at
life itself, and Peter, who had never heard him so eloquent,
was too surprised to interrupt.

Johnnie is ranting at life in the dungeon of tenement
society. He is suggesting that hope is a fraud, his eyes are
open to the truth: want offers no alternative but to take the
path of violence and crime.

The 'hoose' Johnnie Stark lived in drove him to the
streets . . . poverty and sheer monotony drove him . . .

He needs a position that will enhance his self-image. He
needs self-respect, and with no 'Notre Dame' alternative
available to him, he believes his razors are the answer. It is

a deep-down drive. The psychologist Carl Jung wrote that a deep sense of inferiority is always balanced by unconscious compensating megalomania, delusions of power or grandeur (and vice versa). It was apparently inevitable that the fittest would rise from the bottom of the pile in so terrifying a fashion as this.

'Ah'm Razor King. That's somethin' more than any job.'

What brought less disillusioned youth in employment into street-corner gangs was something of the same, but not a deep-down drive so much as peer pressure. For young members of the shipyard black squad the macho culture of the shipyard spilled over into their life on the street after work. I have already quoted the experience of one such squad: 'A big group of us, about sixteen to eighteen, would meet at the corner, so they called us Corner Boys. Corner boys were considered loafers and hard men.' Such lads as these would meet up and go to the pub and to football games, and inevitably they would get into a fight with a neighbouring gang – all much more innocent than McArthur and Long's Johnnie Stark. Yet 'the Corner Boys' was one of 174 names of street gangs that Robert Jeffrey came across in the course of research for his classic compendium, *Gangs of Glasgow*.

Some names reveal the almost childish nature of these gangs' conception – such as the McGrory Boys (after Celtic player Jimmy McGrory), and the Milligan Boys (after the boxer Tommy Milligan). But many of them were neither small nor disorganised nor childishly ineffectual, the Billy Boys in particular, as we shall see.

The Penny Mob, first recorded as far back as the 1880s, allegedly took its name from its members' tradition of contributing a penny a week as an insurance fund to pay fines. The Cumbie gang was named after its home territory, Cumberland Street in the heart of the Gorbals. The Cumbie was fingered in the *Evening Citizen* (one of three evening papers in the city) as a real danger, their war cry: 'Cumbie ya bass!' (literally, 'you bastard') heralding the immediate onset of head-buttings, kickings, and slashings. The name of the infamous Baltic Fleet is reputed to derive from that of a warehouse in their district. The Tongs, originally from the Calton, claimed in a 1968 interview with a *Daily Telegraph* reporter to have taken their name directly from *The Terror of the Tongs*, a violent Hammer Horror movie.

The arms these gangs raised against rival gangs – lists of weapons were drawn up after police clamp-downs or the occasional armistice – have a quaint, mediaeval quality, makeshift, though lethal enough. Hammers, sticks swathed in lead, iron bars, a bolt on a string, beer bottles, billiard cues, metal shaped into a dagger, hatchets, bayonets, Indian clubs, bicycle chains – sometimes with razor-sharp steel fixed into the links – and from the 1920s the cut-throat razor. Imagine the mayhem such instruments could cause.

As for Johnnie in the fiction, so in reality, you didn't arrive completely until you had seen to someone. We can take it from Jimmy Boyle, who wrote in his autobiography:

> I was fighting this guy who had a hammer that kept bouncing off my head and during the struggle we ended up in the close mouth with me on top of him. I hacked the butcher's knife into his face and slashed him. Between the blood coming

from him and from my head, we were covered in it.

This was the first time I'd slashed anyone and really I didn't feel any remorse or pity for the guy as my head was sore and cut . . . Within days I was a force to be reckoned with and some kids were saying that I was as 'mad as a brush'. There was a sort of hero worship about all of this and I was placed on a higher pedestal by all my own gang.[10]

Consistent with this notion that, at bottom, a sense of inferiority was driving these gangsters, 'Vanity,' McArthur and Long tell us, was 'the very core of ruffianism'. With all the cinemas around, Hollywood also extended its influence over the gang culture, to cover dress and mannerisms, says Rena Silvestro, resident in the Gorbals during the worst years of gang activity:

Gorbals and Hutchesontown men considered themselves very macho and lots of them acted like James Cagney or George Raft. A lot wore black shirts and suits like Raft. Of course, at that time we were fed on a diet of American gangster films and a lot of the young boys thought they were the Dead End Kids.[11]

Dressing the part was a must, as Johnnie Stark confirms. Men and women were very much judged by their appearance. A good suit of clothes wins a certain respect . . . Johnnie wore 'a whole suit' (when he went out at night) – that is to say, the coat and trousers were of the same navy-blue cloth and had been sold together *as* a suit. His shoes were well polished, a bright 'tony-red'. In the language of the Gorbals, he was 'well put on' and proud of his 'paraffin', meaning his 'appearance' – it probably harks back to the popular use of a paraffin hair dressing, which slicked back hair sleekly, like a raven's feathers.

It was necessary also to walk the walk – literally, according to 'hard man' Jimmy Boyle. In *A Sense of Freedom* he describes arriving at Bonny's (St Bonaventure's), one of the toughest schools in 1950s Gorbals:

> There was a thing known as 'hard men's walks' of which we were all aware and having just arrived at Bonny's we would all try to adopt a walk that was suitable to us. It must have been funny to see us, still in short trousers, swaggering up to school with these exaggerated walks.[12]

So deep ran the desire for a hard-man image and a tough reputation that even the ugly disfiguration of a razor-scar on the face was, chillingly, desired by some youngsters. True, author Robert Jeffrey notes in *Gangs of Glasgow* that a scar – 'Mars Bar' in rhyming slang – could be a mark of status for some. He relates a court case in which a man charged with slashing a female acquaintance with a razor defended himself by claiming that the victim was proud of the mark, and had pleaded with him to, 'Use the razor on me and make me a hard woman'. The judge, sentencing the man, commented that for some, facial scars were a 'badge of honour and a style of living'.

But what of the women at the lowest level, where the street violence was bred – the so-called 'hairies'? A hairy was a slum girl, not because she was hirsute, but because she did not wear a hat, whereas a higher class girl within the multi-layered working class did. A hairy had a characteristic 'slum laugh . . . a high cackle that ends in a kind of wail'. Certain dance halls were more habitually visited by the hairy than by other levels of tenement girl.

Hairies encouraged violence in their men, were often themselves violent, and expected to receive violent treatment. They encouraged their men to fight, often wildly exaggerating their prowess. The men were only too pleased for their reputation in this regard to soar.

Morality was a very low priority among the very lowest class. McArthur and Long's depiction of Ella McBride has the doleful ring of truth at this lowest level. Ella is 'half in love' with George Smith; she is pleased that he is neither intelligent nor moral. George has a job lifting lines (placing bets) for a bookmaker in Bridgeton. She will go around with Johnnie Stark, who mutilates people with a razor and has standing at the lowest level of Gorbals' society. She will have sex with him in the foul cubicles of public tenement landings, and when Johnnie is done with her, as she knows he will be eventually, George Smith will be 'glad enough to have her' as his wife.

After *No Mean City* was published in 1935, many Gorbalites lived the heroically violent legend. There was even a suggestion, guaranteed to enhance its acceptability, that some gangs took a Robin Hood brief from the community, policing it against incoming marauders and troublemakers, as James Baxter, growing up in Springburn in the 1930s, recalls:

At that time, too, if anybody attacked an old person or a kid, the gangs at the street, to a boy, the big chaps, you know, the corner fellows, got a hold of them. They'd give them a

bloody good hammering, you know. So, old people could
walk the streets without being mugged or anything. Safe.
The tough men, although they fought among themselves,
they respected age.[13]

The following generation would grow up to emulate and
bring to life *No Mean City*'s razor-slashing hero in the teddy
boy gang culture of the 1960s. Every child's vision of life in
the Gorbals was affected by the novel, as Colin MacFarlane
recalls with specific reference to the Britannia pub on the
corner of Thistle Street and Rutherglen Road, when he was
a boy:

When we Gorbals street boys looked through the smoke-
stained windows of the Brit [its] vast cast of dodgy
characters looked like they had stepped straight out of the
book *No Mean City*. We often imagined that fictional razor
king Johnnie Stark might walk through the doors any
minute.

A legend had been born, just like the legend of the Kray
twins in the East End of London. Except, of course,
Johnnie Stark was not real. 'All the characters in *No Mean
City* are imaginary and the book itself merely fiction,' his
creators tell us. It was an extraordinary conspiracy between
life and art, nonetheless. A novel, intended to express
something about a community from one man's point of
view (the Gorbalite Alexander McArthur), had become the
inspiration for the area's future, although the newspapers
had done their bit too.

CHAPTER SEVEN

Conflict

_____

It is a fact of nature that everything has its opposite. Without cruelty in the dungeon of life we would not know disinterested love in the highest room.

In the cauldron of raw, primitive emotion in which tenement society whisked up life as a co-operative venture in the face of dire exploitation in the workplace and poverty at home, there was bound to be conflict.

The warmth of Glaswegians which, for Norman White, had washed away the gloom of the weather, had its opposite at the lowest level in the navel-gazing insularity which made people fiercely territorial and nurtured the gang mentality.

In *No Mean City* Johnnie Stark's people don't know 'the

other side of the river' (uptown Glasgow) at all, even though it is little more than a stroll over the bridge.

> The world outside the tenements is scarcely more real to
> them than the fantastic fairytale world of the pictures.[1]

The level of insularity of the tenement communities is difficult to grasp in modern times. John Hamilton, born and raised in Anderston in the 1940s and '50s, could 'count on my two hands the number of times I'd been into town. I mean there was no reason to go into town, the areas were all pretty self-contained.' His wife, Irene, recalled:

> The only time kids got taken into town for definite was the
> week before Christmas when the lights were up – we used
> to get walked up North Street, along Sauchiehall Street,
> down Buchanan Street, along Argyle Street and back into
> the Square [George Square] to see the Christmas lights, and
> you'd get a bag of chips on the way home. When I'd kids
> we used to take them out on the Saturday night, and before
> I went out I'd make soup and leave it on low, and go and
> see the lights and then come home and have homemade
> soup.[2]

> Each street would be like a wee territory.[3]

> You played in your own street, everything was very insular.
> We didnae even mix with people from three streets away. I
> didn't really know the area, though it's only about two
> hundred yards away. You used to have fights with them,
> filling tin cans up with ashes and throwing them at each

other. It sounds stupid now, but we used to hate each other
in the different streets.[4]

One gang alone made loyalty to an ideology rather than to
a locality its cause, but it was no less insular for that. The
Billy Boys, as I have said, rallied their membership under
the Unionist flag and brought the age-old Irish struggle of
Catholic versus Protestant to the streets of Glasgow.

When the Irish arrived in the city in the late-eighteenth
and nineteenth centuries, they brought 'the troubles' with
them, a contagion more virulent than any of the diseases
that consumed the poor. Incredibly, they are still at work
like a cancer today.

One of the reasons the sectarian struggle has persisted
is that in the late-nineteenth century it became enshrined
in football, the most popular expression of working-class
culture in Scotland.

Inevitably, Glasgow Green was where it all began. In
1873 Rangers Football Club (the Protestant club) was
founded there, in Flesher's Haugh, a low-lying piece of
ground near a river (haugh), once owned by the city's
butchers (fleshers). Later, of course, Rangers moved to
Ibrox Park, a walk southwards from Govan, where it raised
the Union flag of the United Kingdom. Celtic (the
Catholic club) was founded in 1888, and now raises its flag,
the Irish Republic's tricolour, over Celtic Park, east of
Bridgeton Cross.

Glasgow is of course the premier city for football in
Scotland. It is the home of Hampden Park, the mecca of all
Scottish football enthusiasts. According to Richard
McBrearty, who runs the amazing, multimedia Scottish

Football Museum there, the stadium's capacity used to be 183,724, a number difficult to imagine let alone calculate, because it was then largely standing only. People used to say that if you had your hands in your pockets at the start of a match, you wouldn't be able to remove them again until you got out, so tightly packed were spectators, and of course the famous 'Hampden roar' could be heard miles away.

The museum's evocative photographs and recordings document the Hampden experience with a kind of Leni Riefenstahl brilliance, which is appropriate because in its glory years Hampden was the visual, sonic expression of working-class spirit – a churning sea of bunnets, rising and falling with the tidal fortunes of the national team – at the very moment that the propagandist film-maker Riefenstahl was filming Hitler's similarly spectacular mass rallies.

In 1937, when Glasgow was in the deepest throes of economic depression, football was never more popular. It was at Hampden in that year that a European record for attendance at a football match was set when 146,433 spectators paid to see Aberdeen and Celtic in a Scottish Cup Final. That is the figure you will see printed in books and newspapers and even in one of the Scottish football museum's display panels, although as curator Richard McBrearty confessed, 'the official crowd for this match was actually 147,365. It was in its day the world record crowd for a club match or a national cup final and is currently the European record for these specific categories.'

Such figures beggar belief at any level today. However, just seven days before this match a larger crowd watched the 1937 fixture between Scotland and England at

Hampden Park. 'The official crowd was 149,365, the official world record up until 1950 and still the overall European record,' says McBrearty. Even so, this gigantic attendance may be an underestimate, for the turnstiles shut early that afternoon, leaving some 20,000 to 30,000 supporters locked out, many of whom clambered in over the low East End wall. Moreover, it was rumoured that some of the turnstile managers had pocketed a proportion of the takings on which the record breaking figure had been calculated. There was also the consideration that it was the birthright of every Glasgow boy to be passed over a turnstile free of charge. In the end, no one argued that the stadium was in fact close to being filled to capacity, and McBrearty believes that it is possible 'that the actual crowd in the stadium for *both* games may have been as high as 180,000.'

The legendary English centre forward Stanley Matthews was playing in that extraordinary international in 1937. He heard the Hampden roar, and the deafening silence when England scored:

> People were so tightly packed into Hampden there couldn't have been a fag paper's width between them. The terraces heaved and swayed like the menacing swell of an ocean from which a monster of Godzilla proportions is about to surface. For a moment it unnerved me . . . When the referee's whistle got the game underway, the sound of a tearing hurricane swept down from the stands and terraces . . .

More unnerving still was the moment England scored:

I wouldn't have thought it possible for 149,000 people to be silent all at once, but it happened. For a split second the only sound in a packed Hampden was that of the wind sweeping from one end of the pitch to the other. I heard George Male's voice from somewhere behind me shout, 'It's there!' his voice as strident and piercing as a scream in a cathedral . . . [5]

In the end, England, who were playing eleven men plus the Hampden roar, lost 3–1.

So much for the fever of international matches. Even more intense may be the feelings for home teams, as is strikingly demonstrated by the novelist and screenwriter Alan Sharp, born in Greenock in 1934 and famous for writing such as Peter Fonda's *The Hired Hand*, Robert Aldrich's *Ulzana's Raid* and Arthur Penn's *Night Moves*.

In 1982 Sharp wrote the script of Sam Peckinpah's last film, *The Osterman Weekend*, and in 1995 Michael Caton-Jones's *Rob Roy*, which returned him to his roots. Then, in 2000, he produced arguably his most heartfelt work, a short chapter entitled 'A Dream of Perfection' in Trevor Royle and Ian Archer's *We'll Support You Evermore: The Impertinent Saga of Scottish Fitba'*, the first page of which is a passionate expression of what his home team, Greenock Morton FC, means to him.

Picture the scene. Sharp is sitting outside his home in Los Angeles wearing a Scottish International jersey with a No. 14 on the back, watching 'a tall bearded man called Hal Moseley from Texas' go into his house to sleep with his wife. What has led up to this diabolical scene we don't know, except that while Sharp was away watching Scotland play in a World Cup qualifying match at Hampden Park, his wife met Moseley and he has been in her life ever since.

Moseley, possibly a little embarrassed to have found Sharp at home, stops and asks him whether, 'in the light of my attire, I was planning to play soccer'. Confused, fraught with painful emotion about what is about to happen between this man and his wife, and by his own admission very stoned, Sharp becomes instantly convinced that Moseley has struck at the core of his identity, that this is a moment of Judgement-day profundity, that even though Moseley is unaware just how significant it is, his question must be answered with no-holds-barred honesty and dreadful truth.

> I know that unless I told him about Cappielow[6] and Charlie Morton's horse and Tommy McGarrity and Jimmy Cowan,[7] and beyond such specifics, of Calvin and 'geegs' and 'the lonely prisoner who was in hisel', then nothing would be understood.[8]
>
> As I said, I was stoned, but I wasn't that stoned, so I just said, 'No, I'm waiting for Charlie Cooke',[9] which would have been a great title for the Scottish version of Godot, but which happened to be true.[10]

It is a (stoned) writer's way of expressing the intensity of feeling, the rapture that attends a Scot's relationship to football and his home team in particular. We know that whatever the cuckold Moseley takes from Sharp's soul by sleeping with his wife, he will not touch the core of him, and that Moseley, who knows Scottish football not at all, will never be able to give Sharp's wife the fulfilment he can.

The Scots, let it be said, are 'fitba' crazy, fitba' mad'. The sport is bound up with their libido, the fundamental drive.

So, when one comes to a game of football between Rangers and Celtic, the teams that represent both sides of the struggle that has preoccupied the collective unconscious of Irish Glaswegians for hundreds of years, we can expect the emotional investment to be at its fiercest.

Celtic goalkeeper [1964–70] Ronnie Simpson was that rare thing, a Protestant on a Catholic side. Ronnie's father had been captain of Rangers and Scotland in his time:

> There was a lot of rivalry . . . it is much more intense, the rivalry, than between say Newcastle and Sunderland [Simpson had also played for Newcastle]. It's THE game in Glasgow. You didn't feel any different until the day of the match, and then you could feel the tension from the minute you left home. They were big games, not so big now because there are so many foreigners playing. In those days they were local players all the time, and they were big, intense games. The religious side of it was not important for the players, it was just for the spectators. The players were just there to play football. I mean, I was a Protestant . . . but I was there to play football, that didn't matter as far as I was concerned.
>
> [My father] coped with my signing for Celtic wonderfully well, he thought it was the best move I had made. He was very pally with the manager, Jimmy McRory, who played for Celtic against my father.

Birmingham-born Mark Walters couldn't believe the tensions between the two clubs when Rangers signed him from Aston Villa, 'If you are asking me if it's healthy, the rivalry between Celtic and Rangers, me being an outsider sort of thing, I have to say of course it isn't.'

Walters was with Rangers in 1989 when Maurice (Mo) Johnston, who played for Celtic from 1984–87, was signed for Rangers under Graeme Souness, which made Johnston the first Roman Catholic to play for the Protestant team:

> The first day [Johnston] came we had a bomb expert underneath the cars, they must have had a bomb threat and were looking at the cars, it was an eye opener, but that's life in Glasgow. Whether it's right or wrong, that's life in Glasgow.

There had been a tradition never to trade players from these two teams. How did those players for whom Rangers was their life react to Johnston's signing?

> I can say a couple weren't happy, there's no doubt in my mind, although they sort of laughed it off. *I* didn't not pass to him because he was a Catholic, do you know what I mean? I would like to think that it was the same for the players I'm thinking about, but only they can tell you the truth. He scored a few goals in the end . . . I think the business had a bigger impact than Souness and Rangers expected, and I think some supporters didn't come back. Maybe some supporters didn't come back when they signed me, me being a black man, but the religious issue seemed to be a bigger issue than the colour.

Even those whose role it should have been to fight the

prejudice that haunts Glasgow's football heritage were not immune to bigotry. Sickeningly, the police themselves were known to discriminate, sometimes adding to the ills that they were supposed to be curing. Retired detective Les Brown describes in his memoirs his own experience of bias in policing an Old Firm (Rangers–Celtic) derby in the 1960s:

> As a young beat cop I regularly attended Hampden Park, that iconic temple of sport that towers over parts of the South Side. I remember once when 600 uniformed officers were addressed before the game by a Chief Super who told us that the world record for arrests at a football match was created in South America where 166 supporters were arrested. 'We'll beat that today,' he said.
>
> It was a Rangers v Celtic game and crowd trouble, at one point or another, was certain. I was patrolling the track at the north terracing when violence started between the rival fans. The Super appeared from nowhere and said, 'Right, lads, get in among them – but don't arrest anyone with a Rangers scarf.' That, sadly, was the face of prejudice in the old days.[11]

Taking a taxi out of Hampden Park last summer, I asked the driver whether he supported Rangers or Celtic? He said, 'I love football, but it's not worth it. You lose too many friends.' He then began telling me about a murder that had taken place that morning in Govanhill.

Scottish comedienne and writer Janey Godley knew 'a young boy who was stabbed to death just for wearing a Celtic scarf and walking along our street':

He was eighteen years old, studying history at university, and his mammy had bought him that scarf for his birthday. He died with fifteen stab wounds underneath a parked car. The young guy who murdered him demanded he be put in a prison which held Protestant UDA terrorists because he claimed the killing was part of a political struggle against the Pope, the IRA and all Catholics.[12]

There are of course many less extreme examples of how the sectarian side of football can get in the way of the famous Glaswegian friendliness. Joe Pieri was surprised by the reaction of a usually helpful bouncer – a supporter of Celtic – when approached by an opposition fan:

One night after a rather bad defeat of Celtic by their Ibrox adversaries a small inoffensive man approached us. He wore a cloth cap, or bunnet, the trademark of the working man, and sported a blue and white scarf, an article of clothing which gave the clue to his team preference.

'Where's Killermont Bus Station?' he asked. The bus station in question was about three minutes' walk away. Big Steve looked down at the man, fixed his basilisk stare at the Rangers scarf, paused for a moment, then leaned down and barked at me from the side of his mouth, 'Tell the c**t nuthin'.' And gazed disdainfully into the distance over the enquirer's head.[13]

Football violence has been so interwoven with bitter sectarian feud for so long that several respondents in a recent survey[14] believed that football plays a bigger part in sectarianism than religion. What is clear is that sectarian strife in Glasgow has absolutely nothing to do with the religious beliefs of the people who are engaged in it. No one that I have met here would disagree with that.

Q – Was religion important to you when you were young?

A – No, just that you werenae Catholic. That was all, that was all.[15]

No one would argue that there is a doctrinal point at issue at a Celtic v Rangers match, or that those who have 'a square go' in a pub on St Patrick's Day, are philosophers rather than 'widoes' (hooligans). It is of course a psychological expression of chronic insularity in the collective unconscious of a beleaguered people, and it had its origins not in religion as such, but in politics:

My mum was Orange, but she wasn't a Protestant, she was Orange – which is totally different, it's nothing to do with religion at all. And my mother went the whole hog as far as the Masons were concerned, but she wasn't very religious. And the Catholics, with the IRA and all the songs they're singing, that's nothing to do with religion – it's politics.[16]

The politics take us back to Oliver Cromwell's conquest of Ireland (1649–53), when Irish Catholics were stripped of their lands and their religious and political rights. Half a century later, in an attempt to retrieve their land and rights at the Battle of the Boyne in Ireland on 1 July 1690, they backed the deposed British Jacobite king, James Stuart – known variously as James VII of Scotland and James II of

England and Ireland – against his nephew and son-in-law of Dutch extraction, King William III.

Some persist in the mistaken belief that this was a religious scrap, but it wasn't. It was James's last attempt to regain the British throne. True, the Irish Catholics backed James, a Catholic, but only because they believed if he was restored to the throne they would get their lands back. The battle itself was not between Catholics and Protestants. There were in fact Catholics and Protestants on both sides, and it was almost a century later, in 1795, that the Orange Institution, a secret society known as the Orange Order or Lodge, was founded in County Armagh to honour the House of Orange-Nassau of the Dutch-born King William (who had died many years earlier) and to exercise and uphold British and Protestant supremacy over the Irish Nationalists and Roman Catholics.

This was the dire political picture when the Irish first flooded into Glasgow. By 1835, as I have said, there were twelve Orange Masonic lodges in the city and conflict between the thousands of immigrant Irish Protestants and Catholics was assured.

The Battle of the Boyne is celebrated annually still by Orangemen, but on the twelfth rather than the first of July because eleven days were lost in the change from the Julian to the Gregorian calendar in 1752.

In Glasgow, however, the proddies, as the Protestants are known, marched not only on 12 July, but on every Catholic holiday, simply to upset the Catholic faithful, and from 1924 the Bridgeton Billy Boys turned the heat up on their Catholic rivals, the Norman Conks. (When you put it like that it becomes increasingly difficult to sustain a pretence that the troubles are truly even political any longer.)

The derivation of the name Billy Boys is obvious, a celebration of King Billy's victory at the Battle of the Boyne. Through happenchance the name was also appropriately deferential to their leader, Billy Fullerton.

The name of their traditional enemy, the Norman Conks, apparently a reference to a famous eleventh-century turning point in British history, is in reality merely a pointer to the gang's original base, Norman Street in Bridgeton, just west of Dalmarnock Station.

The Billy Boys was formed after a football match on Glasgow Green between a team called Kent Star and some boys from Bridgeton. Billy Fullerton made the mistake of scoring a goal and was later set upon by Kent Star supporters armed with hammers. Fullerton vowed revenge and the Bridgeton Billy Boys was formed. So successful was it that it could eventually claim a membership of 800.[17]

Sam Gilmore, a native of neighbouring Calton, whose family were also residents of Bridgeton grew up in the 1940s and '50s, when the gang was still exercising its power over the area:

The Billy Boys ran a protection racket – shopkeepers and householders. They used to come around and collect for 'the cause', a shilling or two shillings. Normally they were Catholic houses they went to, and let them know, 'If you don't pay, your windows go in' . . . unspoken.

The gang was operating in an area originally designated as Protestant by the eighteenth and early nineteenth century

Irish weavers, but which was now partly a Catholic stronghold, with significant Protestant pockets in Bridgeton.

It was in the context of living in the Protestant community of Bridgeton that Tommy Gilmour's father changed the spelling of his name from the Catholic to the Protestant form. It has been a talking point ever since, as his cousin Sam records:

> My father never really forgave his brother [Tommy's father] for spelling his name Gilmour, because it was for business purposes. 'M-o-r-e' was Catholic. He was in the heart of Brigton, where the Billy Boys congregated. He decided to change it.
>
> Our grandfather wouldn't have bothered. There were six brothers living in a one-bedroom flat – (there were bigger families doing that!). My father was farmed out to a maiden aunt and she made sure that Gilmore was the name.
>
> The Gorbals was a Celtic stronghold. The Calton was a Celtic stronghold, as were small parts of Brigton. From Glasgow Cross to Abercrombie Street was staunchly Catholic. From Abercrombie Street up to near enough Celtic Park was all Protestant – the Billy Boys.

It was Belfast ready-made, a tinderbox waiting to be ignited:

> The Billy Boys were royalist, Protestant, right wing: they used to try to stop the Labour Party meetings. But they didn't go into the Gorbals and they didn't go in the Calton, and they certainly didn't go into the Garngad, up by the Royal

Infirmary, which was more a hundred per cent [Catholic]
than the Calton.

Ninety per cent of the Billy Boys didn't come from
Brigton. Yes, there was a pub in Brigton, the Mermaid, it was
infamous, where you could see King Billy riding on his white
horse. And the Toll at Brigton Cross was more or less their
headquarters. But they came from all over to be associated.

This made sense. When, in *No Mean City*, Johnnie Stark's
brother Peter is beaten up by gangsters from Plantation (by
Prince's Dock, far to the west of the Gorbals and
Bridgeton), his assailant says, 'Tell him Cameron did that
tae ye! Cameron frae the Toll!'. This is the Bridgeton
Toll, as Bridgeton Cross was known locally, that Sam
remembers:

At the time of the Coronation [1952], there were
decorations all over the Toll in Brigton: Union Jacks . . . that
was long before the UDA or UFF.[18] And the Catholics from
the Gorbals and the Calton and parts of Brigton all
descended on the Toll. They were doing a lot of road
renovations at the time, so with the pick shafts from the
roadworks they went to dig up the Toll. There wasn't
enough Billy Boys to stop them. They had scarpered.

You treated the gangs as part of life. For example, on St
Patrick's Day. You understand up here we still have Catholic
schools and Protestant schools. The Catholic schools have six
weeks' summer holiday, the Protestant schools have eight
weeks. But there are also holidays of 'obligation' [Catholic
saints' days]. So the Catholics had a half-day on St Patrick's
Day. You went to school in the morning and you were taken

to Mass. In Calton, a Catholic stronghold, there were people outside selling shamrocks. Afterwards we used to congregate and go and attack the Protestant schools.

The kids were in the playground when we were off for half a day. This was before Maggie Thatcher's time [as Health Minister she did away with school milk] and we used to store up milk bottles of milk and then hail them down on them. Now, think on that. It was bloody nonsense, but when I was eight or nine, that was the way of it.

Catholic Gerard Coyle remembers that for kids the fighting itself was probably more important than the Catholic or Protestant cause:

I remember one day me and a wee guy . . . I can't remember his name . . . we got chased [by Protestants] past the primary school and we thought we were safe, [but] we met these four guys who were at St Francis, the other big Catholic school over in the Gorbals, and they said, 'You guys from St John's?' 'Aye.' 'We're gonnae gi' you a doing.' So, we had to run from them as well, so it was very ecumenical [laughs].[19]

Tony Jaconelli grew up in a mixed family, 'with a double background' as he put it. This released him from extremism in adulthood, but the issue remained a live one. His Italian-born father, though not a practising Catholic, had gone to a Catholic school in Bridgetown 'and all the rest of it'. His Irish-Glaswegian mother, meanwhile, was Orange.

My granny was quite bitter, and it must have been hard for her when her daughter married a Catholic, but she never seemed to try and stop it. All the time I was growing up, particularly on a certain date in July, I was reminded by my mother that, 'because of you I missed the Walk'. She was referring to the annual parade by members of the Orange Lodge to celebrate the victory of William of Orange at the Battle of the Boyne in 1690. She missed the celebrations because I was in the process of entering this world. All my fault? I don't think so.

When we entered the computer age someone gave me a small program which would tell you which day of the week you were born on. I duly typed in my date of birth expecting the day to be designated as a Saturday [day of the march]. It came up Sunday! I mentioned this to Mum and all she could say was, 'Yes, but I was in labour for a long time!'[20]

For adults, the conflict had more serious implications. When the Orange Order first led marches through the city streets in the early-nineteenth century, most authorities in Glasgow were opposed to the idea, including even the Glasgow *Herald*, newspaper-of-choice for the mainly Protestant middle class. The paper was resolutely opposed to an 1822 Orange parade through the centre of town, as can be seen from the tone of an opinion piece run in July of that year:

We have been threatened for some time past with a Grand Orange Procession on this day, the throngest [the busiest and most crowded] in our Fair Week. The Magistrates very properly gave early intimation that none would be permitted. Notwithstanding that prohibition, the office-bearers of seven lodges assembled at nine o'clock in the morning opposite

the barracks, from which they marched to the number of
127 in procession to Fraser's Hall in King Street.[21]

From the outset, these organised marches led to problems, whether instigated by the marchers themselves or by opposition encountered in the streets through which they paraded, sometimes with horrific injuries and even death.

When the Billy Boys marched on some day of obligation, it was always down Catholic streets, more often than not provocatively in Norman Conks territory.

As soon as the offensive music was heard by the Norman Conks, they manned the upper windows and even the roofs in their streets and when the Billy Boys band tried to march past, it was met by a downpour of bricks, missiles, buckets of filth and broken glass. If the Norman Conks could have made boiling lead I am sure they would not have hesitated to use that, too. It was certainly all that would have been needed to complete the picture of a medieval siege.[22]

The Billy Boys were drilled in military fashion. They were organised administratively, raised money effectively and had secret bank accounts, and their drum and flute band was trained by professionals in Belfast. Sam Gilmore's judgement on the Billy Boys that they were 'just a bunch of poofs' should be taken with a pinch of salt. Glaswegians never lose their affiliations. The Billy Boys were quite different from most gangs, who acted spontaneously and any booty was immediately enjoyed in the nearest pub.

Sometimes hundreds of men would be involved in a street-fight, so many that it was impossible for the police to find out how or why it had started. Conflict might be sparked by a quarrel over something quite unimportant, a slight perhaps, or it might be deliberately provoked, gang members hanging around 'the buroo' and setting upon rival gang members collecting the dole.

The Glasgow *Evening Citizen* reported a Billy Boys wedding in 1926 raided by a neighbouring Catholic gang, the Calton Boys from Sam Gilmore's neck of the woods. The aggressors pelted the wedding guests with bottles, but the Billy Boys' bridegroom and best man were armed with a gun and a sword, and there was a running battle between church and the reception at a masonic hall in Struthers Street.[23]

In the 1930s the police met fire with fire. Seán Damer refers to the police of the interwar years as 'always the biggest and most successful gang in Glasgow'.[24]

Sir Percy Sillitoe, Chief Constable of the City of Glasgow Police Force from 1931–43, is remembered by many as a great gangbuster. During his tenure he favoured heavy-handed tactics in tackling violent crime, forming an undercover 'Untouchables' squad to infiltrate gangs and gain information, and on several occasions employing the technique of launching preemptive strikes against impending gang activity. Whether or not everybody would agree now with such violent police tactics, at times more reminiscent of a vigilante gang than a modern police force, Sillitoe's legacy was to last even into the post-war years.

Retired police officer Joe Pieri records a colleague's account of working the beat in a rough area near Saracen Cross in 1946:

> You, as a cop, were supposed to protect the public and we
> did just that. We sorted the neds out. No mercy, pick out the
> biggest of them, pick out the leaders and give them a good
> tanking and show them who was boss . . .[25]

The strict, often physical, justice meted out by the police was largely condoned and even encouraged by local magistrates. One particular judge, Lord Carmont, is remembered to this day by Glasgow criminals. Infamous amongst the underworld fraternity, the harsh sentences he dished out in the 1950s gave rise to the phrase 'copping a Carmont', still sometimes employed nowadays when a lengthy jail term is given. Even within the last few years, authorities in Glasgow have called for a return to the Carmont style, to put the message across that violent crime will not be tolerated.

Pieri laments the loss of Lord Carmont's brand of justice:

> I would say it was safer to walk the streets back then
> [1930s–50s] than now. By and large the neds wouldn't
> bother a passer-by, they used to fight amongst
> themselves . . . with other neds. The big weapon amongst
> them was the razor, a most dangerous thing. But there was
> a judge, Lord Carmont, who cured them of that habit. Put
> the skids under them he did. Every time someone came up
> with a razor charge he would show no mercy. Swish, ten
> years. Swish, ten years. Swish, ten years. Ten years meant ten
> years then. That stopped them using razors. It used to be
> that up Lyon Street, up the Garscube Road, all the neds had
> the mark of Zorro, slash, across the face, but Carmont
> stopped that.[26]

It is difficult to say how successful the hard-line approach adopted by Lord Carmont and the men of the City of Glasgow Police Force was, given that so many crimes went unreported or were dealt with by the police in an off-the-record manner, but no one can pretend that the problem of gang violence and knife crime went away. In fact between 1950 and 1973 the incidence of (recorded) crimes against the person more than doubled, from 950 to 2,498 per year, and by 1996 the figure had almost tripled again, to 6,953 incidents per year.

The police were not the only people tackling the gang problem, however. A more astute strategy may have been that of certain priests in the community, who recognised some of the qualities celebrated in gang culture as being useful in less antisocial activities.

Loyalty was one of the qualities that characterised gang ethos. You wouldn't grass up your worst enemy if the police were involved. It was part of a code of honour. As Sam Gilmore says:

> You would never report even an enemy to the polis. The Catholics saw the polis as all Masonic bastards. I don't know what the Protestants thought of them. I didn't understand that breed. You understand your own breed, but . . .

Three priests – J. A. C. Murray of Park Church and S. H. R. Warnes of St Francis-in-the-East in Bridgeton, and J. Cameron Peddie of Hutchesontown church in the Gorbals – noted the gang members' loyalty, independence, competitive spirit, organisation, and the ability to work within a team, as worthwhile and decided to do something for them. They set up clubs that would divert these qualities into sport and other activities. Peddie told his story in the Glasgow *Evening Citizen* in January 1955.[27]

When he first arrived in the Gorbals he found a friendly congregation and real sense of community in the impoverished tenement societies. He also discovered that the local street gangs were not, as in Bridgeton, fired up by the Protestant/Catholic question.

First, he tried to get them involved with church clubs, and they told him where to go. So he started up clubs for them to run on their own, and in which he had a sort of honorary position as leader. Drinking, gambling and swearing were forbidden; dancing, singing, concerts and boxing were encouraged. Thirty clubs, with some 4,000 members, were formed.

If tensions ever reached breaking point, Peddie would intervene and such were his negotiating skills that serious trouble was always averted. Once, he managed to resolve a problem between a man who had killed another in a fight and someone he believed had grassed him up. Peddie wrote:

> I talked to them in what I imagined the founder of our religion would have said in similar circumstances. Thus the man who had killed and the man whose evidence had condemned him were reconciled. It was a thrilling moment for me.

These priests looked not for the bad in gang members, but for the good. Said Peddie:

The first thing that impressed me deeply about the boys was their amazing loyalty to their class. 'Supposing,' I asked them, 'someone is killed in a fight and one of your men, though innocent, is charged with the death and you know the guilty man to be one of the other gang, would you not save your man by giving away the guilty person?' 'No,' they replied. 'If you are to mix with us, sir, you must understand we never give anyone away, even an enemy. This is the first principle of our code of honour.'

I was profoundly impressed with this and though I did not swear allegiance . . . I resolved not to let them down. I never gave away any of them and they knew it. What a magnificent spirit they had if only turned to other channels.

Peddie never broke their code, nor did he foist his religion on them, or ever attempt to preach it to them.

Today, in no small part due to the increased incidence of mixed marriages, cross-party understanding and appreciation is growing in Glasgow and sectarian incidents are becoming rarer, particularly as various authorities have started to take the problem seriously. Headline-grabbing court cases have forced local authorities and national government to tackle the problem, and both Celtic and Rangers football clubs have launched high-profile initiatives to stamp out bigotry from Glasgow life.

The Catholic–Protestant conflict was far and away the most important alignment in the city over the past two centuries. But, as I have shown, in the Gorbals there was the possibility of another religious–political divide and a group whose appearance was more obviously foreign; they even spoke in a foreign language – the Jews.

Jews suffered in London's East End from violent racist attack, meeting the full force of fascism in the shape of Mosley's Blackshirts in the 1930s and again in the late '40s and '50s, many of the aggressors local right-wingers from Bethnal Green and neighbouring areas.

During the pre-War period Mosley travelled Britain looking for support for his anti-Semitic politics, holding meetings and rallies, making rousing speeches and marching through working-class ghettoes.

In Glasgow, many workers had been left wing, even communist, for a generation by the time he turned up, so that, for example, Monty Berkeley's anti-fascist work on the part of fellow Jews was done under the aegis of the Young Communist League:

> We in the Revolutionary Youth Movement were the only people who were opposing the Mosley fascists and carrying out anti-fascist activity, disrupting their meetings, first not allowing them to settle down. When one of the Mosleyites was holding a meeting at Queen's Park gates we had arranged that we would all go and not allow them to speak. He was standing on a platform . . . and we had arranged that four of us would come and lift a leg [of the platform] and toss them up in the air and throw them out . . . This was frowned on by the official Jewry.[28]

Monty recalled six or seven Blackshirts on the platform, 'all with their swastika armbands'.

One may conclude from this that Glasgow was not a very anti-Semitic place. Some, however, would disagree, citing the fact that even recently Jews weren't allowed to join the Golf Club. But Ellis Cohen holds no grudges:

> We have our own golf course now, but the anti-Semitism
> was there from Day One. You always get, 'Bloody Jew'. I
> remember years ago when I was married, my children came
> up to the house one day and said to my wife: 'There's a new
> family come into our street and they told us to go home.'
> What they meant was, 'You're Jewish, go back to Palestine.'
> The ignorance in the Glaswegian was that they thought if
> you were Jewish you were born in Palestine. I never heard
> anything so absurd in all my life. We are from all over the
> world. It is a way of life.

Generally, the perception is that the Catholic–Protestant
strife served to eclipse any violent anti-Semitism in the
city, but that is not to say that there wasn't discrimination against the Jews, or that there were not instances of
racism.

The joke was, says Rosa Sacharin, curator of the archive
at the Jewish Museum in Glasgow, that of every new face in
the city, officialdom asked: 'Are you a Protestant or a
Catholic?' If you replied, 'I am a Jew.' They would say, 'Yes,
but are you a Jewish Protestant or a Jewish Catholic?'[29]

It didn't matter who you were, at every level of life you
had to choose – Protestant or Catholic.

> Going up to school, you heard them shouting out: 'Are you
> a Billy or a Dan [Protestant or Catholic]?' If you said the
> wrong thing, you got hit in the head.[30]

In time, in the Gorbals, there were not only Billies and Dans, but 'old tin cans'.

> If you were an old tin can you were a Jew.[31]

Exclusive to the Jew-Goy discrimination was the fact that there were no dedicated schools for them. Unlike the Catholics, they had to brave their tormentors every day. Delia Berkley's first taste of a non-Jewish environment was at Hutchesons' Girls' Grammar School. There were three Jewish girls out of ninety in her year:

> There were three sections and in each of them was put a Jewish girl. We could only be together in the breaks. There was a fair amount of anti-Semitism, because I was the unknown . . . There were drawings on the blackboard, notes in your desk – Jewish caricatures and 'Get out of our school', type of thing. Very hurting. After a year I was able to answer the questions of the other pupils: why I did not eat the meat they ate, and why I took different holidays. And they understood. They became interested and by the third year, half of them wanted to convert, because they had worked out that I got some amazing amount of holidays which they did not get.[32]

Alec Bernstein, born three years before the First World War, recalled quite frightening episodes:

> Oh, during the war I was knocked around like hell. The kids used to crowd round me, pinch my piece, and shout, 'You German Jew! You German Jew!' It made me a very timid

child. [But] I remember one time I was going out of the
playground and another kid stepped alongside me and said,
'I saw you being hit, did they pinch your piece?' I said, 'Aye,
they pinched my piece and it had sugar on it.' Brown sugar
at that time you didn't get. He said, 'Come home wi' me
and I'll gie ye a piece and jeely.' And I went with him . . . I
can remember to this day the steps that led up to a
house . . . standing on their pavement . . . I remember it
taking about ten minutes. He must have been making it! It
was quite a while, you know? And he came down and
handed me the piece and jeely and that was it . . . Times
were hard. It was a kind thought.

**Alec was, in fact, Russian, not German. He lived in
Stockwell Street, just over the Clyde from the Gorbals:**

It was a wee mini Gorbals. Our street into Clyde Street is just
one big block. There was quite a number of Jewish families,
and the kids used to play together and with the non-Jewish
kids as well. Come the Passover or the Jewish New Year we
got into our nice togs, and the other kids, the non-Jewish
kids, recognised that this was our thing, you know. We got
along together, there was never any anti-Semitism. It's only
when you get older that this is thrashed into you.

As we've seen, discrimination also became more serious for
Catholics after they left school. They could not get
employed to learn a trade. When Alec Bernstein was
fourteen he went to work for a Jewish manager in a
warehouse. The first day was the last he was called by his
true name, which is Isaac:

> The Jewish manager said, 'That's a helluva name. We'll call
> you Alec from now on.' So, since I was fourteen I've been
> called Alec . . . I was quite happy about it.[33]

The manager was introducing Alec to the reality that as an adult a Jew could expect, as a Catholic could, if not persecution, certainly discrimination in the labour market. The same was true of housing, as Joe and Rosa Sacharin found out: 'We don't rent to a Jew,' a friend was told. 'Oh,' she said. 'Was that why Christ was born in a stable?'[34]

CHAPTER EIGHT

Glasgow at War

The Calton weavers' strike in 1787 may be said to have been the start of the workers' movement in Scotland, and throughout the nineteenth century there were eruptions of discontent, but, come the 1890s, workers in Glasgow were ready finally to cast off the shackles and speak out, not in poetry like the weaver William Billington, but in highly organised worker politics. As the nineteenth century gave way to the twentieth the forces to be known as Red Clydeside began to take shape; the new politics precipitated by the monstrously successful workers' revolution in Russia.

In the vanguard was John Maclean, who, in the early years of the new century preached socialist revolution in Glasgow and to the west of the city, in Paisley.

In 1903 James Maxton, his first disciple, an eighteen-year-old student from Pollokshaws, an affluent district on the South Side of Glasgow, began attending Maclean's open-air meetings and was won over. For the next two years the pair ran an evening class together at Pollokshaws Academy; called 'Citizenship and the social classes' it had Karl Marx's *Das Kapital* as a set text.

Then came William Gallacher, born in Paisley in 1881, who also owed his 'awakening' to the many open-air Marxist and socialist meetings at this time. First a member of the Independent Labour Party (ILP) – an organisation with a socialist constitution – he too came under Maclean's influence and in 1909 joined the more radical Social Democratic Federation.

These three men did much to create the ferment of far-left politics which characterised Glasgow in the first half of the twentieth century.

Maclean ran up against the law many times for his anti-war activities, and in 1916 was sentenced to three years in prison for sedition, only to be released fourteen months later after a massive campaign on his behalf. Demonstrating the respect with which he was held at the highest level, in January 1918 Vladimir Ilyich Lenin himself, first premier of the Soviet Union, appointed him first Bolshevik Consul for Scotland to the new government in Russia.

In 1920 Maclean established the Scottish Workers Republican Party in Glasgow and declared that 'we can make Glasgow a Petrograd, a revolutionary storm centre second to none'. The following year saw him – effectively 'the first native representative of Soviet Russia in Britain' – contesting the ward of Kinning Park in the Glasgow municipal elections, but delivering his address from Duke Street Prison. Two years later he was dead, aged only forty-four.

But his disciples pressed on, if not always with the revolutionary zeal he would have liked. Maxton opted for the constitutional road, serving not the Communist Party but the ILP, gaining nonetheless a reputation as a fiery socialist and anti-war speaker at meetings throughout Scotland. Rising to divisional organiser, his work led to the establishment of trade unionism in education, and in the 1922 general election he was one of ten Glasgow candidates elected as Labour MPs; his constituency, Bridgeton.

Gallacher went on to play a more revolutionary role in industrial disputes as a leader of the Clyde Workers' Committee (CWC), a workers' soviet which met to co-ordinate strike action across the region. At this time, so he declared later in his autobiography *Revolt on the Clyde*, 'the workers were in a mood to tear up Glasgow by the roots'.

In 1920 he represented Clyde shop stewards at the second congress of the Communist International in Moscow, where Lenin first advocated a communist party for Britain. He helped Maclean set up the party that same year. Henceforth, the Clyde was the main centre of communist politics in Britain.

A member of the party's central committee from 1922–63 and an elected MP for the mining area of West Fife from 1935–51, Gallacher was the only Communist MP in the House of Commons until 1945, when Phil Piratin, MP for Mile End (Stepney) in London's East End, joined him. Gallacher was, for many years, chairman of the

Communist Party in Britain, and became president in 1963, two years before he died.

Attending the work of these men and others was an explosion of strike activity, and the emergence of a clutch of socialist groups on Clydeside, notably the Scottish Labour Party, the Independent Labour Party, the Social Democratic Federation and the British Socialist Party.

The period 1910–14 is sometimes referred to as 'the great unrest'. Of all the activity, the all-out strike of 12,000 workers at the previously peaceful Singer's sewing machine factory on Clydebank, led by activists closely associated with a movement called the Industrial Workers of the World, signalled the rise in working-class consciousness.

But it was during the First World War (1914–18) that change began to accelerate, and the years to 1922 are usually those associated with the term Red Clydeside. Despite the illegality of strike action during hostilities, in 1915 Glasgow was the centre of the first major wartime strike in Britain, which spawned the CWC.

Further workplace discontent was led by radical shop stewards in 1916, many of them Marxists. The government, nervous that the CWC were orchestrating a plan to impede the production of munitions for the war, responded by deporting nine of the leaders from the city (to Edinburgh!), making several arrests for sedition and suppressing the CWC newspaper, *The Worker*.

In January 1919 a workers' campaign for a radical reduction in working hours to a forty-hour week escalated into a strike involving more than 80,000 workers across Clydeside and a loss of a staggering 1.25 million working days. During the strike a large demonstration occurred in

George Square in the centre of Glasgow, on Friday, 31 January. Provoked by a police baton charge, the demonstrators rioted, cut tram lines and raised the red flag. Fighting raged between strikers, ex-servicemen and the police. In one incident at the Saltmarket two policemen were stripped of their uniforms and had to make their escape naked. The whole affair was famously described in the Cabinet by the Scottish Secretary of State as, 'not a strike, it was a Bolshevik rising'. In response, the government arrested the strike leaders and drafted in troops, tanks and a howitzer, and set up machine gun nests around the city centre. This effectively stabilised the situation, though discontent smouldered on.

The 1915 strike had coincided with the women's rent strike, demonstrating a solid transition of political views to the left throughout the whole body of working-class Glasgow. The women proceeded with their more holistic, altruistic, and utopian vision, a genuine expectation that co-operative principles could create a better world, establishing in tenement society a model of how the new socialist state, to which the militant male activists were committed, might work; the men, however, chose antagonism and confrontation, which is what brought the whole industrial pack of cards down upon them.

But first came the glory. The membership of the ILP tripled in size over 1914–17 alone, whilst votes for Labour and Socialist Party candidates in Clydeside elections increased almost tenfold between 1910 and 1918.

The advance culminated in the landslide Labour victory in the parliamentary election of 1922, when forty-two per cent of the Glasgow electorate voted Labour and the party won ten out of the fifteen Glasgow seats (previously Labour had held just one). The ten Red Clydesider MPs – including the fiery James Maxton – left Glasgow for Westminster to the cheers of a tumultuous crowd of supporters and the chanting of *The Red Flag*.

Politics meant something then. Ordinary people were passionate political animals. There was mass unemployment, something to protest about, and a government which seemed, in its often ill-advised tactics, to court an inflammatory response.

Support for a new workers' democracy was brewing nationally. In 1925, after a dispute between coal miners and mine owners over a reduction in wages, the General Council of the Trades Union Congress (TUC) threatened widespread worker support in other industries. The government responded, apparently benignly, by making available a subsidy to restore wage levels for a period of nine months, during which time a Royal Commission would investigate the problems of the mining industry.

When the report was published, however, it recommended a reduction in wages. Around the same time, mine owners projected further adjustments to wages and hours. And it was this inflammatory situation that led to the General Strike.

The TUC brought dockers out on strike in sympathy with the miners, along with railwaymen, transport workers, printers, builders, iron and steel workers – some three million men – engineers and shipyard workers to follow, if their terms were still not met.

A conference of the Trades Union Congress was convened on 1 May 1926, at which it was decided that the strike would begin two days later. Tensions in Glasgow ran high, as even the tram drivers came out. University students, part of the Establishment in those days, broke the all-out strike in the city by driving the trams. Sam Gilmore:

The tram car was the main mode of transport – you rarely
saw a motor car. The students were all – at that time –
middle class and upper class. It was before grants and so on.
They commandeered the trams and when they came
through Calton and Brigton, the people smashed the trams
and set about the students. That's why on student charity
day my father wouldn't give a penny. He hated the students.
Latterly, you know, they were working class, but not in his
day. Students were the biggest scabs during the 1926 strike.

However, it was all rather short lived. Only days into the strike the chairman of the Royal Commission, whose report on the mining industry had caused all the problems, got in a huddle with the TUC and together they hammered out a set of proposals – a National Wages Board with an independent chairman, a minimum wage, etc., etc. The proposals were accepted by the TUC negotiating committee, who on 12 May called off the General Strike. It had lasted only nine days in all.

The men went back to work, and only then were the proposals rejected by the Miners' Federation, and by the government, who even introduced a Bill into the House of Commons that permitted the mine owners to announce new terms of employment based on an eight-hour working day, which had earlier been reduced to seven.

The miners had been cheated, sold down the river. They

held out on strike on their own until December, when hardship forced them to drift back to work.

The following year, the Conservative government passed the Trade Disputes and Trade Union Act, which made coming out on strike in sympathy with another industry illegal. The General Strike had been an unmitigated disaster.

It later emerged just how duplicitous Stanley Baldwin's Government had been – even the wages subsidy granted in 1925 had been designed simply to give them time to prepare to smash the unions. The government justified its tactics on the basis of the threat worker power posed to national security.

The General Strike, although overwhelmingly supported, had a relatively slight impact on Glasgow. The TUC only called out workers in the engineering and shipbuilding trades the day before the strike was called off.

Nevertheless, following its disastrous culmination, many workers lost their jobs, and employers, with the tacit approval of government, often refused to reinstate trade unionists, choosing the moment to break union power within their workforces.

The two main Glasgow newspaper publishers, George Outram Ltd and James Hedderwick & Son, who published the *Herald*, the *Evening Times* and the *Evening Citizen*, were among the first to adopt an anti-trades union employment policy within the publishing and print industries.

With the Wall Street crash, which followed in 1929, the Great Depression began in earnest, and, as mentioned earlier, unemployment soared to thirty per cent in the city.

We may usefully note three responses to this.

The Communist Party's National Unemployed Workers'

Movement (NUWM) made its presence felt on behalf of the unemployed on marches in London, Glasgow, Liverpool and Manchester in the face of continual police surveillance, harassment, and attack. In June 1933 they organised a hunger march on Edinburgh. Over 1,000 marchers from across Scotland converged on the city, resisting expulsion for three days until they were allowed to present their demands. The only way the town council could get rid of them was to provide free transport home.

The government meanwhile offered a solution to unemployment of a less than sympathetic sort. Between 1929 and 1939, they set up twenty-five secret concentration camps in remote areas of Britain, where some 200,000 unemployed men were sent to break rocks, build roads and cut down trees for up to nine hours a day.

Finally, in 1938, they spent £10 million, not on food and clothing for the Glasgow poor, but on a huge extravaganza, an Empire Exhibition on a piece of green south of Govan and Ibrox Park, called Bellahouston Park. It was opened on 3 May by King George VI and Queen Elizabeth.

The two biggest buildings were the Palaces of Industry and Engineering, connected by Dominions and Colonial Avenues. There were national pavilions from the UK, Scotland, Canada, Australia, New Zealand, South Africa, Burma, Southern Rhodesia, East Africa, West African colonies and 'composite colonies'. The Scottish pavilion included a reconstructed Highland village complete with a chief's castle, a burn flowing into a painted backdrop and clanspeople spinning, weaving and singing in Gaelic. There was also a physical fitness pavilion, fountains, cascades lit up below in different colours,

an amusement park provided by Billy Butlin, bandstands, a
cinema, a women's pavilion, cafés, restaurants and milk-bars,
model council housing, four churches and the three hundred
feet high Tower of Empire . . . At its peak, three thousand
men were employed in the construction of the exhibition.[1]

Whatever the Communists thought about this celebration
of an Empire, won on the sweat and labour of Glasgow's
workers, the ordinary people went mad for it – 12,593,232
visited, many going time and again on the 12s./6d. season
pass or, if you were as small as John Milloy, squeezing
through a railing.

As a young resident of Govan in 1938, I watched with great
interest for a long time many of the preparations for the
Exhibition. Many times we, the boys on Crossloan Road in
Govan, walked up Helen Street or Craigton Road to see
what was happening . . . For the kids around 43 Crossloan
Road there was an added interest. One of their own, Leading
Signaller Johnny Brennan, RN, from their very own close,
would signal by semaphore from atop the Exhibition Tower,
and set in motion the parade that would lead the royal
couple to open the Exhibition.

On the day the Exhibition was due to open, various
military detachments formed up on Helen Street near the
White City dog racing track. The streets were absolutely
jammed with spectators. There were many bands, brass and
pipe, and all kinds of military orders being barked hither and
thither. Our vantage point was right beside the band of the
Royal Air Force, a very smart looking lot attired in uniforms
more like those of hussars than airmen. Shortly before the

parade got under way the air was rent asunder by the flypast of about twenty heavy bombers of the RAF, heading towards the city centre – a sight not at all common in 1938 Glasgow.

We never did see Johnny's signal from atop the tower, but the parade did set off and we followed it up onto the Paisley Road and along to the main entrance. The crowds were so thick that even we Govan urchins couldn't make our way up to the main entrance and got bogged down well out of sight of the royal couple opening the Exhibition, but very much in the grip of the unbelievable excitement.

It was truly a fantastic summer's entertainment, and I recall feeling at times that it was just unbelievable that all this world-class stuff was taking place here in my Govan. Young and all as I was, I still felt a great sadness when it was all over . . . Not long after the Exhibition's closing, things changed quite a bit. Some of the Exhibition's infrastructure was used to accommodate French Alpine troops evacuated from Norway in 1940, then by German POWs in 1943. Leading Signaller Johnny Brennan, RN, whose signals set the opening cermonies for the Exhibition in motion, went down with all his shipmates in the Cromarty Firth, aboard HMS *Exmouth*, torpedoed on 21 January 1940 . . .[2]

Britain had declared war with Germany at 11:15 a.m., on Sunday 3 September 1939. Immediately what this meant for Glasgow was increased prosperity for the engineering and shipbuilding industries. A steel boom was slung across the mouth of the Clyde to stave off invasion by U-boats, and men went to work with fresh purpose. The Clyde also became a major embarkation point during the hostilities and, though it suffered badly over a few days in 1941, its

OUR GLASGOW

position in the far north-west meant that it avoided the constant bombardment that inflicted London's docks.

To facilitate the sudden expansion of industry and make up for the drafting into the armed forces of men not protected by the Reserved Occupation Schedule, it might be expected that women suddenly came into their own in hitherto jealously guarded male occupations. But, amazingly, even during the wartime emergency the macho domain of industry – coalmining, iron and steel manufacture, shipbuilding, and the chemical industry – was jealously and rigorously guarded by the male workforce, despite the women showing that they were more than up for the challenge, as here at Hyde Park, one of the Springburn works, where they were now making tanks instead of locomotives.

> I'll tell you a story about that. Fourteen years old I was during the war. And they brought a lot of girls in and the boys found out they were getting more money. Fourteen of us went on strike, and they locked us in. But, you know, we were boys, and we climbed over the railway to get out . . . And then when we were out, they sent all of us a letter saying we had to go back or they would take special action, cos it was during the war. All the boys came back . . . We'd discussions with the representatives – I think it was the shop stewards then – the boys never got the chance to represent themselves anyway. And they decided to bring the boys up to the same rate as the girls. But the only thing about it was . . . they paid about fifty per cent of the boys off!

What were the girls employed to do?

They were heating rivets. And after that they started to teach
them to weld too. There were quite a lot of ladies in and a'
like, [you] know. Working and that. In fact, it finished up
that some of them were just as good as the men. Well that,
that was my history in Hyde Park.[3]

In wartime shipbuilding, women accounted for only about seven per cent of the workforce, and they were quickly pushed out again in the aftermath of war, which is a pity, not least because women tend to have more altruistic and optimistic priorities than men, rare qualities in wartime especially:

I worked in Gray, Dunn's biscuit factory. We made biscuits for
the soldiers – they were called 'hard tack' because you'd to
steep them in water for a while, for about an hour, before you
could eat them, they were that hard! I had a small family then
as well, and my mother looked after them while I worked.
Everybody had a different part of the process, and I was at the
bit where you solder the lids on. And we used to put wee
notes in, before we soldered the lids on! Oh, aye, love an'
kisses on the bottom of the notes! And S.W.A.L.K! We'd put
in the wee notes so it would cheer them up, opening the tins,
having a wee laugh and finding a wee note.[4]

Ellis Cohen noted in particular that beyond industry, much had been going on by way of preparation for war, long before hostilities started:

The one thing I admire about this country is that we were
the only ones to prepare for war. The French were so stupid

you couldn't believe them. They built the Maginot Line, a dug-out! The Germans marched over it. How long did it take the Germans to capture Europe? It was because the Europeans had no defence! In 1938 you had an extra class at school, from three to four p.m. Girls usually did knitting, boys did handiwork. But what did we do in 1938? We assembled gas masks and put gas mask cardboard boxes together. At [aged] ten I was doing that.

For Maria Fyfe, born in 1938, there was a special reason for remembering these preparations:

Every child of that time remembers their Mickey Mouse gas mask, but when you are a baby or a small infant, you need something specially designed to prevent small hands, in ignorance of what they are doing, pushing the mask aside. There was such an invention, and you can see it in Glasgow's People's Palace today. It consisted of a bag big enough to hold an infant body, the gas mask itself, and a wide clear panel to allow the baby to see out. My mother had to carry it everywhere she went with me in case there was a gas attack.

In fact, the government had been trying to prepare people for defence against bombing since 1935, and some local authorities, Clydebank among them, had refused to co-operate.[5]

Six months before war was declared, Anderson shelters[6] were erected in back courts. Purpose-built, these air raid shelters measured 1.8 metres high by 1.4 metres wide and 2 metres long, and were made out of corrugated iron. They cost seven pounds to buy, but were free to families earning less than £250 a year. By September 1940 2.3 million of them had been distributed throughout Britain. But many Glaswegians felt safer sheltering in their closes, the entrance halls leading to the back courts of the incredibly well-built tenements, and this was encouraged. Ellis Cohen explains the drill:

> If there was an air raid you had to come down and stand in the close, and at the back of the close, three or four feet from the back of the close, they put up a big wall of bricks, and at the end of the pavement they had a wall up too. So, if a bomb blast came it couldn't blast through the close. Bomb blast killed you. A lot of people died in the war without a mark on them. If you got caught in a bomb blast it damaged your brain. If you were inside you were all right. Our house was destroyed by a bomb blast, but we were alright, we were just blown to the floor. The blast affected the building and cracked it and eventually it fell down, but we survived. But if we were somewhere outside, the blast was so fierce it destroyed your brain.
>
> The problem with these blast walls was that people used to walk into them and damage themselves. It really happened. They were painted white at the side, but during the blackout, with no light to reflect off them, you simply couldn't see them.

These blast barriers, which prevented the possibility of bomb blast tunnelling up the close, were known as baffle walls. Some closes were also reinforced with steel-like scaffolding or with sturdy wood shafts, like pit props.

Listening to the BBC nine o'clock news became a ritual,

and when war broke out, a prearranged evacuation strategy was set in motion nationally, with mixed results.

Eileen and Harry Soppitt lived in New Aberdour in Aberdeenshire, and were hosts for a series of Glaswegian evacuees:

Our village had its usual quota of evacuees at the start of the war. Most, if not all of them from Glasgow and that area. It must have been quite a culture shock for them coming [in 1939] from a city where all amenities and shops of all sorts were available to them. Our village had no amenities of any kind. Not only that, we had no bakery, no chemist, no doctor, no chip shop and no cinema. So they must have felt as if they had arrived in the last place on earth, and as a result of this isolation, apart from one or two families with children, they gradually returned to their homes 'down south'.

However, after the blanket bombing of Clydebank [in 1941], they all streamed back to where they thought they would be safer. This return lasted until again the isolation and the lack of things to entertain them made them seek – I can't say the bright lights as it was blackout time – but certainly a civilisation they were more used to.

But one summer evening – during the second influx – one of the mothers had a distressing and to her a terrifying experience. It was about seven-thirty at night and she had gone to the beach for a walk with her toddler son – about four – and her little girl, who was not quite old enough to walk. They had been gathering shells and pretty stones and were now on their way home up the steep hill that led up from the beach. It was getting near the little boy's bedtime and he was dawdling on behind – every now and then being urged on by his mother. At one point she stopped to wait for him to catch up with her and while she stood she looked out to sea. She noticed an unusual disturbance on the water and then rooted to the spot she saw a submarine start to surface. It wasn't until she saw the black cross on the conning tower that she realised it was a German U-boat and when she broke her stupor she grabbed the toddler by the arm and struggled up the mile to the village where she arrived screaming, breathless and almost speechless.

We could hear her in the house and my father (Harry Soppitt) the village policeman, ran out to see what was the matter, and when she got her breath back she yelled, 'That bl***y Hitler. He chased me out of Glasgow and now he's followed me up here!' She must have felt the war had turned into a personal vendetta.[7]

From the evacuees' side, memories are very mixed:

I was evacuated to Dumfriesshire [and] the lady I stayed with, she was awful good to me.

. . . In Glasgow we lived in a tenement building. She had a bungalow and a bathroom and everything, so, in some ways, it might have seemed quite a good move. But oh, ye missed yer mammy! And you'd get lonely, you know. You gret [cried] every night. Well, I gret every night, though nobody knew you gret.[8]

My sister had two sons evacuated to Lochranza [on the Isle of Arran] during the war. It was a big terraced house, two sisters and a brother or something, but they were elderly and they couldnae take care of the children, the children were left . . . There was maybe half a dozen children with them, and they couldnae look after them, couldnae clean their heads or anything like that. They came back in an awful state. [My sister] took them home . . . She went to see them and she broke her heart, she brought them away again. They were old, the people, and they couldnae look after them.[9]

It wasn't until June 1940 that anyone in Glasgow had a sense of the reality of war. After the fall of France, on 26 May, the order went out for the complete evacuation of the British Expeditionary Force, almost 340,000 men who had been fighting in France, and around 118,000 French soldiers. It was the sight of a battalion of these that first brought the war home to Ellis Cohen:

One day on South Portland Street, which is a very, very broad street, all of a sudden, we are out playing in the afternoon, and soldiers came marching up the street – about twenty broad, right across the street – and as they came closer we saw they were French soldiers, they had a wee helmet, we could see they were French. They had come out from Central Station, marched over the bridge [towards the Gorbals] and come up South Portland Street. Some had helmets like firefighters' helmets, but they all had bandages around their heads, red with blood. What happened was, when they landed from Dover, when they brought them in . . . You know, they took over the whole railway . . . And sent them right across the country, because the Germans would have followed us over to kill everyone. As soon as they came across the Channel on boats they were loaded onto trains. There were WVS girls here giving them out cups of tea, no worries. So when they come off the trains, those who were fit to walk, walked up our street . . . I would say, three or four hundred of them. There wasn't one that didn't have blood on them, because they'd been in the fighting, on the beaches, with the bombs . . . This was the first taste we had of the war, because the bombing didn't happen until 1941.

On the tenth of the same month, June 1940, Mussolini declared war on Britain and caused a particular problem in Glasgow. The long night that followed – the darkest for the Italian community in the city – will never be forgotten.

The Italians famously ran the ice cream cafés and chip shops in the city. They settled in Glasgow just after the end of the First World War, and were a thoroughly integrated, relatively prosperous community.

Tony Jaconelli, whose Italian father had lived in Glasgow since childhood, describes the plight in which his family found itself:

My father came here from Italy when he was eight, so he's never really been an Italian, except during the war when he got stuck in an internment camp for his nationality . . . He came here when he was eight years old, and went to the Sacred Heart in Bridgeton for schooling. After a couple of years his accent was totally gone.

When the Second World War broke out he got interned, so did the rest of the family. There was a knock on the door at night, and he got arrested. My mother was frantic – what had he done, you know? – and they took him down to Tobago Street in Bridgeton for a while, and then eventually they took him up to Maryhill Barracks, where everybody else was. There were a few escapades going on up there – everybody wanted to know what was happening. There was some locals looking to cash in on the circumstances, shouting 'Anybody in there wanting anything?' So people were throwing down money and going 'Get me a paper', or 'go and call my wife', you know? And of course they never came back once they got the money in their pockets.

So these poor characters up there didnae know anything, poor guys stuck up there, most of them were shopkeepers in Glasgow – they'd a business to run – but what they didn't know was that there were people out there knocking lumps out their shops and everything, crashing windows out, breaking in, stealing things. A lot of that went on. There was one little fellow, worked with my dad, called Joe Rea, and he had five sons in the British army and a daughter in the WAAFS and they still trashed his shop. I don't think he ever forgave the Scots.[10]

In Maryhill, to the north-west of the city on the River Kelvin, a mixture of industrial tenements and 1920s 'garden suburb'-type housing, young Robert Douglas recalled vividly just such a scene at Cocozza's Blythswood Café on the corner of Maryhill Road and Trossachs Street. He describes it in his book, *Night Song of the Last Tram: A Glasgow Childhood*:

Old Peter (Pietro) Cocozza, Italian-born, had been taken away that afternoon to be interned for 'the duration'. His two sons, Bertie and Rennie, born in Glasgow, were not subject to internment.

The mob stopped outside the café. As usual, a few local

boys were standing blethering under the streetlight on the corner. At first they just watched developments.

'Hey Eyeties! We're here tae put yer windaes in. You're no' gonny get stabbed in the back like Mussolini would dae it. We're gonny fuckin' dae it right in front of ye!'

There was a chorus of shouts, threats and other oaths from the rest of the vigilantes. Inside the shop, Rennie, the youngest, looked out at the gang from behind the counter. The family had feared this might happen after the previous day's treacherous act by Mussolini. Rennie ran out into the street to confront them.

'Look, ye have nae cause tae put oor windaes in. My brother, Bertie, wiz called up a month ago intae the RAF. Ah've already registered for the call-up. Ah'll be away maself as soon as ah turn eighteen. Ah'm daeing fire-watching at nights until they send for me.'

'You're fuckin Eyeties just like the rest o' them. Anywye, they've locked up yer auld man, huvn't they?'

'He's only locked up 'cause he wiz born in Italy. My father disnae support Mussolini; he's got nae time for him. Honest.'

'Aye, so ye say. C'mon, lads, let's put the bastard's windows in!'

The mob was about to surge forward when Rennie, in a futile attempt to stop them, spread out his arms.

'My brother's already daein' his bit in the forces and ah'll soon be away. It's bad enough havin' my father locked up for nothing. It's jist no' fair tae smash oor windaes.'

So frustrated had Rennie become while trying to reason with his tormentors, he burst into tears. The gang of youths halted. There were murmurs of dissent from some of them: 'Och, mibbe we shouldnae dae their windaes.' 'It's a bit much tae dae their shoap when the two boys will soon be in the forces.'

The ringleader was still for it.

'The auld man's been put in the jail, huzn't he? They widnae lock him up for nuthin'. Ah'm for putting their windaes in!' . . .

As the confrontation unfolded, the four or five local lads continued to watch from under the streetlight. One of them, big Mick Hoban, now decided it was time to try and tip the scales. He strode over and stood beside Rennie.

'Look, ah've grown up wi' these two boys. We went tae school the gither, played roon the streets the gither. Them, and their faither, have nae mair interest in that bastard Mussolini than ah huv.'

As he spoke, the rest of the small group he had been standing with ambled over and lined up either side of him and Rennie.

Mick continued, 'So if ye want tae put their windaes in, lads – your gonny huv tae get by us.' He looked at the leader. 'These are oor Tallies!'[11]

We have an idea of what happened to the many sons left behind by their interned fathers, from Tony Jaconelli, who was just six years old at the beginning of the Second World War:

I learned to survive because I was a 'wee Tally bastard' for a time. People passed me in the street, they'd give me a wee slap on the heid – 'Away back to Italy'. I would say, 'Whit wid ah want tae go tae Italy for? Ah'm fae Shettleston!'

For a long time I took my granny's name, Anderson, I was

Tony Anderson. That's how I felt about it – I was honestly quite ashamed to be a Jaconelli because of what they put me through at school, but gradually it disappeared. By the time I was a teenager I was proud of my name. I'm proud of being a Scot. I'm proud of having Irish connections and proud of having Italian connections. I'm definitely a patriotic Scot.

Tony's father, grandfather and Uncle Jack were, like many other Italian nationals, interned on the Isle of Man, while two other uncles went to Canada 'on the boat behind the *Arandora Star*,' Tony told me. 'The one that got torpedoed with quite a loss of life. My cousin, my uncle's daughter, said that they sailed through the wreckage of the *Andorra Star*, it must have been quite disturbing.'

Renzo Serafini was almost certainly on the Isle of Man at the same time as the Jaconellis. Serafini recalls that it was football that kept them sane:

We were shifted to the Isle of Man, so we started playing football with a small ball and then afterwards we started making teams up to pass the time away. We were locked in. We just had our walk in the morning, or a walk in the afternoon, one or the other. It was either an hour-and-a-half on the football field or an hour-and-a-half of a walk. In my house there was four hundred and fifty people, so we had about four teams there. House two had more teams, and house three had more teams. There was about seventeen hundred of us there.

We used to play inter-camps, sometimes we played the Jewish camp, but then there was four Italian camps there, you see, and we used to play against each other, too.

Sometimes we played the sentries and sometimes in our own camp we used to play Scots-Italians against English-Italians. I always thought this was great, there was me playing for Scotland!

Oh, by the way, we had a person there who was one of the directors of Birmingham FC, and he sent to Birmingham and we got their jerseys so we used to play in their colours, that's how we got our jerseys.

We used to train . . . You see, our camp was eighty-eight yards in length, eight yards across, and I used to gather the boys, you know the boys for the first team, and we used to train after roll call at night. We used to run back and forward, and then the hotels that we were staying in, there was stairs up three or four storeys. And we used to run up the stairs from one side and down the other side, up and down, up and down. We used to do that for about an hour, an hour-and-a-half, just to keep fit.[12]

Tony Jaconelli remembers that his father's forte developed in a different area. He ran the black market in the camp: 'They had a casino and everything, a home from home. You put a Glasgow man anywhere and he'll make the best of the situation – if there are loopholes he'll find them.' Then, somehow, Tony's father found a way to join the British army:

He got accepted to the Pioneer Corps, they were going to go round the country building Nissen huts and camps for the troops. He finished up a full corporal. My uncle Jacky, his older brother, he heard about it and applied. He had to come to the mainland for an interview, so they put him in the charge of two squaddies with their 303 rifles.

So, they're waiting at the station for the train to wherever they're going, and one of the guys says, 'I could murder a pint,' and Jack says, 'There's a pub over there.' The guy says, 'How the hell could we go into a pub with guns and you?' So, Jack says, 'I'll watch your guns!' So there's Jack left sitting on the railway platform with PoW gear on, holding two rifles! The squaddies never even thought about it for a minute!

When he got to the interview, my Uncle Jack had a photograph from when he was working at the Aberdeen Infirmary, and he had a photograph of himself taken in a bay window, with his jacket on back to front and a moustache painted on him, giving a Hitler salute. When he went to the interview they wanted to know why he was carrying a picture of Hitler in his wallet, but they wouldn't believe it was him. So he never got into the British Army.

First blood in Glasgow's war was drawn in September 1940, in a tragic quirk of fate. HMS *Sussex* was shored up under refit in the Clyde. Being prepared for Murmansk convoy duty, the ship was undergoing last-minute repairs in her engine room and was lying in the short basin at the end of Yorkhill Quay, Fairfield's Yard. In the early hours of 18 September, all of a sudden a plane came over and dropped a bomb which fell through a hole in the deck left by the removal of a few plates to allow access to the engine room:

I was a nineteen-year-old Royal Navy Able Seaman and had been onboard HMS *Sussex* since October 1938. I therefore knew pretty well every part of the ship. [The bomb] went through the lower and platform decks and burst in the engine room near oil fuel tanks.

Four members of the crew were killed, and twelve others died later of wounds. The lower deck at that point was destroyed, fire and bilge pumps were put out of action, the fuel tanks caught fire and flames were soon spreading fore and aft. But the worst part was the fact that all the magazines were full of ammunition, torpedoes, shells and depth charges, as well as eight torpedoes in the tubes on the upper deck. If the fire reached the magazines, a large part of Glasgow would have been threatened with death and destruction.

The crew that was on board that night started to fight the fire, but due to the lack of the fire and bilge pumps as well as the thick, black oil fuel smoke, we were struggling. However, the fire brigade soon arrived and we, the Navy lads, were glad to have some help. We got more than that. They took over and soon had pumps going and water being sprayed just where it was required in the fire.

I was ordered to help the firemen by guiding them around the ship and assisting with the hoses. It was a long, dirty and scary night. The plates were buckling with the intense heat and black slippery oil was everywhere.

Quite a few, including Navy men, were sent to the Western Infirmary with severe burns. It was then noticed that the torpedoes in the tubes were getting very hot and would probably explode with the heat. Although we tried to pull them out it was a hopeless task, and all we could do was to spray them with water to keep them cool!

It was then that the Fire Chief called for the vehicle ferry to be used as a fireboat, and they manned it with fire engines. She arrived about five thirty a.m. on the nineteenth, and soon had sixteen powerful water jets playing on the *Sussex*.

It was not until the nineteenth, twenty-three hours after the bomb had hit, that the fire was brought under control and the ship was sunk alongside the wall, so that she was flooded to extinguish the blaze and prevent any explosion of the ammunition.[13]

Peter J. Petts's first-hand account of the sinking of the *Sussex* is an important document, perhaps the only witness statement that exists, for the story of the *Sussex* being destroyed in the heart of Glasgow 'was kept secret till long after the war had ended. Even we Navy lads were told "not to discuss it", so we didn't.'

As John Milloy wrote in response to Peter's account when it first appeared on the internet: 'Everyone in Govan thought the bomb had gone straight down the cruiser's funnel. I thought too that it was Stephen's yard rather than Fairfield's, who did the repairs on the *Sussex*, since the father of one of my pals, a Stephen's employee, worked on the repairs after the bombing. A great piece of history Peter! Cheers.'

Milloy, from Govan, had an adventure of his own that day. Having seen the plumes of smoke he ran with his mates to see what was going on. Together they 'waited around until lunchtime when all the workmen from the yards would be crossing on the ferry' and mingled with 'the crowd of dungaree-clad shipbuilders in boarding the ferry'.

We managed to cross over [on the ferry] without any difficulty, but as it turned out we could have seen more from the other side as there was a six-feet high fence all round the dock.

To us this fence presented no great problem. Big Angie gave wee Dugald [Milloy] a pucky up onto the top of the fence and Dugald helped Angie up. We both dreeped over the other side and hid behind a shed, right beside the massive hulk of the *Sussex*. Many people – firemen, sailors, marines, policemen – were working frantically on the still-smoking bombed cruiser. Important-looking people in all sorts of uniforms ran to and fro in front of us, far too busy with the task at hand to be bothered with two Glasgow urchins in short trousers gaping in awe from behind a shed.

There was a row of clear wooden boxes alongside the shed we were hiding behind. I don't know what they contained. I know what they looked like, but we never did ascertain if they were body boxes. In the height of the excitement we didn't dwell on them too much.

A steel helmet, thickly covered in black oily muck lay at the foot of a gigantic heap of oily sludge that was being removed from the ship. While Angie kept watch I crept over to the heap, grabbed the helmet and scurried back to watch while Angie did the same. The steel helmet bore the name of a captain (rank, not the captain of the cruiser) and other hieroglyphics that left no doubt that it had been a part of this tragedy. This steel helmet became mine, to be treasured and used through all the air raids Glasgow ever had afterwards.

Having made a couple more dashes over to the heap to each get an officer's cap we then made our way out by the way we had come in. There was no trouble getting over to

Govan with the ferry and onto the tram car and home to
hide our loot, now safely hidden in a cardboard box. We
spent that night in Angie's back court wash house boiling
everything to try and get rid of the black oil. We never did of
course, the padding in my helmet always stank of oil – a
constant reminder of where it had come from. The officers'
hats fell completely apart with all our boiling but we were
able to save the gold-leaf-thread badges (I wore mine on a
Clyde Navigation Trust cap and it looked just like a navy
officer's hat).[14]

On the afternoon of 13 March 1941, another young lad,
called Duncan Thaw from Riddrie, way east of the city and
up by the Monkland Canal – tagged along with two
midden-raking older boys, later following them into
Blackhill as they took their haul in a pram to a rag man
called Peely Wally ('pale and unhealthy looking' in Scots'
parlance). The adventure left Thaw miles from home.
Suddenly finding himself alone and realising that he had
to get back he panicked and ran sobbing down a street past
'staring children and men who paid no attention'. By the
time he reached the familiar canal, a moon was up and he
heard a siren sounding.

He ran down the path between the nettles and through the
gate and past the dark allotments. The siren swooned into
silence and a little later (Thaw had never heard this before)
there was a dull iron noise, gron-gron-gron-gron, and dark
shapes passed above him. Later there were abrupt thuddings
as if giant fists were battering a metal ceiling over the city.
Beams of light widened, narrowed and groped above the

rooftops, and between two tenements he saw the horizon lit orange and red with irregular flashing lights.[15]

Thaw was witnessing the start of the Clydebank Blitz. The description comes to us from the classic novel *Lanark: A Life in Four Books* by writer and artist Alasdair Gray, a book that finds special resonances in the minds of Glaswegians because in both an autobiographical and poetic sense it is so very true.

Gray was himself born in Riddrie, in 1934. Fellow Glaswegian writer Hardeep Singh Kohli wrote of *Lanark* that it first lifted his 'eyeline above small-town minutiae to see my hometown as a thrilling, exciting, vibrant and meaningful place'.

The planes that Alasdair Gray heard that night as a seven-year-old, and describes through his semi-autobiographical character Duncan Thaw, were coming in low over Glasgow from Beauvais in Northern France, Stravanger in Norway, Aalborg in Denmark, and the main force from Holland and Northern Germany flying in over Hull.

At the same moment Gavin Laird and his mates Nicky and Eddie Doyle were at a cinema called the Palace in Clydebank, pinned down by the waves of bombers:

> During the night as the time went on, there was a lull in the bombing and Nicky, Eddie and I got off our marks and shot past the man at the door and ran like hell up Kilbowie Road. We were about halfway up the hill when the incendiaries began to come down. It was like looking at falling flames or rain that was on fire, raining down on Clydebank and the

graveyard, and if you were an eight-year-old, it was like some kind of horror film.[16]

Ellen McAllister was lying in bed in the Gorbals with her young sister, when a landmine fell and blew out the side of a local school and church:

> Bombs also fell on Logan Street, Rutherglen Road, Ballater Street and Chapel Lane and that was only some of them. That night I thought we'd had it. The bed lifted about three feet in the air, wooden shutters were blown open and all the glass in the windows shattered. I thought the whole world was on fire. Incendiary bombs were dropping from the sky like fiery raindrops.[17]

Elizabeth Bailey had been playing with her school friend Esther in the early evening of 13 March. The siren had sounded and Esther had decided to go home.

> I remember there was the most beautiful of sunsets in the sky away down the River Clyde above the dark rock of Dumbarton where the ancient castle stands. The weather being so mild, we played on much later than usual, I then went with Esther to see her to the bus for her short journey home, it was just too late for her to walk. I normally walked part of the way with her.
> The bus drove off, a smile, a wave, 'See you tomorrow' . . .

When Elizabeth returned home she saw that Esther had left her school bag and gas mask behind. For a moment fear struck her that Esther might be killed if there was a raid, but she dismissed it. On every occasion the siren had sounded, it had been a false alarm.

On this night, however, there was no false alarm. The Bailey family go into their Anderson shelter.

> This was going to be a nightmare night. Mum, my two young sisters, my baby brother, our widowed neighbour and our little spaniel, Maisie, all crushed down as we tumbled in. I was so stiff in the morning when the raids were over, but we were all very lucky to be alive.

In the cold light of day, Elizabeth discovered that her worst fear had been realised: Esther had indeed been killed in the bombing.

> She lived in a tenement house on a hill above [the] Singer's factory. So many of these houses had direct hits and were razed to the ground, causing a terrible loss of life. Esther's dad also lost his life . . . I remember how surprised I was to read that Esther's dad was only thirty-three years old (only twenty when Esther was born). I would like to add this little poem as a memory of Esther: It's called To Esther with love, Betty:

> It was goodnight under a setting sun
> with all the joy of years to come
> before the dawn terror tore the sky
> you to die; I to cry
> for our sweet goodnight was a sad goodbye.

The number of citizens killed in the Glasgow Blitz was never released by the government in case of panic. It was to prove one of the most controversial issues connected with the war locally.

> In the end, after great prevarication . . . it was shown that 528 had been killed and 617 seriously injured on Clydebank, considerably fewer than were killed outside Clydebank.
>
> It may be added that in the list of civilian dead published by the Imperial War Graves Commission in 1954, the total number of deaths of Clydebank people is only 448.[18]

A more reliable estimate is that 647 people were killed, with 1,680 injured and 6,835 tenement buildings damaged throughout the city, particularly in Maryhill to the north-west, and Scotstoun to the west, which was home to the famous Yarrow shipyard. The yards were of course the main target.

Part of the problem in fixing the number of dead lay in the confusion that followed the bombing:

> Very quickly it became evident that one of the problems that was arising was the official registration of the dead. Many people came inquiring about where and how to register their dead relatives. I had inquiries made and found that the Registrar's Office was untenable and that it was quite impossible to obtain death certificates in Clydebank . . . There were large numbers of people wanting advice and help.[19]

William Smillie, a fire officer, saw for himself the tragic circumstances:

I went to Second Avenue and saw three incendiaries lying on the road. I was earthing them over when I heard someone shouting, 'For God's sake, come and help us!'. The shelter had collapsed and there were men in it trying to hold the roof up with their backs. I put my crew in and ran for a rescue squad. A gas main was leaking and when I got back four of my crew were unconscious. I got them to the stage where they were vomiting but on their feet and then we tackled a burning tenement in Montrose Street. Before we had got far with that, a screamer came down and blew me over the wall into the churchyard unconscious. When I came to, the pump was dry, the bomb had taken half of Kilbowie Road and the big water main with it and left Clydebank without water. The hydrant was dry so we used the crater. I got the men together and we had another go at the tenement and then after that a four-storey tenement in Kilbowie Road and then some villas. We did these jobs and then we reported in.[20]

There was many a tale of heroism, but also inevitably of cowardice. On the first night of the bombing (13 March 1941) one official, a local police superintendent, was with his family in an Anderson shelter in the garden of his house when a bomb destroyed the house and blew in the shelter. He evacuated with his family out of town. The following day, Brigadier Dudgeon, Inspector of Police Forces in Scotland, advised the chief constable to transfer the man temporarily and replace him.

Coping with casualties and the homeless was a specially trained emergency squad of social workers. The morning after – on Friday 14 March – seven of the ten rest centres in the city were reported habitable, full of people but inadequately staffed. An administrative centre was set up at the Pavilion Theatre, Kilbowie Road. Delivery of 4,000 hot meals was expected, along with a large number of mobile canteens. One A. M. Struther was the man in charge of operations:

> Few I spoke to had had anything to eat or drink since the previous night. An incident occurred which indicates the plight people were in. A woman brought a boy of eleven to me, he had bruised the side of his face, his spectacles were cracked and he had hurt his leg. Aged eleven he had extracted himself from the rubble which had covered his father, mother, brothers and sister and was just wandering about. I asked the lady to find the nearest first aid post and to have him attended to there. This lady came back later and was one of our ablest voluntary workers.

Before long the number of rest centres had been reduced to six, the remainder had to accommodate from three to four times the number of persons expected in each. For example, the Boy Scouts Hall, South Douglas Street, scheduled to hold 150, held between 300 and 400 people on the Friday, and on the following day nearly double that number.

Food soon became sparse. Tea, bread and margarine and a good supply of milk for children were the order of the day. But there was also an administrative nightmare:

> Registration Forms had to be completed in duplicate for each family and particulars given of names, address and occupation and also reason for having to leave homes, for

example 'completely bombed out', 'awaiting time bombs', etc. There were no type-written forms ready nor was there carbon paper, this meant that each form, from heading to the completion of the particulars, had to be written by hand and filed in duplicate.

The majority of people concerned were workers from John Brown's shipyard and their families, also a percentage from the Singer's and the Ordnance factory. The men were anxious to know where they were to stay after their wives and children had got away [been evacuated], as they must remain at their work if Brown's was to carry on.

Many of the men wished to go home to fetch what personal belongings they could salvage and said it would take half an hour. Permission to do this was granted. Later in the day, the men went for their pay and many of the women missed the first chance of evacuation while waiting for their husbands to return.

By five o'clock on the Friday evening, a number of buses had arrived to take people to the Vale of Leven. On the Saturday, 15 March, a Mr Gunnet at the Ministry of Information, telephoned Struther to tell him that there had been another serious raid on Clydebank. Struther expected the day before him to be even more difficult than the last, and he was not disappointed:

Shortly after arriving in Clydebank, I met Mr J. Collet of the Ministry of Labour whom I told that I had sent a message to Mr J. W. Clark about the need for tackling the problems of transport, feeding and billeting of workers. He asked what business it was of mine.

There was by now the additional problem of 4,000 evacuees in the Vale of Leven, and the number was increasing every minute. Again there was a shortage of food, other than bread and margarine, and of plates, cutlery and cooking utensils. But on the plus side, a great feeling of community was beginning to be generated, with a particular councillor, Horace Francis of Clydebank, giving encouragement to his people by example:

> His wife and baby of a week old had been rescued with him after being buried for four-and-a-half hours. After he had seen his wife safe he had insisted on his going back. He was a councillor and his place was among those who had suffered. He had a damaged leg and a bruised head. Another councillor who had not shown such heroic qualities [was] reported to have referred to him as a 'bloody communist trying to win favour'. I heard a local person of standing say, 'Let's have more such bloody communists'.

By the Sunday, there was a scarcity of blankets everywhere. Five hundred had been brought down, but it was now estimated by the Public Assistance Officer that there were 9,000 people in the Vale of Leven.

Another problem, inevitably, was sanitation:

> The automatic flush-type WCs at Renton School Centre were quite unable to cope with the numbers using them and added greatly to the worries of the already overtaxed janitor [even babies' chamber pots were being used].

For others more fortunate, their homes and lives were relatively intact, as Maria Fyfe recalls:

> I remember, I have a bit of a memory of, going to the air raid shelter when I was very small. My mother actually kept the newspaper out of my sight. She had read somewhere that children were getting some kind of mental effect of fear from the war and she tried to keep the fear from me!
>
> If we went out at night we needed a torch with a tiny pinpoint light to find our way in the blackout, but I was not afraid when I had my two big brothers, Jim and Joe – known to me as Dim-dim and Do-do – to swing me along . . . If there was even a chink of light coming from your house you would get a knock at the door from a man in black, the ARP (Air Raid Precautions) warden. I was nine months old when the Second World War broke out in Europe, and by the time I was two I thought the bombs were coming when we were merely hurrying to get out of the rain.

Whereas in the memories of children during the even harsher blitz in London's East End[21] I discovered a dimension of excitement about the whole affair, in Glasgow this was completely absent. As Ellis Cohen recorded, misery characterised the experience, in particular the morning after an air raid, when you turned up at school and there were tragic absentees.

> My [childhood] experience was war time, so you wouldn't go out in the street and play. We would just listen to dance music. But of course I was very interested because at that time I was building crystal sets. I was interested in wireless

since the age of nine. War was no fun for boys. You get to school the following day and the headmaster says, 'George so-and-so was killed last night. Mary . . .' People were dying around you. It was a nightmare and it looked like it would never end.

Rationing, introduced in 1940, meant that food was scarce for everyone, of course. Maria Fyfe spelt out what you were allowed:

The weekly limit for each person at first was 4 oz (113 g) raw bacon or ham, 3.5 oz if cooked; 4 oz butter, and 4 oz cheese. But you got three pints of milk, scarcely a hardship, and 12 oz – yes, three quarters of a pound – of sugar. What did they do with all that sugar? . . . You could have a pound of jam – with a lot of turnip in it – every two months . . . [Later] the butter ration went down to 2 oz, margarine 4 oz, and 8 oz sugar. Imported fruits like bananas, oranges and grapes became impossible to get, and it would be six or seven years before they were seen again. Meat of any kind was limited to 1s./2d. worth (six and-a-half pence) for every person. At early 1940s prices that would buy half a pound of mince. Sweets had special coupons of their own at the back of the ration book. You got a mere 6 oz every four weeks, and this scarcity lasted until 1953 [the rationing of all foods ended finally in 1954].

With a little bit of ingenuity, however, Ellis Cohen's mother found an alternative supply:

We would go into the country. My mother would take a bus into the country and go to farms. They'd sell us an extra dozen eggs. In those days you could get a certain sort of varnish, and you could varnish the eggs and they would last for months. It kept them sealed, so they wouldn't go off. So we would go into the country and buy this, buy that, and stock up.

When people are on their uppers, people will find new ways.

Eventually the war came to an end and, suddenly, the streets were garlanded with bunting, and for a while at least the world was a wonderful place:

Like every other city in Britain, Glasgow was bursting with excitement. We knew the war was over and were just awaiting official confirmation.

Then, in the morning [8 May 1945] came the voice of Winston Churchill over the radio . . . The entire city went a little mad. Schools were closed for the day. It was a day of celebration! I was fourteen and wanted to join these celebrations too, but not by myself. I looked around and took up with the nearest female at hand.

She was an older girl, perhaps sixteen or so. Still, she was to be my companion for the rest of the day. We made our way hand in hand from where we lived in the Cowcaddens part of the city in order to find the main celebration in George Square. Every street we went through was holding some party or another.

The tram cars in Hope Street were filled with servicemen of all nationalities – American, Canadian, Australian,

European; all of them commandeering the trams and singing and dancing up and down the length of Hope Street, singing all kinds of songs I had never heard before.

At the bottom of the street the dance was the 'eightsome reel' – this of course took precedence over all the other carousing. This was Scotland's national dance, and everyone could join in. The music was relayed from the old Kemsley House, former home of the Glasgow *Daily Record*, who also supplied the lighting for the parade. To see the lights go on again was a miracle in itself.

I didn't see too many drunks, now that I think on it. There was no need. The spirits were lifted high enough as it was. It was quite wonderful to see all the men and women in uniform hugging, kissing and generally flirting with the civilian population.

During all this time I never once let go of my companion's hand. I danced with her, hugged her, kissed her too, I don't know how many times. I never did find out what her second name was. All I knew was her name was Norah, my lovely Norah. In all my life I have never forgotten her, and although we were as close to being intimate as was possible, there was never any impropriety. We actually stayed together until four a.m., when we finally kissed and said goodbye, each hugging the other. I never saw her again, and to this day I wonder sometimes whether or not Norah remembers as well. My lovely Norah, with you I shared the most memorable day in my life. My thanks forever to you.[22]

CHAPTER NINE

Glasgow on the Move

———————————

Clem Attlee's post-war Labour Government (1945–51) promised the New Welfare State; a national insurance system that meant pensions for all, free medical care, family allowances, and means-tested national assistance. But could the government afford to deliver?

The war came to an end, soldiers were reunited with their families, but money and day-to-day goods remained in short supply. Rationing continued until long after the war ended. Queues were commonplace even for essentials. While nobody went hungry, supplies were pretty basic. Bread rationing was introduced in July 1946 and lasted for two years; potatoes were rationed in 1946–7; a major fuel shortage due to declining productivity, inadequate transport and the bleak winter of '47 closed factories across

Britain and left houses without electricity for five hours a day.

We went cap in hand to America, trading on the sacrifice Britain had made for world peace in the war: they felt they had won the war, and were not impressed. The deal we came away with was not enough and tied Britain to America as a poor relation. Then America awoke to the wisdom of a speech by Winston Churchill about the danger of Joseph Stalin, who had succeeded Vladimir Lenin in the Soviet Union on his death in 1924 and whose power was spreading into Eastern Europe, and billions of dollars came into Britain to ensure that we would be on the right side; many Americans viewing the rise of socialism in Britain as tantamount to communism, and communism in Glasgow and East London with special concern.

This money underwrote the Welfare State and the fabulous fifties, which saw the start of television, ventures into space, and Tory Prime Minister Harold Macmillan's era (1957–63), when apparently we never had it so good.

In Glasgow the new affluent society was less apparent, but there were radical plans already afoot for a new city, one that would take power away from the communist unions and break up tenement society. Soon the Gorbals, Hutchesontown on its east side, and even the shipyards would be history.

The idea was to tidy up Glasgow and create a new urban environment, which would make available a mass of space in new developments for prospective tenants who would not be put off by the dark fortresses, and want to come and create the wealth that would obviate the need which had given rise to the socialist tenement society. The plan was to throw a lot of America's money around, along with a lot of its capitalist ideals.

Immediately after the Second World War community spirit in the tenements was never stronger. Revived and sharpened in the face of hostilities, it showed in the welcome meted out not only to men returning from active service, but also to Italian internees, much maligned in the nationalist fervour at the start of the war, as Joe Pieri and Renzo Serafini recall:

Remarkably enough, when I did go back . . . I found that attitudes seemed to have been transformed. Complete strangers, ex-soldiers who had fought in the Italian campaigns and who correctly assumed that I was Italian, would regale me with their stories of the war in Italy. Of how they were treated as liberators, of the hospitality received from Italian families, of the help given to escaped British prisoners and of the friendliness of the population in general. For whatever reason, the war seemed to have broadened attitudes and increased people's tolerance. Paradoxically, after all that had happened, for the first time in my life I began to feel welcome and part of the society in which I lived.[1]

It was unbelievable from a prisoner of war camp, coming back . . . I mean you didn't know what the people were going to say to you, after all I was an enemy. I came walking up platform one, and there was a taxi driver who used to work for a firm across the road from my father and mother's chip shop. He was there, not waiting for us, but as soon as he'd seen myself and my brother, 'Hurry up,' he says, 'I'm

here for a run, but I'll take you home first.' So, what more
beautiful welcome than that![2]

The people had not gone soft, however, and when it was
supposed that one section of tenement society had taken
advantage of the rest, they were still able to bare their
teeth, as Ellis Cohen remembers. Jewish tailors had been
co-opted by government to turn out scores of military
uniforms during the war, an important reserve occupation,
but there had been suggestions that the Jews had made hay
while others put their lives at risk, for example by moving
in on their market stalls and businesses while they were
away and by taking advantage of a stagnant property
market – not the case with Ellis and his friends, however:

In 1947 I was in Iraq. There was a lot of people saying what
the Jews are doing to British soldiers, blah, blah, blah. So,
they really got the people's back up in Glasgow and they
said what we'll do is we'll go into the Jewish Institute and
really sort out the Jews. I was one of the Jews in the Jewish
Institute. Anyway, I am dancing and one of the committee
members says, 'There's a wee bit of trouble outside. Do me a
favour and escort two nice ladies down to the bus stop.' We
come out of the Jewish Institute and in front of me was
about say thirty or forty policemen on horseback. In-between
the police on horseback was a huge policeman holding up
his baton. You could hear a pin drop. My eyes took me
straight across the street and it was black with people. All
the tenements, which were non-Jewish, had people hanging
out of the window. Not a word! What really sorted them out
was that every one of us was in uniform! These bloody Jews

who don't fight in the war! Everybody, older guys, younger
guys. I had a WAAF and a Wren either side of me.

All the boys were in the forces because conscientious
objector isn't in our vocabulary. I mean they were all
surprised when they saw that. What happened when you
walked round to a side street it was detectives, it wasn't
police, it was big, big tall detectives. Time you got to
Eglinton Street, which was maybe a hundred yards away,
there was nothing at all. Everything was normal.

This general feeling of togetherness also spurred the
community to express itself ever more lucidly in workers'
theatre. I have already mentioned this great tradition from
which the Glasgow Unity Theatre evolved, and its political
edge. North of the Firth of Forth in Fife, for example, after
a six-month lock-out in 1927 following the General Strike,
the local mining community had celebrated its experiences
in Joe Corrie's *In Time o' Strife*, first performed locally by the
Fife Miner Players. Now, post-war, this form of theatre
found its widest audiences.

The Unity Theatre movement was part of the great
Glasgow socialist movement. 'Didn't some get into it
through peace work?' Maria Fyfe asked rhetorically when
she first wetted my interest in it. 'There was that woman, I
think she was a communist woman [Ena Lamont Stewart],
who wrote *Men Should Weep*. I think that's one of their
plays.' Maria continued:

The biggest theatrical thing in my lifetime was the creation
of the 7:84 Theatre Company. They were a socialist group.
Bill Paterson was one of the founder members. This theatre

group was famous because it brought socialist messages to the stage in Scotland. I'll never forget their first play. It was called *The Cheviot, the Stag, and the Black Black Oil*, and it began with a group of people singing a Scottish patriotic song that goes, 'These are my mountains and these are my glens . . .' and then someone strides on and says: 'They're not your mountains, they're not your glens, they belong to landed gentry and you are not allowed to set foot on them!'

The Cheviot, the Stag, and the Black Black Oil was written in 1973 by John McGrath, founder of 7:84 and author of *A Good Night Out*, the bible of alternative theatre, the company's name derived from a statistic revealed in *The Economist* that seven per cent of Britain's people own eighty-four per cent of the country's wealth. The play begins with the atrocities of the Highland Clearances from 1746 and develops its central theme of dispossession through North Sea oil exploitation up to 1974. Audiences were moved, amused and endorsed the play.

More relevant to our theme, *Men Should Weep* focuses on life in the Glasgow tenements of the late 1930s. Written by Ena Lamont Stewart for Unity and first performed in Glasgow in 1947, it was revived successfully in the 1980s by 7:84, in a production directed by Giles Havergal of the Glasgow Citizens' theatre.

The Citizens' in the Gorbals [or Citz, as people know it today] was originally the Royal Princess's Theatre, everyone's favourite pantomime venue.[3] Then, in 1945, it was taken over by playwright James Bridie, who turned it into 'the people's theatre'.[4] The Citizens', where all seats were priced the same, became massively popular, especially in the 1960s when a late license permitted the bar to stay open after 9:30 p.m.

Of *Men Should Weep*, theatre director Dominic Dromgoole wrote:

> I picked it up, expecting a Brechtian epic of incendiary agit-prop. What I read initially confused me. This was no speechifying call-to-arms, no pained argument about sexual politics. This was a gentle and human tale about a group of people living a life in extraordinary circumstances. This was recorded experience, not manipulated experience. My confusion soon turned to admiration . . .[5]

Ena Lamont Stewart was the middle-class daughter of a Church of Scotland minister from the Highlands. In the Gorbals, where her father kept open house to the community, Stewart lived a life of uplifting optimism in the midst of great material want:

> We laughed a lot, talked a lot and read a lot. We also sang a lot and had, in addition to the piano (which was played a lot), an organ, two sets of bagpipes and a penny whistle.

What touched her to write the play were the 'shawly women', the rag-wives we have already met, who were at the bottom of the vast economic trade in cloth, which started with the gathering of the material at, among other places, Stewart's father's church jumble sales, and continued in Paddy's Market and the Barras (Barrowland).

Concluded Dromgoole:

> Rereading the play today reinforces the impression that *Men Should Weep* is a classic of 20th-century theatre . . . [it] speaks about more than recession. It is also a timeless play about family, survival, delusion and dignity.

It is the story of the community with which we are dealing, Glasgow's tenement society, as is the other famous play associated with the Unity Theatre from this period, Robert McLeish's *The Gorbals Story*.[6]

McLeish was born in Eglinton Street in the Gorbals in 1912. He apprenticed and qualified as a heating engineer, but was thrown out of work in the Depression. The Unity Theatre drew all sorts in. That was its purpose and modus operandi. McLeish helped out backstage and front of house and in his spare time began writing. The culture of the place was such that writers at the theatre began sharing with him their experience.

Eventually, McLeish came up with *The Gorbals Story*, which became a massive success from 1946, as I have said, and which in 1950 was turned into a feature film written and directed by David MacKane.

The play was really the forerunner and true precedent for the whole 'Angry Young Man' movement of the 1950s. Although there is nothing angry about it, the play expresses a poetic truth lacking in the coffee-table socialism of its imitator, John Osborne's *Look Back in Anger*. Why? Because it is authentic. It is difficult to think of anyone more middle class than John Osborne or more working class than McLeish.

Perhaps ironically it also succeeds because, except very subtly, it goes absolutely nowhere. Its sheer lack of plot took getting used to for one or two critics. There is a story of sorts, a young impoverished couple try to find a place to stay, and there's a romance between a girl and a young Asian (Asians were just then coming onto the scene in Glasgow, as we will see), but McLeish manages to cover every theme in *The Gorbals Story* and more, without letting the plot divert our interest away from the inter-relationship of all the various, fantastically portrayed characters.

You are there in his tenement 'hoose', you could be drinking a cup of tea at the kitchen table, while the whole thing – all the voices in this book, if you like – is going on around you. There is movement, but it is subtle and thematic; it moves us to conclude that this way of life cannot ultimately be recommended in a civilised world, but the community values inherent in it at all costs must be.

The Gorbals Story was hailed as a classic and the people came in their thousands to see the play. But, as ever in a country where the 'lessons' of art seem always to be kept an unhealthy distance from life, the authorities' actions flew in the face of received wisdom. They uprooted the community that was at the heart of the play, they broke it up and moved it to places far away from the hub to eternal limbo, its presence now appropriately ethereal, in the Gorbals myth and on chat-room websites like ourglasgowstory and gorbalslive.

The density of human habitation in the Gorbals, the lack of civilised washing and sanitation facilities (only three per cent of the houses on the east side, in Hutchesontown, had a bath), the ill-kempt back courts, scruffy old wash houses, and the now disused air raid shelters, combined together with the capitalist conditions attached to the

American money that was bulging their pockets helped to convince the authorities after the Second World War to smash whole areas of tenement buildings and launch a comprehensive redevelopment, the largest of any city in Britain.

The strategy came to be known as the Bruce Report, after the Corporation engineer, Robert Bruce, who came up with it and formalised it before and during the Second World War. If Bruce had had it all his own way, Glasgow today would be without many of its most historic and architecturally important Victorian and Georgian buildings. His proposals to re-build the city fifties-style called, for example, for the demolition of Glasgow Central Station, the Kelvingrove Art Gallery and Museum, Glasgow School of Art (designed by Mackintosh), and the City Chambers, priceless memorials to Glasgow's industrial past.

In the event, thousands of tenements were demolished, particularly in the Gorbals and Hutchesontown. In 1947, councillors visited the French port city of Marseille to inspect new tower blocks devised by Le Corbusier, the *nom de guerre* adopted by Swiss-born architect Charles-Edouard Jeanneret. By 1979 Glasgow had more than 300 multi-storey tower blocks.

The early publicity convinced people that they were witnessing a great new age.

Over the next twenty years, Glasgow will have started a series of redevelopment schemes like the Gorbals. These will cost at least 200 million pounds and will give a new look to one twelfth of the city. As with people, so with factories. Haphazard sprawl of industry will be checked and new

factories will be built only in specialist zoned areas. The
changing face of Glasgow. Glasgow on the move. These are
two phrases which will be heard a lot in the days to come as
the city pushes ahead with more and more of its
redevelopment schemes.[7]

Tenements, well built – the popular cry was 'too well built,
they have outlived their day' – and historic buildings alike
were destroyed in the flurry of excitement, while the odd
library and Catholic church sat absurdly, anxiously
speculating on its fate, amidst the monster blocks that
sprang up in the wasteland around them.

Yet, within a few years, many of these same blocks were
themselves rubble, like the notorious Hutchesontown E
project – a twelve-block maze of precast concrete wind
tunnels – (built in 1968 and demolished as early as 1987)
and the Queen Elizabeth Square tower blocks which
earned Basil Spence his knighthood and which bit the dust
in 1993.

The nightmare scenario didn't stop there. Built to the
north-east of the city during the mid- to late-1960s the Red
Road flats at Balornock and Petershill were, at 26, 28 and
31 storeys, the highest in Europe. Not only did poor
planning and cost-cutting result in a lack of amenities,
poor services and a high incidence of vandalism and other
social problems, these blocks were built with steel frames
clad in asbestos panels. The Red Road joiners – the 'white
mice' – were, as I noted earlier, martyrs to the cause.

These ten joiners worked for Cape Insulation cutting up
boards, asbestos boards you know. And I got a complaint

from my members who were up there working for an insulation company, and when I went up there they were complaining about the dust they were making with the rip saws and the boards. Now, the climax is at the finish of this. Now they says to me – well they used abusive language, which we can a' can use if we want – they used abusive language and told me to 'Get to f***!' in a nice abusive manner: 'You're always moaning and groaning about something yous.' We were complaining about the dust, but they wouldnae listen to us. So, I went away and phoned up a factory inspector, and he created and made them polythene it off. Do you know these ten joiners I warned? Every one of them's dead. There's the climax. Now, they got a warning and wouldnae take it. Now ten of them's dead!

Where was that?

The Red Road Flats.[8]

In recent years some of these flats have housed asylum seekers and refugees from Africa, Asia, Russia, Iran and Iraq. Since 2003 they have been owned by Glasgow Housing Association. As I was writing this, it was announced that they are set for demolition in a £60 million re-housing initiative.

All this aside, these high-rises created a social problem for their tenants, due to the fact that the planners hadn't understood that they were not simply building buildings, they were constructing communities, or, as it turned out, they were deconstructing them and leaving a vacuum in their place.

Families in the tower blocks no longer connected as they had in the tenement closes. In a high-rise there was nowhere even for women to enjoy a natter of a fine evening. The whole social, co-operative basis of living – what made working-class life special – had been ignored and lost and replaced by locked doors and heads turned away.

Adam McNaughtan wrote a song, *Skyscraper Wean*, lamenting the impact of high-rise blocks. It became a Glasgow classic. Nan Tierney's lament from her own personal experience, *High Living*, while less well known, is as important a document:

> I was the first tenant in the high flats, Dougrie Place [on the Castlemilk housing estate on the city's south-east]. I moved in with my husband in October 1964. We balloted for house allocation and got the thirteenth floor – we could have changed, but I'm not superstitious. When it is stormy, it can be noisy. You can't hear the TV when the wind is high – but you get used to it. There are two lifts in the flats, one that stops at odd number floor levels and the other which stops at even number floor levels. In the early days, I found it a wee bit difficult to get to know my neighbours. We only met on the lift. Gradually I got to know more people. I got to know the people on my own landing – they were balloted the same time as myself. The middle of the three blocks has a common room. In the early days the Tenants' Association used to organise socials – they were good. They are improving again.

In November 1974, the city's Labour council leader went public acknowledging that high-rise blocks were a disaster in social planning.

> In Glasgow we will not be building any more high flats after this. It is just not worth the candle. We have had a large number of complaints from both young and old people. The planners should have told us about the difficulties before they were built – but they did not. We had to find out for ourselves . . . They are socially undesirable.[9]

Out of the Bruce Report came the so-called Clyde Valley Plan of the late 1940s, which blueprinted the wholesale movement of hundreds of thousands of inner city tenement-dwellers to areas to be developed on the far boundaries of Glasgow, places like East Kilbride in the south and Cumbernauld miles away to the north-east. Glasgow Corporation [renamed Glasgow City Council in 1975], perhaps alive to the likelihood that Gorbalites, Bridgetonites and the like were going to find it a bit overwhelming suddenly to become suburban, or even countrified, argued for keeping the working population closer to the city centre.

The Corporation did not altogether succeed in ditching the Clyde Valley Plan, however. They uprooted May Hutcheson's family from Shields Road and transported her 'to the outskirts of Glasgow, where new houses had been built. We were really overlooking the country, looking out at cows and fields, and my brother used to deliver milk for the farmer. So it was totally different, and we didn't like it. As children, we didn't like it, (we were ten) we wanted back to the slum!'

People who had lived for generations in cramped conditions with outside toilets and no bathrooms needed better housing, but they didn't want to leave the areas where they had grown up and the close communities they lived in. It became a common sight to see sad little groups watching bleakly as their former homes, and those of their parents and grandparents were demolished.[10]

The old tenements had a character to them. The wee shops! Every shopkeeper practically knew ye. They knew ye fae ye were local. And ye went in, and they knew ye . . . It had that wee one-to-one. You got service. But you go into a big supermarket, you don't even get civility, never mind service. Naebody wants tae know ye. They just want the money at the till. That's no' a nice world![11]

Well, I'm not the first person to say this. Lots of people say that the sense of closeness in the tenements was something. People moved out to different areas, families were broken up, the aunts and uncles no longer just stay near. Improved conditions certainly, but something has been lost.[12]

You were a prisoner, there was nothing round about. If you went up that street and down that street you were just seeing a replica of the street you lived in.[13]

One alternative to the plan to send everyone to the farthest limits of the 1945 city boundary, was to clear housing areas like Mosspark and Knightswood, which, as I mentioned, had been created earlier in accordance with the 1919 Housing Act, and build high-density housing there.

In the end there was a compromise between these two positions, and they parcelled people off to new estates halfway, like Castlemilk (to the south of Bridgeton) and Easterhouse (eastwards beyond the East End).

Initially the Corporation found everyone very keen on the move. If you canvass a community with serious overcrowding, poor sanitation, no hot water or electricity, and ask them whether they would like these things, naturally they will say yes. No one ever asked whether they would prefer them to do up the tenements in the Gorbals and Bridgeton, clean them up and sort out the sanitation, which the city is now doing to tenements that remain in Govanhill.

There were, to say the least, a few teething problems with the new developments.

I'm one of the first tenants in Castlemilk . . . Everybody was very happy to come out of the old tenements into new houses with facilities they had never enjoyed in their lives before. But Castlemilk was just in the process of being built. When we moved in, the houses were ready, but the pavements were totally unusable; there was no bus service; there were no amenities whatsoever . . . You didn't even have any shops in the scheme . . . There was very little except the houses, no schools to speak of. They had put down the houses and that was it.[14]

I often wondered about those folk who moved in, stayed for a wee while and then disappeared, leaving the house empty. There was always quite a few houses empty, brand new as well. There was no amenities, no shops, practically no schools, and extra bus fares. When people came to Castlemilk, there was a tremendous change to their lives. Some people couldn't take the shock. Others couldn't afford it. We were like early settlers. We needed an extra wage for bus fares to get to visit our families, who were all away in another part of town. Children had problems too. They had to be bussed all over to their old schools. Some kept up social activities in their old districts – the Boys' Brigade for instance. That meant more bus fares.[15]

The nearest shops were six or more miles away at Spittal, and more than double the distance to the bigger shops in Rutherglen. No one had a car. It was a hike through the countryside to where you could catch a 46 bus. That was the way if you wanted to go to the cinema or theatre, too. 'People used to say it was a week's wages for travelling, you know . . .'[16]

There would be a resident bookie in Castlemilk before a shopping centre opened up. 'He stood in the spare ground. He took in lines there.'

Nor was it only Castlemilk that was ill equipped. Boyd Calder remembers his mother being thrilled about moving out of their old tenement house in Springburn, into the 'brave new world' of Corporation housing in nearby Barmulloch. It turned a 'house-proud housewife into a cleaning zealot'. But it would be years before even basic amenities were put in place.

My mum had either a long walk to the 'local' shops . . . or a bus trip into Springburn for any provisions the various [grocery] vans which came round every day could not provide. The primary school wasn't built till I was six or seven, my first years at school were spent in the old prefab school at the top of the scheme. The house which we were so proud of turned out to be a shoddily built, non-soundproofed, cold, badly thought-out post-war fix to the housing problems of Glasgow when remembered in later years.[17]

Rose McLean had been apprehensive about the move to Castlemilk, and having three children and a baby of nine months had relied on her husband and two eldest daughters to view the place before arriving:

In fact, I didn't see the house until the night we moved in. When they came back and said the house was on the ground floor I thought I was getting a back and front door you know – but it was a corner house with a big garden in Ardmaleish Road. They talked about the white sink in the kitchen and the BATHROOM – we only had a toilet on the stair. They were all thrilled . . . To this day I've been happy and I haven't regretted moving to Castlemilk.[18]

Rose is not alone in enjoying her new home. In particular, many speak of their surprise and love for the gardens that had fallen into their hands – a far cry from the rubbish-strewn back courts. Suddenly, people could grow their own vegetables and fruit. It was as if 150 years of industrial revolution fell away and the long-lost joy of working the soil proved to be instinctual. Mary Cairns found herself in Priesthill, near Pollok, where we have already seen Maria Fyfe's family enjoying their garden:

> How my parents loved that garden – they were always trying
> to get cuttings from people (because we had no money to
> buy plants) and my mother discovered she had green fingers
> as she encouraged the most unlikely specimens to grow and
> flourish. Priesthill in the late forties was a big adventure
> playground for me. I learned to go my brother's bike and
> explored all around. I climbed trees, paddled in burns
> catching minnows – it was like being on holiday.

So what if Mary had to go back to the Gorbals every day
to Abbotsford School because 'the City Fathers did not
have the foresight to build schools'? She thought it
was worth it. As did Rose McLean, although she did not
underestimate the nature of one loss that the move
involved:

> All this was a very big step for us, you know. I was the only
> one of my family moving to the south side of the water.

Tenement life was often extended family life – grandparents, uncles, aunts, cousins: generations all living close
by – a fact not accounted for in the Corporation's
transitional strategy.

For Tazza Macleod, life in inner-city Cowcaddens had
become 'horrible', with 'rats and sewage everywhere, a
breakdown in basic needs for folk'. She had been drafted
into Easterhouse with her parents:

> I can still remember the flitting, packing up our small
> belongings and the very long journey in a van to the
> promised land of new tenements. This was the country,

farms with cows and stuff. Places to play, ride bikes and
explore . . . At last we had space, three bedrooms, bathroom,
kitchen and a veranda. A back court to hang out the
washing. We were toffs indeed.

Our neighbours came from different parts, redeveloped
areas in Glasgow, and it took a while to build up
relationships. Many people were apart for the first time from
family and social supports. There must have been many
social problems at that time and an incident was when a
neighbour gassed herself. She was found with her head in
the oven. I think she survived but it was a talking point in
our close for a long time. My mother counselled us by saying
it is good that we were all-electric.[19]

The Macleods didn't stay. They moved back 'to be closer to
Glasgow'.

Before the 1950s housing scheme, Easterhouse had
been a cluster of small villages. Its people worked as
farmers, miners, weavers and on the canals. Easterhouse
village itself was a mining village, with small cottages on
either side of the street, general stores and a bar. It was a
favourite place for inner-city children's outings. The Co-op
ran an annual trip for children from Glasgow's South Side;
they came in horse-drawn carts as far as Riddrie, where a
horse-drawn barge took them up the canal to Easterhouse
for a picnic.

What the planners never appreciated was that when
they transported the impoverished inner city slum
populations into such places, they transported the gang
culture with them.

When variety star Frankie Vaughan, a veteran mover

and shaker in the Boys' Clubs of Great Britain, was performing in Glasgow and heard the horrendous tales of violence in Easterhouse, he decided to do something about it. He raised money from his concerts to set up the so-called Easterhouse Project, working with the locals to organise a weapons' amnesty and clear the ground for the gangs to set up a club of their own:

> We must stop the violence and I have told the lads that I will
> have nothing to do with them unless this is done. I will stand
> up for them against anyone and will come up here anytime
> they feel they need me – but the main part of the work is up
> to them.

The scheme was assured a high level of publicity not only by Vaughan's celebrity and, later, by his flying gang leaders to Blackpool for a conference, but also initially by the opposition of the police to his plan. In desperation, the song-and-dance man contacted Prime Minister Harold Wilson personally by telegram:

> Yesterday I went to Glasgow and persuaded leaders of
> feuding gangs to end the bloodshed. They agreed to turn
> their weapons in on Saturday evening to a spot where we
> will build a youth centre. Have just been told the police will
> not agree to a one-hour armistice. Results of this could be
> disastrous, even tragic. I appeal to you to intervene and let
> our peace efforts continue unhindered.

Wilson backed him and the gangs handed in their weapons, the episode attracting no small amount of criticism on account of the publicity it gave to gang culture, which many a Glaswegian, with a mixture of shame and Presbyterian primness, preferred the outside world to believe was a fiction, a media myth.

Frankie Vaughan sympathised with and understood the gangs and publicly focused his attention on the coming generation:

> The reason for the fighting is because of the conditions these kids, these children, live in. They are not men, they are children. I know for a fact that if I lived there with my family my children would run around with these kids and be involved in these gang fights.

But hang on a minute, wasn't 'new' Easterhouse built as the promised land?

Rubbing home the intangible sense of loss, the community was then denuded of its favourite mode of transport, its trams. Just when tram services into the countryside might be appreciated more than ever, the Corporation decided to discontinue the service.

Quite apart from the almost mythic status of trams in this loco-loving city – 'All during my early childhood Ma just had to say, "Dae ye fancy a wee run on the tram?", and my pals would be abandoned, games left unfinished, comics folded to be read later'[20] – the service had operated twenty miles into the countryside, even as far as Loch Lomond. It might have been handier for the Corporation to enhance the tram service to areas of the wider city where they were so busily relocating people, but modernisation was by now an infection in public quarters.

When Glasgow said goodbye to its last tram on 1 September 1962, there was desolation, as if something had died. A quarter of a million Glaswegians gathered in the streets in torrential rain to wave goodbye. Even the publicists supped the milk of sentimentality:

> For the people of Glasgow the tram is a symbol of the hard years. It was one of the few amenities they could afford – (you could travel an amazing distance for 2d. right up to the end) – and one of the few pleasant memories they retain. Now prosperity chokes the streets with private cars, chain stores and supermarkets replace local industry and the little shops. Glasgow enters the 1960s at the expense of its character . . .
>
> Now it's Friday night, the shipyards on the Clyde are closing for the weekend. When the workers return, they will be travelling by bus.
>
> What was the attraction of the tram car? The smooth, straight rails gave a sense of security no other vehicle on the road could provide. A sense of cosiness too as the passengers rattled home in a warm atmosphere of steamed-up windows, of damp coats and mackintoshes. This feeling was heightened by the friendliness of the crew . . .[21]

Interestingly, the tram service was one of the few areas of work where men didn't have a stranglehold. Conductresses abounded, and even some of the drivers were women (they were not allowed to drive buses!). Many cities recruited women for tram work during the First World War, Glasgow alone retained them to the end. The trams were part of the mother culture of the city which the 'real men' of Glasgow never much liked to admit. Now they were rooting the women out of the tenements and the trams out of the streets.

The final and fundamental dismantling of Glasgow tenement society came with the demise of the shipbuilding industry, which had been planned by government as assiduously as it had planned the fragmentation of the working-class community, long before it occurred.

Following the Second World War, during which the Clyde shipyards had been so busy, the industry was hit by low reinvestment and the emergence of new competition from Japan, Sweden and West Germany, together with cheap, reliable air travel from the 1960s, which whittled away at the staple trade on the Clyde in ocean-going liners.

The industry was further eaten away by dissent from within. From the start of the Industrial Revolution mechanisation and automation had diminished the allure of work in the workforce. Increasingly stripped of opportunity to express their skills and themselves in their work, and exploited financially, inevitably men adopted an instrumental attitude towards it.[22]

A prevailing theme in oral testimony from workers is the erosion of their skills; and with conditions of work no better or safer, and confrontation between Management and Union now creating its own bitter aspect of the working environment, men increasingly worked to live rather than lived to work.

The warped culture of work is nowhere better expressed than in the issue of safety. Employers provided no safety hats, masks or clothes until the 1960s, and occupational health facilities in case of accidents were minimal. Workers were also misinformed about potential dangers.[23] In the 1980s, when it became apparent how lethal working with asbestos could be, it emerged that insulating engineers and the like were deliberately misinformed that only the blue form of asbestos was dangerous and that drinking milk was an antidote to any ill-effects of such toxic dust inhalation.

> We were continually told, if you complained about working
> in a dusty environment, that it didnae dae you any harm,
> that it contained magnesia which was good for the stomach.
> [laughs] I mean we're only talking about foremen on jobs,
> you know, they were usually thickoes, but eh . . . Anyway,
> you were told these things . . .[24]

As another factory worker observed, ruefully:

> When you went in the door of Turner's Asbestos there was a
> Factory Act [poster on the wall] with all the stuff. The only
> problem was that you couldnae see through it with the layer
> of asbestos cement on the glass you know.[25]

Grim, dangerous working conditions fossilised as the heavy industries contracted and money was scarce and the will was lacking to improve occupational health and safety, until the oil industry showed the way:

> The oil refineries were the start of us getting a wee bit more
> safety conscious, you know . . . overalls, water to wash
> ourselves. But the shipyards have carried on the same old

way for a long number of years when the places like
Grangemouth [on the Firth of Forth] and the ICI were
settling down a bit to give you canteen facilities. Well you
never had that in the shipyards.[26]

The trades unions did what they could to improve wages
and conditions and undoubtedly played a positive role
overall in protecting workers from the worse excesses of
exploitative capitalism. In other respects, however, they let
the workers down. For example, they did nothing about
the misogyny that pervaded the Glasgow Labour movement well into the 1970s, and union bureaucracies and the
bullying behaviour of officials were deemed by many a
worker to have made them 'as bad as the employers'.[27]

Whilst workers retained their most vociferous criticisms
for exploitative management, still the deficiencies of some
unions did not go unnoticed. One shipyard lagger referred
to the Transport and General Workers Union as 'an arse-
hole of a thing . . . it's always been run by a shower of
would-be gangsters'.[28]

Since the heady years of Red Clydeside, when tanks were
sent into the city to quell the unrest, Glasgow workers had
had a reputation for militancy. Management and men were
frequently at loggerheads on the Clyde, and nowhere was
this more evident than in the shipyards where the foremen
and supervisors were evocatively described by shipyard
workers as 'the bastards in bowlers'.[29]

The tradition of having a union for every type of worker
persisted. As a result, inter-union conflict was never far
below the surface:

307

> We had fifty-six shop stewards in Fairfield alone and fourteen different trade unions.[30]

Sam Gilmore remembered one very good example of the kind of senseless inter-union dispute which sapped men's will to work and self-respect:

> Up to forty years ago the unions were all different, with the welders Johnny-come-lately. Piece by piece they amalgamated. But for years although they were members of the same society, they were still jealous of their own craft. There was a strike one time at Alexander Stephen's shipyard. The men were trying to get a straight line on a steel plate; there's a plater and a shipwright, one at one side, one at the other side, and a line with chalk on it between them, and somebody in the middle to 'ping' it. They had a sixteen-week strike over who pinged the chalk line. The pinging of the chalk line took fully two seconds. Sixteen weeks! Nobody was giving in! Those nonsenses . . . Oh aye, the demarcation disputes.

The whole culture of the shipyards was dissipating. The camaraderie, once born of mutual pride in skills, was now down to solidarity between men toiling together in often extremely dangerous environments, faced with authoritarian and sometimes blatantly anti-union bosses.

Co-operation, the ideal at the heart of tenement society, now had no place at all in the workplace. Men now competed with another as often as they co-operated. A heating engineer, commenting on the dangers of working with a toxic paint in the confined space inside a boiler, described how the job attracted a higher 'abnormal conditions' wage rate and intense competition among the men to undertake it:

> Everybody was squealing to get inside the tank, you know
> for the dough, you know?

In such an atmosphere, the new Welfare State was bound also to be exploited. Electrician Sam Gilmore was finding it difficult to get a permanent position, on account of having been active in the trade union in the construction industry. 'I was doing OK on the sites and home jobs, in the black economy so to speak. I was doing OK.' But he was claiming state benefits at the same time, and this meant that he would have to go to the Employment Exchange and take any job they offered him, say in the shipyards, which was the last place he wanted to work. So, knowing that the shipyards were a closed shop – 'No card, no job' – he told the Exchange he didn't belong to a union:

> I didn't want a job with the yards. I told the Unemployment
> Exchange I didnae belong to a Union, but they must have
> checked it out, because they said, 'Come here you!'

Gilmore arrived at Fairfield's shipyard in 1967, at twenty-eight years of age. In the cable store the big lengths of electrical cable used to be handled by about twenty people. 'Then they invented a machine to do it,' Gilmore told me, 'and part of the deal [with the union] was that they employed two men to look after it, and I fell into that job. Let me put it this way, I worked in the shipyards twenty-three years and never worked on a ship. The only time I went on the ship was for TV appearances.'

He again rose quickly up the union ranks:

There was absolutely no co-operation with the bowler hats [management]. It used to be a laugh. They were not very intelligent guys. They stood there waiting for the horn to go. They moved forward, the men moved forward, then the horn went . . . ! That was on the way out. Now coming in you came in individually, clocked in. You were allowed to be twenty minutes late. If you come in twenty-one or twenty-two minutes late you had to get a foreman to sign you in. You might have to go all over the yard, over maybe three or four boats to find a foreman. You could be in the yard all morning and no get paid. And you couldnae get out the yard because you had to have a pass out. So once you were in and you had to get this foreman's signature, it was lunchtime.

In his autobiographical account, Hugh Savage remembered that the shipyard owners used to hire work detectives, who became the natural butt for worker humour.

One cold morning the guys decided to get this one. There were steel plates on deck and the detective had steel heels on his boots. So the guys welding managed to manoeuvre him close by them and zip zip they welded his boots to the deck. Across from him a couple of welders started to brew up so he starts to go over and kick over the billy cans – that was what they did if the men were making tea, they kicked over their billy cans. But this one was stuck to the deck, they had welded his boots, so he couldn't move. All the guys had a nice brew-up, and a good laugh.[31]

Shipyard closures and redundancies characterised the 1960s and 1970s, leading at length to the closure of all yards other than Fairfield's in Govan. But there had been one final attempt to turn the hopelessly antagonistic situation between worker and employer around. In 1966 George Brown, as First Secretary in Harold Wilson's Labour Government, agreed what was known as the Fairfield Experiment, a new form of capitalism: part-union, part-employers; part-government, part-private share-holders. It seemed to be a wonderful proving ground for new industrial relations in shipbuilding – a parley between bunnets and bowlers without precedent in the industry, as a rigger who worked in Fairfield's for eighteen years and was one of the party instrumental in setting up the Experiment, explains:

[We] went down to London and we lobbied all the MPs and it was Harold Wilson [who was prime minister] at the time. We met Harold Wilson and we put the case forward, and he sent George Brown up to Govan with us. And he came up and we explained the situation and he spoke to all the managers and he spoke to all the shop stewards and we set up a united [front] to try and keep the place going. See, the banks had stopped the flow of material coming into the yard, and [George Brown] decided to put up a million pounds to keep things moving. And eh, we did.

We set up a tripartite. There was eh, government money,

trade union finance, and private finance, you know? . . . It was the Fairfield experiment in industrial relations . . . We were trying to break down demarcation barriers and all the things that were being held against us for years . . . We had all our shop stewards trained in industrial 'engineering' you know. Time and motion study. We sent them down to Esher in Surrey on courses and everything . . .

[We were] working with the employers . . . None of this having to go up and see the managing director. You just went up and chapped at his door, you know? No barriers at all. We had things going really well . . . It was going great and we set a target for five years, but after about the third year we had reached our five year target you know . . .[32]

The Fairfield Experiment made huge strides not only in employer-worker relations, but in other areas where there had been dissent. Safety hats were introduced: black for quality control, a red hat for a foreman, a white hat for a manager. 'A senior manager had his name on it,' Sam Gilmore told me with a wry smile. 'Then the safety specs came in. All part of the Experiment. It went on and on. Everything improved; new toilets and things like that. And there was a lot of bonding between the management and the workforce, because the management discovered theirs wasn't a job for life after all and realised they'd better get down to it.'

But then, in 1968, the Labour government committed to the idea that they could halt industrial decline on Clydeside by amalgamating the Upper Clyde yards, created Upper Clyde Shipbuilders (UCS) – a consortium of Fairfield, Alexander Stephen, Charles Connell, John

Brown and Yarrow. It was a fiasco, which led to higher wages and decreased productivity, and finally, in 1971, to the famous work-in.

This quite remarkable worker-provoked mutiny involved men taking over three shipyards and controlling who and what went in and out of the gates. Although the yards' liquidator had declared many men redundant, the workers stayed put, their wages (at their peak, £6,000 a week) paid by funds raised by themselves from all over the world.

Eventually, the government was forced to do a U-turn, forced to admit that there was at least some viable shipbuilding left on the upper reaches of the river.

Sam Gilmore was, by this time, a senior shop steward, a convenor and right-hand man to Jimmy Airlie, leader of the work-in – 'I was a shop steward. Airlie and I were in Govan and I was more or less his sidekick':

> The best thing that ever happened to the yards was the work-in. By this time there was a joint shop steward committee, rather than each negotiating on its own. We were up at a bonus meeting. The managing director, Heffer, was down in London for more money. We had a full order book; he was only looking for a pittance of money to tide us over. We were sworn to secrecy, but someone at the DTI must have leaked it. The Glasgow *Herald* came out wi' it. We called a meeting on the Saturday morning and it was a spontaneous thing. Airley came up with the idea: 'There's no fuckin' point in coming out on strike cos they want us oot anyway.' So it was Airlie's idea to work in.

Said fellow leader Jimmy Reid later:

> It was the only logical effective form of opposition to closure.
> Strike action was unthinkable, we would have left the
> factory, the yards and that would have delighted the
> government because they would have put padlocks on the
> gates.

Jimmy Reid was the spokesman for the work-in, and very
effective, but Gilmore says that Airlie was more than a little
concerned about Reid's love of exercising his oratorical
skills:

> Airlie told him to stop getting involved with the employers'
> logic: 'Ignore the employers' logic.' Reid would give you the
> semantics, quote Homer, all that fuckin' crap. But he was
> good on the telly. And Jimmy is such a two-faced – ten-faced
> – character that whoever was watching him, they all thought
> he believed the theory. Awful lot of platitudes. As a
> propagandist he was brilliant, but Airlie's philosophy was,
> 'Be decisive'. Whether it was decisively right, or decisively
> wrong.
>
> When the work-in started there was only a few weeks
> before the holidays. We weren't guaranteed wages . . . We
> started raising money. We collected at that time over two
> million pound worldwide. Sympathisers. We had levies: thirty
> [new] pence a week levies, in factories. At the end we had
> half a million pound left. We then set up a fund with the
> TUC to assist people who fought for the right to work. The
> strikes over the wages, they got nothing out of it. It was for

the right to work. The miners benefited. They fought for the right to work. We had John Lennon. He sent a bouquet of red roses. I said, 'What do we want roses for?' But he also sent five thousand pound. That was big bucks in that time. We had charity concerts, the Dubliners, Jack Bruce, Eric Clapton.

Reid was giving a press conference when the flowers arrived.

So you get this crowded press room and they're answering the questions and some of the stewards that were guarding the gate as it were, I don't mean guarding in any sense except making sure what was going in and what was going out was acceptable.

So they come in and they said, 'Hey Jimmy you've got a big wagon wheel out there of roses for you.' I'd never received flowers from anybody, not the done thing in Clydeside for a man to get flowers and so I said, 'Who's it from?' He says, 'I don't know but there's a cheque here.' And he looked and all he could see was Lennon, L-e-n-n-o-n. He said: 'Lennon, some guy called Lennon.'

One of the old communist shop stewards from Dumbarton, he says, 'It cannae be Lenin, he's dead.'[33]

I asked Gilmore whether at the time he felt there was a big change afoot, a political revolution happening which the working classes might win?

Not me, because Airlie kept me on the straight and narrow. He said, 'We are getting support from most political parties.

We are here fighting for the right to work.' He kept it . . . To begin with the official trade union movement were very wary of us. The Scottish TUC wanted to take control, they wanted to organise a demonstration in two weeks. We said, 'We are having a demonstration on Wednesday.' Over two hundred thousand people demonstrated, the biggest there'd ever been. Then the STUC couldn't get in quick enough, into the front line. The greatest supporter was Tony Benn, he finished up a personal friend of mine. Then they all wanted to get to know him, [Hugh] Scanlon and all the trade union leaders.

The biggest boost we got was a letter from Nicholas Ridley. His choice of words . . . we'll 'butcher the yards'. We could never have invented him. He was manna from heaven.

The Tories were now in power – Edward Heath had been prime minister since 1970. Parliamentary undersecretary of state for industry Nicholas Ridley's leaked letter was dated some while before the work-in, proving that it was mainstream Tory strategy to get rid of the shipyards on the Clyde. 'That's right,' Gilmore confirms:

John Davies was Minister for Industry, another godsend, he had nae personality. And then that other plonker, George Younger. I met most of them.

Ted Heath, he was up at Glasgow, the Central Hotel. He was up for a lunch at the Glasgow City Chambers. I was leading a delegation to make our presence known. I went in to see Heath there at the Central Hotel. I hadn't realised he was such a big guy. He was sitting down, but he was built, y'know. He had that idiot Younger sitting next to him. Then the two heavy guys with the bulges sitting at the back.

So I went in. He says, 'Like a cup of coffee?' I says, 'No.' I started to make oor case. He was looking, not at me, but oot of the windae. So, I lost my rag. I say, 'I'm obviously boring ye.' 'Oh, no, no.'

At that time, he was getting stick for *Morning Cloud*, yachting and that. Some people were thinking that he spent too much time at sea, discussing the nation's problems wi' dolphins and such like creatures. I mentioned this, perhaps he'd prefer to be fishing. And he jumped oot of his seat and he said, 'I spend twenty-three hours out of twenty-four thinking aboot the problems of state. Fishing is my hobby and a relaxation . . .' By this time he'd got his cool back, but he really blew it, y'know. I says, 'Look Minister, instead of that, I think you should spend more time at sea.'

What were you trying for at that meeting?

I says, 'We are no claimin' the world owes us a livin'. But we are claimin' there is a right to earn money.' I says, 'We've got all this work. The nation is totally reliant on imports and exports. If we don't have the capacity and are reliant on other countries, we'll get held to ransom.'

The BBC made a documentary, the producer was Richard Taylor, and it was very, very sympathetic. I was nominated to go on the documentary as a shop steward. I was twenty-nine, thirty, with a young family. We lived in a one-bedroom flat, with no bath or inside toilet, in Dennistoun. I was ideal.

At that time the cameras were huge and had to be set up, y'know, and they couldn't get in the door. He says to me – now the living room was about three-quarters the size of this and the bedroom was the same – 'What are you going

317

to do if you get any more family?' I said, 'We'll get hooks put up on the wall and hang them up on them.' He kept in touch and it seems the government tried to kill it, but the technicians stole a copy of it, and it was eventually transmitted (1970–71) and was a lot of success. He wrote me a letter, 'Don't let the bastards bring you down.'

Mrs Gilmore came into the room. 'The wives were a hundred per cent behind us,' says her husband. 'Everybody was, the whole of Scotland . . .'

I asked Mrs G: Was it an exciting time or a scary time?

'A scary time.'

Did you think there'd be a whole new order, a big change, as a result of what was going on?

'At the end I knew they'd win, but it was frightening. The support was tremendous.'

You were a young mother at that stage, you were worried for your family's future?

'Yes, I was worried.'

Did you think the shipyards would go under eventually anyway?

(Quick as a flash) 'No. I always thought we would win.'

Sam concluded: 'As far as I was concerned it was oor finest hour. We brought out our own record.'

Mrs G: 'We can't play it, it's an old seventy-eight.'

The work-in reversed the decision of the British Government to close the shipyards. Ted Heath took a U-turn and announced a £35 million injection of cash into the Fairfield, Alexander Stephen, and Charles Connell yards. Within three years, shipbuilding on the Upper Clyde had received around £101 million of public grants and credits, with £20 million going to the UCS.

It was quite a victory. Although the work-in didn't save all the yards, Fairfield itself survives to this day, as does Yarrow on the north bank of the Clyde, both eventually falling into the hands of Marconi (in 1999 and 1985 respectively) and thence becoming part of BAe Systems. Fairfield, founded in 1867 and one of the oldest yards in the world, defied Nicholas Ridley's plan to 'butcher the yards' and, much modified and modernised, is today the main assembly yard for the Royal Navy Type 45 Destroyer programme.

CHAPTER TEN

New Lamps
for Old

Had anyone spared a thought for the city's authenticity
there would have been nothing like the movement of
tenement dwellers out of the city that there was, for the
areas to be depopulated were those that defined the real
Glasgow, and the people they were moving around were
the flesh and blood character of the city.

The main effect of redevelopment in the Gorbals was to
turn what was once Glasgow's most cosmopolitan inner city
area into what is now probably its least. Among those who
made it so colourful were many who truly connected with
the spirit of the place, indeed were its spirit: they wrote
their life narratives on the closes and back courts and
recreated their lives as myth, which became the stuff of so

many books, plays, films, comedy sketches, and are the object of reminiscence groups in Glasgow and on the internet even today. The myth – the collective story and substance of working-class Glasgow – is irrepressible. There is no defining Glasgow without reference to it.

It withstood more than simply the bulldozers. After the 'big flit', when some 750,000 people were moved out of the inner city, the political purpose was to create a brave new city that would no longer be dependent on shipbuilding and the like. Glasgow was, instead, to become a European leader in art, tourism, fashion and shopping.

This ambitious strategy and loss of the old world created great anguish within the city, not least because it was perceived as insubstantial, a triumph of PR spin, with the untruth and gullibility that that entails.

A decade after the attempt by Westminster to destroy the Glasgow shipbuilding industry, the city council launched 'Glasgow's Miles Better', a public relations exercise designed to re-brand Glasgow as a tourist's haven.

> Throughout the 1980s, image, art and culture were used to refashion the city centre, along with new shopping centres, new warehouse-type housing in parts of the central city, including the newly remodelled Merchant City area, lying to the immediate east of the city centre.[1]

To begin with, of course, there was little or no actual tourism, fashion or shopping to be had. There was not even much left to excite nostalgia about old Glasgow, and many who knew the city viewed the campaign with incredulity. But it gained momentum and support nonetheless.

Part of the reason it did so was its emphasis on art, which has long been a highly visible and credible part of the city's international reputation, thanks partly to the Glasgow School of Art, Charles Rennie Mackintosh and the 'Group of Four', as I have described. It became a common riposte that to deny the political PR of 'Glasgow's Miles Better' and subsequent campaigns was to deny the artistic aspect of 'what Glasgow truly is', which was patently undeniable and a dimension of the city too often forgotten in people's identification with its industrial past.

This confused and polarised the situation further, with one opposition group, Workers' City, which included writers and workers and excited great popular support, being labelled 'Stalinist', and proponents of the new Glasgow being accused of 'yuppifying' the city.

After 'Glasgow's Miles Better' came the 'National Garden Festival' campaign, which drew hundreds of thousands of tourists into the city. This was followed in 1990 by the 'European City of Culture' project, and in 1999 they promoted Glasgow as the 'UK City of Architecture and Design'. Then came the most recent re-imaging: in 2004, 'Glasgow, Scotland with Style' claimed the city as the largest retail fashion centre outside London.

These PR campaigns cost many millions of pounds, but fifty years after the Bruce Report their champions claimed to have produced a new city, with art, tourism, fashion and shopping – not shipping – to the fore.

Yet, when heir to the throne Prince Charles opened the Glasgow Garden Festival, he chose to quote from Adam

McNaughtan's great lament for what the new Glasgow had replaced:

> Oh, where is the Glasgow where I used to stay
> The white wally closes, done up wi' pipeclay
> Where you knew every neighbour frae first floor to third
> And tae keep yer door locked was considered absurd . . .

Many felt that the money would have been better spent on restoration rather than invention, and on low-profile, self-generated management of the communities of the disappeared.

Certainly today there is fantastic shopping, clubbing and eating in Glasgow, and there are great centres of art, music, drama, and dance in the city – Tramway, The Arches, the Centre for Contemporary Arts, the Citizens' Theatre, The King's and the Theatre Royal offering amazing diversity, from cutting-edge to classical. And there are contemporary Glasgow theatre groups offering hilarious redefinitions of what being Scottish is.

But where is the art that expresses the new Glasgow, a population that has fallen by almost fifty per cent? Where is the community that might inspire its particular art? *What* is Glasgow community, at root, today? What does it mean to be Glaswegian? What does it mean to *belong* in Glasgow today? Has the city council managed to redefine that with its PR campaigns from the top down?

These are questions that were never asked before the Bruce Report, nor at any time since the nineteenth-century comedian William Fyffe asked a particularly drunken fella in Glasgow Central Station where he hailed from, and the man replied, 'At this very moment, sur . . . At this very moment, I belong tae Glesgae.' Then, after a pause, 'Aye, an' d'you know something, sur? Glesgae belongs tae me!'

It was how the famous song was born: I like to think not out of drink, but out of the insight, the *à côté* view of the world, that being drunk occasionally brings. For although Fyffe never developed my theme, this man's view of Glasgow was not, nor ever would be, Buchanan Street shopping mall. Glasgow was something that had developed within, something particular and inspiring which belonged to him, that in a way was him.

Amazingly, as the Glasgow corporation was driving the working-class community into exile in the 1950s and '60s, another set of people was moving in, a set that today provides a tidy lesson in why publicity-hungry politicians should leave community evolution well alone.

The vanguard had arrived as early as the 1930s in the neighbourhood of Roslin Place and Maitland Street, in the Cowcaddens/Port Dundas area on the northern side of the city centre, and in the Gorbals and Anderston areas, often in dilapidated properties where you could live for virtually no rent and the support of your friends was essential to survival.

I came to Glasgow in 1932 . . . there were between sixty and seventy men from India in Glasgow then, all engaged in peddling. They were living in groups of four to eight, depending on the size of their particular house, in the Cowcaddens/Port Dundas, Anderston and Gorbals areas . . . Muslims, Sikhs and Hindus all lived together. We had a common kitchen; food was cooked in turn by one member of the group for all, and all ate together at one table from one pot. There was a lot of regard, affection and regard for each other in those good old days. A newcomer was fed, clothed and looked after by the members of the community without any regard to his caste or creed until he was able to stand on his own feet.[2]

The strength of this early Asian community should not be underestimated, for a sense of class or caste is more deeply ingrained in the Hindu even than in the British, and in this new community the drive for survival conquered class prejudice.

When tenement dwellers were being relocated after the war, the Gorbals became the main area of settlement for Asians in Scotland, with up to 10,000 living there. The ghetto even boasted its own newspaper, *The Young Muslim.*

Niklas Schier was living in the Gorbals at the time and remembers vividly the first Asians appearing. They taught him how to play cricket:

They set up their businesses very fast, mostly grain and poultry stores in those days.

One day I visited the store of a new-found Asian friend and observed his Granddad taking live chickens from a basket containing quite a few of these agitated birds and plucking them and despatching them by wringing their necks.

As boys are with these things, I watched fascinated for about an hour and then asked my friend if he could ask his granddad if I could have a go!

He duly asked and presented me to the old man, who peered at me, gave a grunt and a nod and lifted me onto the tall seat he was using next to said basket of unfortunate chickens and gestured with both hands for me to choose my victim. Thrusting my hand into the basket I was attacked by what seemed to me like every bird in the basket.

I drew out my hand like lightning.

I can still hear the laughter of this old chap and see him in my mind's eye holding on to his turban whilst doubled up with laughter, and my friend [too] to this day.

Later I was informed by my friend that for this job speed really was of the essence. Nor did they let me live it down. Every time I went to play with my new neighbours (they were teaching me cricket) they would on arrival do a rather funny impersonation of a chicken that made my cheeks red.

The Gorbals of those days was a brilliantly multicultural community that enriched the lives of all who shared their lives in it.

Cricket, an English invention, had gone round the world and come back again. The poultry dealer will not have missed the irony. How this came about is a fascinating story, the consequence of British greed, and guilt. The British had had a field day in India for centuries. The British East India Company, given its first Royal Charter in 1600, was set up to market indigenous Indian industry worldwide, and might have brought tremendous prosperity to the impoverished subcontinent. Instead, it not only profited unduly from marketing Indian goods, but also sought to extract land revenues from the impoverished Indian landowners, and to trap, sell and kill elephants, tigers and rhinos, keeping the money it made for itself and the British individuals who ran it.[3]

Bengal was regarded by the British public in the light of a vast warehouse, in which a number of adventurous Englishmen carried on business with great profit and on an enormous scale. That a numerous native population existed they were aware, but this they considered an accidental circumstance.[4]

In time dissatisfied with its remit as a mere commercial trading venture, the East India Company came virtually to rule India with its own army, right up to 1857, when the Indian Rebellion – instigated initially by a mutiny of sepoys (local recruits to the British East India Company army) – led ultimately to its dissolution. The situation was tidied up politically in 1858, when effective rule was transferred from the East India Company to Queen Victoria, who was proclaimed Empress of India eighteen years later.

What this meant was that from 1858 until India's independence from the British in 1947, the period of the British Raj, *all citizens of India were British.* Good from a British point of view because they could be called up to fight under the British flag, which they did in two world wars. Good from the Indian point of view if you happened to be of a high-ranking caste, in which case the British would teach you how to play cricket.

The first Asian settlers came to Britain in the 1920s from Assam, but more than a hundred years earlier, Bengali people were used on East India Company boats virtually as slave labour.

To get work on a British merchant ship you had to find your way to Calcutta, where serangs (foremen) found you a place at an extortionate cost of three months' wages.

Likely, you would be given the job of fireman in the mistaken belief that an Indian could withstand the massively high temperatures better than a white man. If so, you would work four-hour shifts, then eight hours off, round the clock. Lascars,[5] as the Indian seamen came to be called, were increasingly in demand. Conditions in which they lived at sea were horrendous. Disease was common, as was death, the seamen's exploitation culminating in 1832 in the Lascar Act, which did little to help. In 1804 a ship's surgeon wrote that the lascars were—

> A class of men whose labours have been employed, to a greater extent than ever before, for the advantage of the British nation and of the Honourable East India Company.

Lascars would take lodgings in a British port while their boat was docked, and many did jump ship and seek to settle here. Gradually, the legend persisted that migration was possible and that there was money to be made by coming to Britain.

It is important to realise just how poor these pioneers will have been in India.

> In their own country they would most probably have been unemployed and living in abject poverty. In this country they were, on an average, making about one pound and ten (old) shillings (£1.50) a week. They lived frugally on approximately one third of this and saved, more or less, one pound per week. That was about five pounds a month, equivalent to seventy rupees in India. A monthly income of seventy rupees in India in those days was a great boon, as the average

income of a labourer there was then about ten to fifteen
rupees, or just about one pound, per month. They were,
therefore, quite happy and content to be in Scotland.[6]

As time went by, the barest of infrastructures began to be
built so that it was possible, just possible, to make a life
here. As well as sending a proportion of their incomes back
to their homelands, the Asians in Glasgow saved among
themselves to strengthen the blossoming community and
pave the way for their families to arrive from India.

Until the 1950s, the Indian and Pakistani people in
Britain were almost exclusively male, with female family
members left behind until suitable accommodation could
be provided in Glasgow.

Bishen Singh Bans, who arrived in Glasgow in 1936 after
his studies in London were disrupted, helped set up a
community support organisation for Indians:

In 1937 we formed the Hindustani Majlis, the Indian
Association, to look after the welfare of Indians living in
Scotland. This Association also took care of the burial or
cremation arrangements of its members who died here. We
contributed three (old) pence each to make up these
expenses for our dead comrades.[7]

With such concerted efforts to look after their welfare and
establish themselves, it took only a few decades for
Glasgow's Asians to move on from their impoverished
beginnings.

Back home in India, as the first migrants were settling in
Britain, moves were being made towards independence of

the mother country. Mahatma Gandhi, who played a pivotal role in this and was frequently imprisoned by the British for organising acts of civil disobedience, had visited London in 1931 for the Round Table Conference which looked at changing the constitution of British-governed India.

When war came in 1939, politically astute Gandhi demanded independence as the price for supporting Britain. Meanwhile, contact between Asian immigrants and the British Government developed. In 1947 independence was won for India, but to Gandhi's horror the country was partitioned into two sovereign states, India and Pakistan, the latter itself subdivided as West and East Pakistan (later Pakistan and Bangladesh respectively), with India geographically between them: a political separation that marked a religious distinction between Hindu (India) and Muslim (Pakistan and Bangladesh).

Émigré Shah Abdul Najid Qureshi described the distinction this way: 'Hindu people were the cultured society – the student community . . . people who were studying law and philosophy and medicine and all that.' But the more fundamental difference was described by another settler in Britain, Shafiq Uddin: 'Only Hindu has classes or castes, which dictate social position according to what you do. There is no class distinction in Islam. Islam forbids that. If you are a Muslim you can sit at the same table as anyone; not if you are Hindu.' While the drive for survival among the earliest Asian immigrants to Britain might have overcome that in the late 1930s, not so on the subcontinent a decade later.

Gandhi realised the danger of the separation, and

immediately it was met with Hindu–Muslim riots. Gandhi fasted until the Hindu rioters in Delhi swore themselves to nonviolence, but on 30 January 1948, on his way to pray, he was assassinated by a Hindu infuriated by his success in bringing the two religions together.

Now, independence was not enough. Having prised the greedy fingers of the British from this jewel in the Imperial crown, the subcontinent was looking to their sometime masters for reparation. There was a debt to pay.

After hundreds of years of interference, exploitation and domination the British had left India in terrible poverty, the like of which no Englishman could even imagine. Reparation came in the form of passports.

First, they were granted to relatives or dependents of 'distressed seamen', men left in dire poverty as a result of working for the British, then pressure was brought and others were given passports too, and the massive immigration of Asians into England from the 1950s began. Travel agencies first opened in Dhaka and in Sylhet in Bangladesh, and in London a reciprocal agency was set up.

1956 was dubbed 'the year of the passports'. The pioneers were eventually joined by thousands upon thousands, and whole areas of Britain changed rapidly. Yet the original idea was for the Indian immigrant to work here for a time, build up some capital, then return to the subcontinent with his newfound wealth and inject it into the Indian economy. This rarely happened, as Abbdus Sattar, a resident of Govanhill today, recalls:

> When I came to Glasgow in 1961 we didn't have our
> families here, just single people. The men came first. We

were issued passports for five years, the idea was that we
were going to work for five years, earn some money, go
back home and settle back. I mean we would have more
money, better standard. That was the idea. It didn't happen
because when we came, the facilities attracted us so much
that we didn't want to go back.

When the Gorbals tenements were demolished in the
fifties, the Asians moved on rather than take up the offer of
council houses further from the city centre. Many went to
the neighbouring district of Govanhill: not to be confused
with Govan, which is far away, Govanhill is an area to the
south of the site of the celebrated ironworks Dixon's Blazes
and had better quality working-class housing than the
Gorbals, as Fatima Rafiq and Harbaus Kaur told me.

See it used to be all Asians living in South Side, Gorbals area.
Then they started pulling the tenements down and they
slowly moved to Govanhill. Govanhill was so nice, so good.
When I moved here forty-one years ago, Govanhill was a top
area.[8]

In Govanhill today, Asians whose parents came to Glasgow
in the 1950s and '60s play host. From the beginning of the
twentieth century the area had been home to an army of
Irish Catholics, who worked the factories and built the
tenements; Westmoreland Street was their social, cultural,
economic centre. There was also a large Jewish community,
and Italians. The Jews had moved out by the 1960s, and the
Asian population moved in.

Today there are between 10,000 and 13,000 people in

the area, thirty to forty per cent Pakistani in origin, with numbers recently swelled by between 1,000 and 2,500 East Europeans, Slovakian Roma mainly, but also Bulgarian, Rumanian and Polish. Govanhill is the Gorbals of today, though no resident Robert McLeish is writing plays about the spirit of the community just yet.

What you notice at once is that Govanhill slipped through the net of the politicians' post-war regeneration plan, so there is street upon street of tenements, and people even today are living the 'close' lifestyle that was taken away from them in the Gorbals.

Moreover, a huge effort by Govanhill Housing Association is raising the tenements in the area to golden-sandstoned, City of Bath standard. More than 2,000 tenement flats have already been restored.

Wholesale restoration is however impeded by current housing legislation, which denies private landlords access to grants, as Anne Lear, director of Govanhill's housing association, explains to me:

Private landlords have bought so much of the tenement property round here, and 2006 housing legislation says that there are no grants for private landlords at all. When the landlords are asked to improve the level of the housing, they say, 'No, I'm not going to do it, because you're not giving me a grant to do it, and it's too expensive.'

We have got ourselves into a situation where you have no carrot to offer the private landlord, you have only got a stick – Glasgow City Council Section Repairs Notices. And it's not enough of a stick if they are unlikely to do the work to the standard that we, as a housing association, want to achieve, because of course they have to recover the money, they have to make the figures work.

In addition, there is concern for the emerging Roma community that were the council to force private landlords to invest more in their properties, the landlords would sell them off to the highest bidder and turn the tenants out on their ear.

I wander with Anne Lear through streets of her housing association's reclaimed tenements, and wonder that the Gorbals and other areas of original tenement society weren't given this chance.

She is adamant that I should see the problem areas, for Govanhill has around 750 tenement flats below a 'tolerable' standard, their owners linked to the fixers who are bringing waves of migrant Eastern Europeans in. 'This is Westmoreland Street, the street you will read about in the press,' Lear tells me as she leads me up a close. 'It's just one close of many. The letting agency has got rid of all its tenants, who were largely Eastern European. It's owned by an offshore company.'

Clearly, tenement ownership retains the element of secrecy it has always had. I walk through a dingy close mouth, look up a spiral staircase through three landings to a murky semi-transparent roof. 'The council have just cleared all these closes and back courts, they were full of needles and household rubbish,' Lear tells me.

It would be easy to go away with the impression that this part of Govanhill is a community in crisis, justification for some sort of drastic Clyde Valley Plan. According to Ellis Cohen, who now lives in Allison Street, which intersects

Westmoreland Street, the community around here is dead. He doesn't even know his neighbours:

> Because they are all these immigrants and they keep
> changing, it is a very different Glasgow to the one that I
> once knew.

But Lear insists that the wider Govanhill is 'a vibrant community with a lot happening in it and good people wanting to make a difference.'

Govanhill Community Development Trust is a wholly owned subsidiary of Govanhill Housing Association. It was set up in 1992 to develop initiatives other than housing which, in the rhetoric of regeneration, 'contribute to the social and economic development of Govanhill'. I spoke to a group of Pakistani women in the Community Centre and felt the 'heat' from the Asian community about the new arrivals:

> Recently, people have come from Eastern Europe and that is
> why it has become a bit of a danger area, especially in the
> evening. Ladies don't go out now, not after six p.m.
>   They break into the car on my street.

But a twenty-nine-year-old Community Development Trust outreach worker, Karmjit Badesha, whose mother, a Sikh from the Punjab, arrived in Govanhill in 1969, offered a deeper insight:

> I've spoken to my friends who said that they are annoyed
> with the behaviour of some people on Allison Street,

especially the new migrants and stuff, and I just try to say to them that if you compare that to what happened with us when we came over in the 1960s . . . I'm sure a lot of people were saying, 'Look at them, look at how they are, look at how they behave, look at the smells coming out of the houses, how they dress . . . '

The Roma are not here to frighten or make Glasgow suffer, they are on an adventure of a lifetime and are about to add their distinctive individuality to the community mix, just as others have before them.

Anne Lear tells me that crime statistics simply don't justify our fear of them.

The police say that the statistics aren't there to support it, but people perceive it and in their minds it is a fact. A lot of the members on my committee say that they don't like walking through the streets when there are big crowds standing on street corners. But I was at a meeting the other day and one of the ladies at the meeting said that she felt more afraid of the groups of young white youths wearing white caps and white trousers than she did of the Roma community. She lives in one of the streets where the Roma community is living.

Of course the Roma community tend to meet outside on corners of streets because when there is overcrowding people come out onto the street. It is part of the tradition to meet on corners and talk to each other, and there is no community facility for Roma use.

There is, as we have seen, a long tradition among young Caucasian lads on Clydeside to gather on street corners; for a century it was a way of life for the image-conscious black squad apprentices from the shipyards. A gang from Blackhill even marked themselves out as Corner Boys, and now the Roma gather and blether in the same way.

Part of the reason for this is that like their Corner Boy predecessors the Roma live in desperately crowded conditions. Just as six or more people shared a single-end in the 1920s and '30s, and it was unthinkable to be in the tiny room together for any length of time, so the Roma youths also need to get out of their overcrowded quarters:

> You have extended Roma families living in one flat because
> [being part of the European Community] they have a right to
> social housing in Glasgow and can't afford to do anything
> else.

When I walked about Westmoreland Street and Allison Street, first with Anne Lear in the afternoon and then alone in the evening, there was colour on the street, lights in late-night Asian shops; things were going on. I didn't find the gathering of Roma on street corners intimidating. Around 9:30 p.m. I was trying to buy some audio tapes. People to whom I spoke seemed up for a laugh not a fight. I was no more likely to meet a Roma mugger than I was a caricature Glaswegian drunk singing his way home to 'I belang tae Glesgae, dear old Glesgae toon . . .'

Right now this part of Govanhill is a cultural frontier, like those 'dilapidated properties in a state of utter disrepair' in the Cowcaddens/Port Dundas, Anderston and

Gorbals areas in the 1930s, home to the first Asians. Community is a process of constant renewal. Everyone in the vanguard of a new migrant community started in this way, and were reviled and misunderstood, and the only question for those with the whole community in mind is how best to encourage the newcomers to make a contribution to it.

There is a clear model in the history of the area of how to make that happen. Original Clydeside tenement society gelled because there was a work ethic which survived from the old days and was encouraged in the achievement of industry: the ships, the locomotives, the railways, etc. Work was the culture, it was a *working* class, and work was other than merely a job, as we have seen.

Today, immigrants to Britain from within the European Community must have documentary proof in a legal format of having worked for a full year before they receive benefits. For Roma, often doing bits and pieces of work here and there, the documentation is hard to get. So that keeps them working. But work itself is hard to get, just as it was for the Italian, Jewish and Asian migrant in times past. Ironically it was no kindness, but that difficulty in obtaining employment which finally integrated them into the wider community.

Employers were loath to offer work to these groups. So what did they do? They were galvanised by lack of work into starting up their own businesses, many of which flourished and became the bulwark of increasingly self-sufficient communities.

The Jews became tailors, furniture makers and bakers, as we have seen, contributing to the community economy and introducing new tastes to the table. Unlike either the Jews or the Roma, Asian men migrated to Glasgow alone, without wives or families. Some, in the fifties and sixties, studied to degree level at British universities, but took jobs wherever they could, particularly in chemical factories and on the buses. Discrimination on the part of employers restricted them to these sort of jobs, which were made available to them partly because no one else wanted them. 'The employers needed labour and they couldn't get their own labour, so they were forced to recruit immigrants,' as Pakistani migrant Bashir Maan, who arrived as a student in the 1950s, and later became a Glasgow Labour city councillor and leader of the Scottish Muslim Council, recalled.[9]

But Asian men also landed these jobs because they worked exceptionally hard, and in the end that is what counts. Later, when they married or brought their families over to be with them, they began to see the benefit of starting up their own retail businesses and became family shopkeepers. There was prejudice against these start-ups, but this time, with the greatest irony, the prejudice played into the Asians' hands, as Bashir Maan explains:

> Now the trouble they found was that no customers would come in during the day, so they had to keep their shops open till late at night to make a living . . .[10]

Late-night opening was a revolution in retail, and the Asians reaped the benefit. According to one group I met in Govanhill, discrimination was the original reason 'why everybody opened their shops here, because nobody pays any attention to jobs for Asians'. But whatever circumstance favoured this development, it is clear that the entrepreneurial spirit came from within the Asian community; benefits – public money – were nowhere to be seen.

> By the 1960s, around seventy per cent of the Asians in the city were employed in the catering and retail trades, while just fifteen per cent still peddled goods door to door as their predecessors had.

In every case, that is to say every new wave of migrants, has met initially a measure of discrimination and racism, but has adapted to circumstance and discovered an entrepreneurial opportunity which has helped not only to bring them to the forefront of but to help develop the local community.

The great advantage of the outsider coming in to a new environment is that he arrives without the cultural preconceptions of the host nation – another reason for low-profile encouragement and non-interference. With the right introductions he may be in the best position to see where new opportunity lies.

Communities create their own momentum. For sure, it will take time for the Roma to achieve what the Jews and Asians achieved, but government cheque books will not make it happen.

Karmjit Badesha is fierce about the downside of political interference in Govanhill:

> The way the government and the councils have handled Govanhill hasn't been great, they have basically let in so

many people and then don't realise how to deal with them. They don't understand that maybe for a lot of these communities it's difficult, or maybe even unheard of, to let someone in [to their home], like a social worker, housing officer, or a doctor to speak to them, that coming in like that may seem intimidating.

Govanhill has been focused on as an area that needs special help, which quite saddens me to think that it's got to that level. I think the council are regretting that they have let Govanhill go for the last five years and now on the run-up to the elections the politicians are coming in, flying their flags and waving their cheque books.

Politicians are making electoral capital out of Govanhill while the dire consequences of their interference fifty years ago are there for all to see, a few miles to the north-east. As Badesha points out:

Areas like Easterhouse are horrendous. There is still a notorious gang culture over there.

Fortunately a mediating organisation with no political brief and a full tank of experience in managing the evolution of communities has found its way into Govanhill. Oxfam was invited here by a charitable organisation called Glasgow Braendam Link and the local health partnership. Once they had nosed around for a while, Oxfam recognised the similarities between the current Roma phenomenon and that of preceding migrant cultures at a similar stage of their evolution.

Jim Boyle, Coordinator at Oxfam, compares the Roma

not to the first Asian migrants, as I have done – though he recognises that there are similar barriers to their integration (language and cultural) – but rather to the Irish who were centred on Westmoreland Street, where the Roma are now. He notes the big families, the over-crowding, the cheap housing and poor condition of it, and the hostile response to their arrival in the city:

It was 'dirty Irish' a hundred years ago, so 'dirty Roma' today.

Significantly, however, Boyle observes that the poor conditions in which the Roma now live were not created by them. The landlords of the poor tenements in which they live are, as I have said, linked to those bringing the Roma in. He also observes that there is a healthy host community, that this Glasgow village of Govanhill is 'a decent sort of place to live, a very vibrant area, which has its local shops, its community . . .'

Because it escaped regeneration, there is still the network of tenement streets and a community feel to the place. I asked Jim Boyle to compare his experience of Govanhill with that of areas which had submitted to regeneration, and were part of new Glasgow:

We also work in Govan and in Clydebank. We asked Chic Collins from the University of the West of Scotland to go into Clydebank, which had twenty-five years of regeneration – basically to draw out what you are drawing out . . . and the same work was carried out in Govan as well. What's striking is that the heart of Govan was ripped out. Where there used to be local shops, and so on, is . . .

'A mess,' I interjected, for I could empathise at once, having become involved with the Govan Reminiscence Group, a really lively mix of people who put aside all their business for the afternoon just to talk me through their memories. But walking through the place to meet them, having just read Alex Ferguson's autobiography and expecting something really tight in terms of community and a spark on the street, was like walking through a bomb site. Jim Boyle could see what I meant, and it wasn't only true of Govan: 'Clydebank again,' said Boyle, ' – post-industrial town, twenty-five years of regeneration – although physically it may look better, socially not much progress . . .'

A terrible consequence of the post-war regeneration-demolition programme was the removal of the root stock on which subsequent inner city immigrant groups – the Asians, the Roma – might be grafted: the respectable working-class families who took their turn in the wash houses and cleaning the steps, who came up with their co-operative ideals, their working-class utopia, who would never dream of not putting rubbish in the midden. There were of course always bad closes, but as Anne Lear pointed out to me, there was, then, a system of people dealing with them.

What seems clear is that current policy needs to be modelled on, and not cut off from, what has gone before, the positive, people-based culture of Glasgow's industrial past, and one breathes a sigh of relief that Oxfam, who can bridge the gap between officialdom and what is happening at grass roots, is now involved. The bottom-up approach is second nature to Oxfam: change happens on the ground,

from the roots up, organically, as in nature. Another
positive that Jim Boyle recognises in Govanhill escaping
the post-war regeneration net is that 'groups on the
ground here have become more self-sufficient, and maybe
with just a bit of support they can drive the agenda now'.

In line with the example of tenement society over 200
years, work is at the centre of Oxfam's strategy; not massive-
scale regeneration of industry along the banks of the
Clyde, but emulating the Jewish and Asian experience by
'stimulating growth and employment locally, supporting
people in their ideas. The other thing we did about five
years ago was research into "home working". It was
predominantly among Asian women.' Above all, Jim Boyle
sees the importance of women in the development of the
local community:

> There isn't an organisation anywhere on the ground that
> doesn't have women driving it. That is what we've got to
> recognise and build on as well. That's why Oxfam promotes
> that gender analysis. Not PC, 'be nice to women'. It's a very
> practical thing: women view things differently, use assets
> differently, have a different take on life . . .

Men are competitive, macho, need to prove themselves.
They will find the areas of entrepreneurial endeavour that
will finance the community. But women are more likely to
be nurturing, collaborative, co-operative, holistic, altruistic,
as tenement society discovered from at least 1915. There is
nothing sexist about this. In the past, women have always
been the fount of community, as Mrs Shewa Kaur Singh,
who came to Glasgow as a young woman, tells me:

I was seventeen when I came from India, just a small village . . . we were farmers. I was to get married to a person who was already living in Britain. (I don't tell everybody that!) I didn't know anything about Glasgow. I did not have an idea in my mind about it. I was worried. When I actually came to England I came to the Heathrow airport. My mother-in-law and father-in-law were living in Kent, so we travelled to Kent. Then, after a month I got married and my husband was living in Glasgow. After two days we travelled to the Glasgow. Eighteen hours or something in the car!

I was suddenly married. With my husband's cousins I was really rather shy, and [on the drive to Glasgow] I was sitting in the back seat, one of them driving and the other sitting next to me and asking me every couple of hours, 'Do you need anything to eat?' Or, 'Do you need . . . ?' you know [laughs], and so we came to Glasgow and I see all the buildings. I just get shocked, because all the buildings were so black at that time with the coal fire.

To begin with I stayed with one of the elders, my husband's elders. I went to Maryhill, old, old, big, big tenements. We didnae have our own house. My husband was living with his auntie and uncle as a lodger, so they had a five or six family of their own and my husband and his two brothers were living with them. We lived there for two or three months.

Mrs Singh and her husband then moved to a house in Battlefield Road, south of the Gorbals, not far from Hampden Park:

We had a small business, a corner shop. I helped my husband, we worked hard. Well in the shop I had a lot of friends. I was friends with everybody, especially the older people. See, the older women always felt for me, because I couldn't speak very well and they always invited me, 'When you have got time, come to my house'.

I had two or three old women [friends]. We had a shop in Govan, on Greenfield Street – they are all pulled down now, you know. I had very, very good old friends. If I had a moment spare I would go to their house. Even if I couldnae speak very well, they treated me like I was their daughter. All the old ones come and they want to chat with me in the shop, that's why they come, they don't come to buy much. They do buy as well, but they come for company.

My husband used to always say to me, 'You know, you should not spend so much time with this and that.' You know, 'Sometimes we have a few customers waiting for a paper, this and that.' But I can't say to that person, 'You can't talk to me, I've got to . . .'

Mrs Singh's priority – a woman's priority – integration into the local community was the key to her happiness, and, despite her husband's view, probably to their shop's success.

If none of the problems Glasgow faces today is new, it stands to reason that there is a responsibility to educate the new migrants about what has gone before, so that they can see how things worked, how other races and nationalities coped and came to contribute, and therefore to belong, to the wider community.

Because the root stock was dug out by the Corporation

after the Second War there is only a vague, almost Dickensian notion among migrant communities since the war about what old Glasgow was like. I asked a group of Pakistani men in Govanhill what they knew about it. They looked at one another and said:

> He's talking about when Jimmy Boyle was here, the community of criminals. It's all changed now. The Gorbals I haven't experienced myself, but I've read the books, we are much better now. About morality I couldn't say, but more selfishness I would say now, these days. Those days the people used to help each other, you know it was different.

They had read the books by and about the sometime criminal Jimmy Boyle and the gangs, and thought they knew what had gone before, which is a bit like watching a film about the Kray twins and thinking you know about London's East End.

It is clear that Glasgow is more than its caricature, and that beneath the cosmetic gloss of Garden Glasgow, and City of Culture Glasgow, and all the other PR Glasgows, the city's strength and distinction continues to lie in the unique experience of its people, which modern living cannot afford to ignore, because in it can be found the true, hard-won values, humour, and the deep sense of belonging that was the best-kept secret of its working classes and is still Glasgow at its core.

Acknowledgements

I would like to acknowledge the contributions of the many people whose memories appear in this book, but my special thanks go to interviewer, researcher and writer Chris Watt, whose relentless application and skills, while yet an undergraduate at Glasgow University, created the initial impetus.

I am also deeply indebted to Arthur McIvor, Professor of Social History at the University of Strathclyde, who immediately saw to the heart of *Our Glasgow* and acted as its editorial consultant, generously sharing his knowledge, experience, and written work, as well as introducing me to the oral histories which fall under his aegis at the university (including the Stirling Women's Oral History Project

Archive, 1986–9), and to the work of Ronald Johnston, with whom he broke the story of the exploitation of asbestos workers in *Lethal Work: A History of the Asbestos Tragedy in Scotland*, and Dr Neil Rafeek, who with Johnston and McIvor conducted some of the most trenchant interviews with industrial workers in *Our Glasgow*.

Where there are life stories being told there are also tireless transcribers, none more so in this case than my wife, Dee Dudgeon, who may now be an expert in the many dialects that make up Glasgow's diverse population.

Among the 'witnesses to history', some of whom elected to remain anonymous, I would like to acknowledge in particular Sam Gilmore, Tony Jaconelli, Renzo Serafini, Joe Pieri, Maria Fyfe, Tommy Gilmour, Mrs Shewa Kaur Singh, May Hutcheson, Tommy Stewart, Sydney Smith, George Rountree, Abdus Sattar, Mohammed Hanif, Asif Ehani, Harinreh Singh, Fatima Rafiq, Harbans Kaur, Rahad of Dixon Hall, Jim Boyle, Karmjit Badesha, Bashir Maan, Ellis Cohen, Monty Berkeley, Philip Berman, Hannah Frank Levy, Alec Bernstein, Delia Berkley, Bill Alexander, Tazza Macleod, Boyd Calder, Doug Heath, Aonghas Mor (Angus MacPhee), Thomas McSorley, Jean Kendal, Rita Moffat, Norman Ross, Annie Docherty, John Milloy, Peter J. Petts, Sam Watt, James Baxter, Eunice Rushton, Cathy Page, Marion Smith, John Wotherspoon, Ina Wotherspoon, Alex McGregor, Betty Knox, Thomas Orr, Amelia Newton, S. Graham Hoey, William McGinlay, Agnes McDonald, Robert Lister, James Kinnear, John Dowie, Mary Preece, Peggy Taylor, Bobby McGee, Gerard Coyle, Crawford Dick, George Fairley, Gurdev Assad Singh Pall, Charles McLaughlin, John McLaughlin, Thomas Scott

Wilson, Paul Kelly, Hugh Cairney, Stewart McIntosh, Jim O'Donnell, Mrs Whelan, Mrs Roper, Mrs Capaldi, Miss McKerrell, John Hamilton, Irene Hamilton, and John Pollock. Their characters make parts of this book their own. I am deeply indebted to all of them.

But there were many other people without whose work this book would not have been possible, not least Dr Elspeth King, sometime curator of the People's Palace, Glasgow Green, and now Director of the Smith Art Gallery in Stirling, whose ground-breaking redressing of the gender balance in her book, *The Hidden History of Glasgow's Women*, came to my attention at precisely the point it fell clear how significant, underrated and generally misunderstood was the contribution of the women of Glasgow to industrial society.

Acknowledgement is due too to the observations of sociologist Dr Seán Damer, and to those who have told their own stories with such feeling in the often bestselling books listed in 'Sources and Endnotes' following: Bill Paterson, Robert Douglas, David Kirkwood, Stanley Baxter, Deirdre Chapman, Hugh Savage, Owen O'Leary, Alex Ferguson, Jean Faley, Frances Kathleen Walker, Jack Clyde, Colin MacFarlane, the singer Lulu (Marie McDonald McLaughlin Lawrie), Billy Connolly in his wife Pamela Anderson's biography of him, Alexander McArthur, Eddie Perrett, Ellen McAllister, Peggy Taylor, Joe Pieri, Agnes Mclean, Maggie Craig, Les Brown, Jimmy Boyle, Stanley Matthews, Iris MacDonald, Ina Lynch, and Bobby McGee.

My gratitude also goes to the many museums, libraries and societies – custodians of the industrial and social history of the city: to Celine Blair, Glasgow Museums; Enda

Ryan, Special Collections at the Mitchell Library; Dr William Kilbride, Glasgow Museum Collections; Mary Frances McGlynn, Local Studies Department at Clydebank Museum; Richard McBrearty, Curator Scottish Football Museum, Hampden Park; Janet McBain, Scottish Screen Archives; Anne Lear, Director of Govanhill Housing Association; Amra Nazim, Govanhill Community Development Trust; Jim Boyle, Coordinator at Oxfam; Harvey Kaplan, Director, and Rosa Sacharin, Curator, Scottish Jewish Archive Centre at the Garnethill Synagogue; Springburn Museum Trust and groups such as the Govan Reminiscence Group, Anderston Reminiscence Group, Gorbals Live, Kinning Park Over Sixties Club; and Iain Russell, late of ourglasgowstory.com, and David Walker of the M74 Dig Oral History Project.

A new section of the M74 motorway, currently under construction, will soon emerge from Rutherglen westwards past Bridgeton, the Gorbals, Govanhill, and on into Tradeston, close to Shields Road and the Mackintosh designed Scotland Street School Museum, to which May Hutcheson, a child at the school in 1925, introduced us.

As part of this M74 Completion Project, funded by Transport Scotland, Glasgow City Council, South Lanarkshire Council and Renfrewshire Council, a public archaeology programme was planned to bring this area of Glasgow's industrial past to life. The programme included excavations, displays, events and activities. As part of the oral history project, David Walker interviewed a number of people who lived in the areas around the excavations and participated in its industrial past. It was from this fund of material that the memories of Gerard Coyle, Crawford

Dick, George Fairley, Gurdev Assad Singh Pall, Charles McLaughlin, John McLaughlin, and Thomas Scott Wilson came to be included in *Our Glasgow*. You can download, read and listen to the full text of these interviews and others at www.glasgowmuseums.com/venue/show Exhibition.cfm?venueid=12&itemid=210

Finally, I would like to thank the publishers who have granted permission to quote from the many books on which I have drawn.

Every effort has been made to trace the holders of copyright in text quotations and photographs, but any inadvertent mistakes or omissions may be corrected in future editions.

Piers Dudgeon, November 2008
(janthony78@ymail.com)

Sources and endnotes

Chapter 1: From Legend to Enlightenment

[1] *Tales Beyond the Back Green*, Bill Paterson (BBC Radio Scotland and Hodder & Stoughton, 2008).

[2] The Protestant William of Orange (1650–1702), stadholder of the Netherlands from 1672 and as William III, King of Great Britain and Ireland from 1689, after being invited by opponents of the Catholic James II to accept the British throne.

[3] These Mercat crosses can be seen all over Scotland to mark places where markets were legally held. The one presently in Glasgow Cross dates back only to 1930, a replacement for one removed from here in 1659.

[4] *Making Ships, Making Men*, Alan Mackinlay (Clydebank District Libraries, 1991).

[5] Bill Alexander, www.ourglasgowstory.com.

[6] *Voices from Work and Home*, I. MacDougall (Mercat Press, 2000).

[7] *My Life of Revolt*, David Kirkwood (Harrap, 1935).

[8] Scottish Occupational Health Oral History Project (subsequently cited as SOHOHP), SOHC Archive Deposit 016 interview A3 by Ronald Johnston.

[9] *Lethal Work: A History of the Asbestos Tragedy in Scotland*, R. Johnston & A. McIvor (Tuckwell Press, 2000). SOHOHP interview A9 by Ronald Johnston.

[10] From Jimmy Reid's speech after being robed as Rector of Glasgow University (1972).

[11] His job was to place the red hot rivet in the hole and, using a heavy tool, take the force as the riveter hammered the rivet head.

[12] The Poor Law: an early version of social security.

Chapter 2: Character

[1] Deirdre Chapman in *Glasgow: A Celebration*, ed. Cliff Hanley (Mainstream Publishing, 1984).

[2] *A Govan Childhood*, Aonghas Mor (Angus MacPhee), www.ourglasgowstory.com.

[3] *Glasgow: Going for a Song*, Seán Damer (Lawrence & Wishart, 1989).

[4] Interview with Bashir Maan by Chris Watt.

[5] Owen O'Leary in *Glasgow: A Celebration*, ed. Cliff Hanley (Mainstream Publishing, 1984).

[6] *Industrial Revolution: 1770s to 1830s*, Michael Moss, www.theglasgowstory.com.

[7] *Tales Beyond the Back Green*, Bill Paterson (BBC Radio Scotland and Hodder & Stoughton, 2008).

[8] Paul Kelly, in search of his forebears, brings him to the Garngad. Paul Kelly was born in Glasgow in 1971 but now lives in Botswana. Investigating his family history a few years ago, he found that 'all roads led to Garngad'. He published his findings on www.discuss.glasgowguide.co.uk.

[9] *Vendetta*, Paul Ferris and Reg McKay (Black & White Publishing, 2005).

[10] *The Indian Eye on English Life*, B. M. Malabari (Constable, 1893).

[11] M74 Dig Oral History Project. Extract from interview with Gerard Coyle by David Walker.

[12] SOHOHP interview A19 by Ronald Johnston.

[13] *Born Up a Close: Memoirs of a Brigton Boy*, Hugh Savage (Argyll, 2006).

[14] Hugh Cairney, interviewed by Dr Neil Rafeek, 26 March 2005 (SOHCA/016).

[15] The largest and oldest chemical works in Europe. Founded in 1797, its chimney, known as Tennant's Lum, was 435 feet tall.

[16] Owen O'Leary in *Glasgow: A Celebration*, ed. Cliff Hanley (Mainstream Publishing, 1984).

[17] John Hamilton, Anderston Reminiscence Group.

[18] SOHOHP interview A9 by Ronald Johnston.

[19] Tommy Stewart and Sydney Smith, Govan Reminiscence Group.

[20] *Making Ships, Making Men*, Alan Mackinlay (Clydebank District Libraries, 1991).

[21] SOHOHP interview A3 by Ronald Johnston.

[22] *Making Ships, Making Men*, Alan Mackinlay (Clydebank District Libraries, 1991).

[23] Tommy Stewart and Sydney Smith, Govan Reminiscence Group.

[24] *Managing My Life*, Alex Ferguson (Hodder & Stoughton, 2000).

[25] *Making Ships, Making Men*, Alan Mackinlay (Clydebank District Libraries, 1991).

[26] Ibid.

[27] SOHOHP interview A3 by Ronald Johnston.

[28] SOHOHP interview A18 by Ronald Johnston.

[29] Hugh Cairney, interviewed by Dr Neil Rafeek, 26 March 2005 (SOHCA/016).

[30] *Growing Up*, Edward Gaitens (Cape, 1936).

[31] *Growing Up In The Gorbals*, Ralph Glasser (Chatto & Windus, 1986).

[32] Tommy Stewart, Sydney Smith, Govan Reminiscence Group.

[33] *The Clydesiders*, Hugh Munro (Macdonald, 1961).

[34] *The Shipbuilders*, George Blake (Faber and Faber, 1935).

[35] *Making Ships, Making Men*, Alan Mackinlay (Clydebank District Libraries, 1991).

[36] *The Shipbuilders*, Martin Bellamy (Birlinn, 2001).

[37] *Work*, R. Fraser (Penguin, 1969).

[38] *A Healthy Balance: Glaswegian Men Talk about Health, Tobacco and Alcohol*, K. Mullen (Avebury, 1993).

[39] *The Shipbuilders*, Martin Bellamy (Birlinn, 2001).

[40] Stewart McIntosh interviewed by Dr Neil Rafeek, 9 June 2003 (SOHCA/016).

[41] SOHOHP interview A6 by Ronald Johnston.

[42] Jim O'Donnell interviewed by Dr Neil Rafeek, 26 March 2005 (SOHCA/016).

[43] *Billy*, Pamela Stephenson (HarperCollins, 2001).

Chapter 3: The Great Change

[1] Hugh MacDonald, *Glasgow Citizen* (18 October 1851).

[2] *The History of Govan*, T. C. F. Brotchie (John Cossar, 1905).

[3] www.glasgowwestend.co.uk.

[4] M74 Dig Oral History Project. Extract from interview with Charles McLaughlin by David Walker.

[5] *Born Up A Close – Memoirs of a Brigton Boy*, Hugh Savage (Argyll, 2006).

[6] *Up Oor Close – Memories of Domestic life in Glasgow Tenements*, Jean Faley (White Cockade, 1990).

[7] The People's Palace permanent exhibition of Glasgow life, Glasgow Green.

[8] *News of the World* (1934).

[9] *Picture Post* (1948).

[10] *Red Skirts on Clydeside* (Sheffield Film Co-op, 1984).

[11] Tommy Stewart, Govan Reminiscence Group.

[12] Sam Watt, the Springburn Museum Trust.

[13] James Baxter, ibid.

[14] Cathy Page, ibid.

[15] Marion Smith, born Marion Russell in 1906, ibid.

[16] *Night Song of the Last Tram: A Glasgow Childhood*, Robert Douglas (Hodder & Stoughton, 2005).

[17] Doug Heath www.ourglasgowstory.com.

[18] John Wotherspoon, the Springburn Museum Trust.

[19] *Night Song of the Last Tram: A Glasgow Childhood*, Robert Douglas (Hodder & Stoughton, 2005).

[20] The People's Palace permanent exhibition of Glasgow life, Glasgow Green.

[21] Tazza Macleod, www.ourglasgowstory.com.

[22] Frances Kathleen Walker in *Gorbals: The Way We Were*, Ellen McAllister (Scotch Mist Productions, 1999).

[23] Tommy Stewart, George Rountree, Govan Reminiscence Group.

[24] M74 Dig Oral History Project. Extract from interview with George Fairley by David Walker.

[25] *A Govan Childhood*, Aonghas Mor (Angus MacPhee), www.ourglasgowstory.com.

[26] Alec McGregor, the Springburn Museum Trust.

[27] Betty Knox, ibid.

[28] *Up Oor Close: Memories of Domestic life in Glasgow Tenements*, Jean Faley (White Cockade, 1990).

[29] Mrs Whelan, Mrs Roper, Mrs Capaldi and Miss McKerrell, Anderston Reminiscence Group.

[30] The Springburn Museum Trust.

[31] Ibid.

[32] Irene Hamilton, Anderston Reminiscence Group.

[33] The Springburn Museum Trust.

[34] Mrs Whelan, Mrs Roper, Mrs Capaldi and Miss McKerrell, Anderston Reminiscence Group.

[35] Sam Watt, the Springburn Museum Trust.

[36] *Born Up A Close: Memoirs of a Brigton Boy*, Hugh Savage (Argyll, 2006).

[37] Interview with Bashir Maan by Chris Watt.

38 M74 Dig Oral History Project. Extract from interview with Crawford Dick by David Walker.

39 M74 Dig Oral History Project. Extract from interview with Thomas Scott Wilson by David Walker.

40 John and Irene Hamilton, Anderston Reminiscence Group.

41 Thomas Orr, the Springburn Museum Trust.

42 Amelia Newton, ibid.

43 Mrs Whelan, Mrs Roper, Mrs Capaldi and Miss McKerrell, Anderston Reminiscence Group.

44 Stirling Women's Oral History Project Archive, 1986–9. Mrs S. 3.1.

45 *Tea at Miss Cranston's*, Anna Blair (Birlinn, 2006).

46 Stirling Women's Oral History Project Archive, 1986–9. Mrs S. 3.1.

47 Ibid.

48 Jean Kendal, www.ourglasgowstory.com.

49 Stirling Women's Oral History Project Archive, 1986–9. Mrs S. 3.1.

50 *Gorbals: The Way We Were*, Ellen McAllister (Scotch Mist Productions, 1999).

51 John Wotherspoon, the Springburn Museum Trust.

52 M74 Dig Oral History Project. Extract from interview with Crawford Dick by David Walker.

53 Ibid.

54 M74 Dig Oral History Project. Extract from interview with George Fairley by David Walker.

55 Ibid.

56 Frances Kathleen Walker in *Gorbals: The Way We Were*, Ellen McAllister (Scotch Mist Productions, 1999).

57 *The Gorbals Story*, Robert McLeish, ed. by Linda Mackenney (7:84 Publications, 1985).

58 *Glasgow: Going for a Song*, Seán Damer (Lawrence & Wishart, 1990).

59 *Up Oor Close: Memories of Domestic life in Glasgow Tenements*, Jean Faley (White Cockade, 1990).

[60] *Managing My Life*, Alex Ferguson (Hodder & Stoughton, 2000).

[61] Lord Rosebery on his opening of the People's Palace on 22 January 1898.

Chapter 4: The Women of the Tenements

[1] S. Graham Hoey, the Springburn Museum Trust.

[2] Professor Arthur McIvor, Department of Social History, University of Strathclyde, Glasgow.

[3] *Red Skirts on Clydeside* (Sheffield Film Co-op, 1984).

[4] Ibid.

[5] Ibid.

[6] Ibid.

[7] *The Hidden History of Glasgow's Women*, Elspeth King (Mainstream, 1993).

[8] Ina Wotherspoon, the Springburn Museum Trust.

[9] Agnes McDonald, ibid.

[10] William McGinlay, ibid.

[11] *The Hidden History of Glasgow's Women*, Elspeth King (Mainstream, 1993).

[12] Marion Smith, the Springburn Museum Trust.

[13] *Glasgow Taxi*, Jack Clyde (Shepheard-Walwyn, 2004).

[14] *A Govan Childhood*, Aonghas Mor (Angus MacPhee), www.ourglasgowstory.com.

[15] M74 Dig Oral History Project. Extract from interview with Crawford Dick by David Walker.

[16] Stirling Women's Oral History Project Archive, 1986–9. Mrs N. 2.

[17] *Glasgow: Going for a Song*, Seán Damer (Lawrence & Wishart, 1990).

[18] Stirling Women's Oral History Project Archive, 1986–9: Mrs N. 2.

[19] *A Govan Childhood*, Aonghas Mor (Angus MacPhee), www.ourglasgowstory.com.

[20] Rita Moffat, www.gorbalslive.org.uk.

21 *The Hidden History of Glasgow's Women*, Elspeth King (Mainstream, 1993).

22 M74 Dig Oral History Project. Extract from interview with Gurdev Assad Singh Pall by David Walker.

23 *A Govan Childhood*, Aonghas Mor (Angus MacPhee), www.ourglasgowstory.com.

24 Tony Jaconelli, www.ourglasgowstory.com.

25 *Oor Wee Shop*, Jean Kendal, www.ourglasgowstory.com.

26 John and Irene Hamilton, Anderston Reminiscence Group.

27 Tony Jaconelli, www.ourglasgowstory.com.

28 John Pollock, the Scottish Football Museum, Hampden Park.

29 M74 Dig Oral History Project. Extract from interview with Charles McLaughlin by David Walker.

30 *The Real Gorbals Story*, Colin MacFarlane (Mainstream, 2007).

31 *Lulu: I Don't Want to Fight*, Lulu (Time Warner Books, 2002).

32 M74 Dig Oral History Project. Extract from interview with John McLaughlin by David Walker.

33 James Kinnear, the Springburn Museum Trust.

34 Norman Ross, www.ourglasgow.com.

35 Annie Docherty, www.ourglasgow.com.

36 *No Mean City*, A. McArthur and H. Kingsley Long (Corgi, 1935).

37 *Glasgow: Going for a Song*, Seán Damer (Lawrence & Wishart, 1990).

38 Mrs Whelan, Mrs Roper, Mrs Capaldi and Miss McKerrell, Anderston Reminiscence Group.

39 John Dowie, the Springburn Museum Trust.

40 Ibid.

41 Mary Preece, ibid.

42 James Baxter, ibid.

43 *Glasgow: Going for a Song*, Seán Damer (Lawrence & Wishart, 1990).

44 Stirling Women's Oral History Project Archive, 1986–9. Mrs S. 3.1.

45 *The Real Gorbals Story*, Colin MacFarlane (Mainstream, 2007).

[46] *The Hidden History of Glasgow's Women*, Elspeth King (Mainstream, 1993).

[47] *Barrowland: A Glasgow Experience*, Nuala Naughton (Cluny Publications, 1993).

[48] Ibid.

[49] *Glasgow By The Way, But: Celebrating A City*, John Cairney (Luath Press, 2006).

[50] *The Magic of the Gorbals: How We Lived, Loved and Laughed, 1914–60*, Eddie Perrett (Clydeside Libraries, 1990).

[51] *The Hidden History of Glasgow's Women*, Elspeth King (Mainstream, 1993).

[52] Ibid.

Chapter 5: Street Magic

[1] Monty Berkeley, Garnethill Synagogue and Museum of Jewish Life.

[2] *Two Worlds*, David Daiches (1956; Cannongate, 1987).

[3] Philip Berman, Garnethill Synagogue and Museum of Jewish Life.

[4] *The Magic of the Gorbals: How We Lived, Laughed and Loved, 1914–1960*, Eddie Perrett (Clydeside Libraries, 1990).

[5] Monty Berkeley, Garnethill Synagogue and Museum of Jewish Life.

[6] Alec Bernstein, ibid.

[7] Monty Berkeley, ibid.

[8] *The Magic of the Gorbals: How We Lived, Laughed and Loved, 1914–1960*, Eddie Perrett (Clydeside Libraries, 1990).

[9] Hannah Frank Levy, Garnethill Synagogue and Museum of Jewish Life.

[10] John and Irene Hamilton, Anderston Reminiscence Group.

[11] M74 Dig Oral History Project. Extract from interview with Thomas Scott Wilson by David Walker.

[12] *Gorbals: The Way We Were*, Ellen McAllister (Scotch Mist Productions, 1999).

13 M74 Dig Oral History Project. Extract from interview with Thomas Scott Wilson by David Walker.

14 Tazza Macleod, www.ourglasgowstory.com.

15 Peggy Taylor, the Springburn Museum Trust.

16 M74 Dig Oral History Project. Extract from interview with Crawford Dick by David Walker.

17 M74 Dig Oral History Project. Extract from interview with John McLaughlin by David Walker.

18 M74 Dig Oral History Project. Extract from interview with George Fairley by David Walker.

19 Stirling Women's Oral History Project Archive, 1986–9. Mrs I. 3.

20 Stirling Women's Oral History Project Archive, 1986–9. Mrs S. 3. I.

21 Tazza Macleod, www.ourglasgowstory.com.

22 Stirling Women's Oral History Project Archive, 1986–9. Mrs. N. 2.

23 Stirling Women's Oral History Project Archive, 1986–9. Mrs S. 3. 1.

24 Ibid.

25 *The Real Gorbals Story*, Colin MacFarlane (Mainstream, 2007).

26 Stirling Women's Oral History Project Archive, 1986–9. Mrs S. 3. 1.

27 Interview with Tony Jaconelli by Chris Watt.

28 *Come Oon, Get Aff*, BBC Radio Scotland, 24.10.1990.

29 First included in a 1960s BBC Scotland series, before it became a book, *Parliamo Glasgow*, now published by Birlinn Ltd (2008).

30 *The Real Gorbals Story*, Colin MacFarlane (Mainstream, 2007).

31 Ibid.

32 Elaine C. Smith, *The People's Patter*, BBC Radio, 31.12.1996.

33 *River of Memory: Memoirs of a Scots-Italian*, Joe Pieri (Mercat Press, 2006).

34 Sam Watt, born 1919, the Springburn Museum Trust.

35 *Gorbals: The Way We Were*, Ellen McAllister (Scotch Mist Productions, 1999).

36 Betty Knox, the Springburn Museum Trust.

37 *Gorbals: The Way We Were*, Ellen McAllister (Scotch Mist Productions, 1999).

38 Interview with Tony Jaconelli by Chris Watt.

39 Agnes Mclean in *Glasgow: A Celebration*, ed. Cliff Hanley (Mainstream Publishing, 1984).

40 *Gangs of Glasgow*, Robert Jeffrey (Black & White Publishing, 2008).

41 *The Dancing Days*, Maggie Craig (Headline, 2004).

42 *No Mean City*, A. McArthur and H. Kingsley Long (Corgi, 1957).

Chapter 6: Class War

1 Chris Young about Norman White in *Glasgow: A Celebration*, ed. Cliff Hanley (Mainstream Publishing, 1984).

2 *A Boxing Dynasty: The Tommy Gilmour Story*, by Tommy Gilmour and Robert Jeffrey (Black & White Publishing, 2007).

3 *Gangs of Glasgow*, Robert Jeffrey (Black & White Publishing, 2007).

4 Tony Jaconelli, www.ourglasgowstory.com.

5 *Up Oor Close: Memories of Domestic life in Glasgow Tenements*, Jean Faley (White Cockade Publishing, 1990).

6 *River of Memory: Memoirs of a Scots-Italian*, Joe Pieri (Mercat Press, 2006).

7 *Finding Peggy: A Glasgow Childhood*, Meg Henderson (Corgi, 1994).

8 *Battered Wives*, Scottish Television (1974).

9 *Glasgow Crimefighter: The Les Brown Story*, Les Brown and Robert Jeffrey (Black & White Publishing, 2005).

10 *A Sense of Freedom*, Jimmy Boyle (Pan Books, 1977).

11 *Gorbals: The Way We Were*, Ellen McAllister (Scotch Mist Productions, 1999).

12 *A Sense of Freedom*, Jimmy Boyle (Pan Books, 1977).

13 James Baxter, the Springburn Museum Trust.

Chapter 7: Conflict

1 *No Mean City*, A. McArthur and H. Kingsley Long (Corgi, 1935).
2 Irene Hamilton, Anderston Reminiscence Group.
3 Mrs Whelan, Mrs Roper, Mrs Capaldi, Miss McKerrell, Anderston Reminiscence Group.
4 John Hamilton, Anderston Reminiscence Group.
5 *The Way It Was*, Stanley Matthews (Headline, 2000).
6 The Cappielow Park Stadium in Greenock.
7 Cowan played in goal for Greenock Morton and Scotland.
8 Similarly relevant to legend and the tradition of Greenock Morton, no doubt.
9 Charlie Cooke played for Aberdeen, Dundee, Chelsea, Crystal Palace and Scotland before ending his career in the US, playing for, amongst others, the Los Angeles Aztecs.
10 *We'll Support You Evermore: The Impertinent Saga of Scottish Fitba'*, Trevor Royle and Ian Archer (Souvenir Press, 1976).
11 *Glasgow Crimefighter: The Les Brown Story*, Les Brown and Robert Jeffrey (Black & White Publishing, 2005).
12 *Handstands in the Dark*, Janey Godley (Ebury Press, 2005).
13 *River of Memory: Memoirs of a Scots-Italian*, Joe Pieri (Mercat Press, 2006).
14 'Sectarianism in Glasgow: Final Report', prepared for Glasgow City Council by NFO Social Research, 2003.
15 Stirling Women's Oral History Project Archive, 1986–9. Mrs S. 3. 1.
16 Interview with Tony Jaconelli by Chris Watt.
17 *Gangs of Glasgow*, Robert Jeffrey (Black & White Publishing, 2008).
18 The Ulster Defence Association (UDA) is a loyalist paramilitary organisation in Northern Ireland. Its military branch has operated under the name Ulster Freedom Fighters (UFF).
19 M74 Dig – the Scotland Street Museum. Extract from interview with Gerard Coyle by David Walker.
20 Interview with Tony Jaconelli by Chris Watt.
21 Quoted from *Irish: The Remarkable Saga of a Nation and a City*, John Burrowes (Mainstream, 2005).

[22] *Cloak without Dagger*, Percy Sillitoe (Abelard-Schuman, 1955).

[23] *Gangs of Glasgow*, Robert Jeffrey (Black & White Publishing, 2008).

[24] *Glasgow: Going for a Song*, Seán Damer (Lawrence & Wishart, 1990).

[25] *The Big Men: Personal Memories of Glasgow's Police*, Joe Pieri (Neil Wilson, 2003).

[26] Interview with Joe Pieri by Chris Watt.

[27] *Gangs of Glasgow*, Robert Jeffrey (Black & White Publishing, 2008).

[28] Monty Berkeley, Garnethill Synagogue and Museum of Jewish Life.

[29] Rosa Sacharin, Archive Curator, ibid.

[30] Lionel Levy, ibid.

[31] Alec Bernstein, ibid.

[32] Delia Berkeley, ibid.

[33] Alec Bernstein, ibid.

[34] Joe and Rosa Sacharin, ibid.

Chapter 8: Glasgow at War

[1] *Glasgow: Going for a Song*, Seán Damer (Lawrence & Wishart, 1990).

[2] John Milloy, www.ourglasgowstory.com.

[3] SOHOHP interview A3 by Ronald Johnston.

[4] Helen in *See, When You Look Back . . . Clydeside Reminiscences of the Home Front, 1939–45*, Margaret Bennet and the Kinning Park Over Sixties Club.

[5] *The Clydebank Blitz*, I. M. M. MacPhail (W. Hodge, 1974).

[6] Named not after the then home secretary, Sir John Anderson, but David Anderson, one of the civil engineers who approved the design.

[7] Eunice Rushton (nee Soppitt), *BBC People's War*. Article ID: A9006969: 31 January 2006.

[8] *See, When You Look Back . . . Clydeside Reminiscences of the Home*

Front, 1939–45, Margaret Bennett and the Kinning Park Over Sixties Club.

9 Stirling Women's Oral History Project Archive, 1986–9. Mrs S. 3. 1.

10 Interview with Tony Jaconelli by Chris Watt.

11 *Night Song of the Last Tram: A Glasgow Childhood*, Robert Douglas (Hodder & Stoughton, 2005).

12 Renzo Serafini, the Scottish Football Museum, Hampden Park.

13 Peter J. Petts, www.ourglasgowstory.com.

14 John Milloy, ibid.

15 *Lanark, A Life in Four Books*, Alasdair Gray (Canongate, 1981).

16 *Untold Stories: Remembering Clydebank in War Time* (Clydebank Life Story Group, 1999).

17 *Gorbals: The Way We Were*, Ellen McAllister (Scotch Mist Productions, 1999).

18 *The Clydebank Blitz*, I. M. M. MacPhail: The Story of William Smillie, sub-officer in the Clydebank Fire Brigade. Available in the Clydebank Library.

19 The diary of A. M. Struther, Officer for Scotland National Council Social Services Scottish Advisory Committee. Available in the Clydebank Library.

20 *The Clydebank Blitz*, I. M. M. MacPhail: The Story of William Smillie, sub-officer in the Clydebank Fire Brigade. Available in the Clydebank Library.

21 *Our East End*, Piers Dudgeon (Headline, 2008).

22 Thomas McSorley, www.ourglasgowstory.com.

Chapter 9: Glasgow on the Move

1 *River of Memory: Memoirs of a Scots-Italian*, Joe Pieri (Mercat Press, 2006).

2 Renzo Serafini, the Scottish Football Museum, Hampden Park.

3 *Stanley Baxter's Bedside Book of Glasgow Humour*, Stanley Baxter with Alex Mitchell (Birlinn, 2003).

4 *Magic in the Gorbals*, Cordelia Oliver (Northern Books from Famerdram, 1999).

5   Dominic Dromgoole's feature, *Revolt of the Washerwomen*, the *Guardian*, 27 August 2005.

6   *The Gorbals Story*, Robert McLeish, ed. by Linda Mackenney (7:84 Publications, 1985).

7   Educational Films of Scotland (Park Film Studios, 1963).

8   SOHOHP, Interview A23, by Arthur McIvor and Ronald Johnston.

9   Glasgow *Herald*, 19 November 1974.

10 *Finding Peggy: A Glasgow Childhood*, Meg Henderson (Corgi, 1994).

11 Betty Knox, the Springburn Museum Trust.

12 Marion Smith, ibid.

13 Bobby McGee, ibid.

14 Iris MacDonald, *The Big Flit: Castlemilk's First Tenants* (Workers Educational Association, Castlemilk People's History Group, 1990).

15 Ina Lynch, ibid.

16 Bobby McGee, ibid.

17 Boyd Calder, Springburn Heritage Group.

18 Rose McLean, *The Big Flit: Castlemilk's First Tenants* (Workers Educational Association, Castlemilk People's History Group, 1990).

19 Tazza Macleod, www.ourglasgowstory.com.

20 *Night Song of the Last Tram: A Glasgow Childhood*, Robert Douglas (Hodder & Stoughton, 2005).

21 *Nine, Dalmuir West* [aka *The Last Tram*], a 12-minute film documentary of the last weekend of the Glasgow trams, directed by Kevin Brownlow (1962).

22 *Workers not Wasters: Masculine Respectability, Consumption and Employment in Central Scotland*, Daniel Wight (Edinburgh University Press, 1994).

23 *Lethal Work: A History of the Asbestos Tragedy in Scotland*, Ronald Johnston and Arthur McIvor (Tuckwell Press, 2000).

24 SOHOHP, interview A14 by Ronald Johnston.

25 SOHOHP, interview A19 by Ronald Johnston.

[26] SOHOHP, interview A22 by Arthur McIvor and Ronald Johnston.

[27] SOHOHP, interview A9 by Ronald Johnston.

[28] SOHOHP, interview A14 by Ronald Johnston.

[29] *Making Ships, Making Men*, Alan McKinlay (Clydebank District Libraries pamphlet, 1991).

[30] Interview by Ronald Johnston with a 77-year-old retired rigger, who worked in Fairfield's for eighteen years and became a full-time union convenor.

[31] *Born Up A Close: Memoirs of a Brigton Boy*, Hugh Savage (Argyll, 2006).

[32] Interview by Ronald Johnston.

[33] Interview with Jimmy Reid, 'UK Confidential' (BBC, 2002).

Chapter 10: New Lamps for Old

[1] Gerry Mooney, *Cultural Policy as Urban Transformation? Critical Reflections on Glasgow, European City of Culture 1990*, '*Local Economy*', Vol. 19, No. 4, pp. 327–40, November 2004 (The Open University (Scotland), Edinburgh).

[2] Khartar Singh Seran in *The New Scots: The Story of Asians in Scotland*, Bashir Maan (John Donald Publishers, 1992).

[3] *Annals of Rural Bengal*, William Hunter (Elder, 1868).

[4] Bengal and East Bengal, with Assam, was a huge area taking in the whole of the eastern side of the continent, bounded to the north by China and to the east by Burma.

[5] 'Lascar' meant soldier in 17th-century Urdu.

[6] *The New Scots: The Story of Asians in Scotland*, Bashir Maan (John Donald, 1992).

[7] Bishen Singh Bans in *The New Scots: The Story of Asians in Scotland*, Bashir Maan (John Donald, 1992).

[8] The Govanhill Pakistani Women's Collective.

[9] Bashir Maan interviewed by Dr Neil Rafeek, 9 May 2003 (SOHCA).

[10] Ibid.

Index

accidents, work-related 25, 46–8, 305
air raids 251–2, 254–5, 265–6, 269–79
Airlie, Jimmy 313, 314
alcohol abuse 51–2, 197–201
Alexander, Bill 12
Alexander Stephen shipyard 55, 308
Anderson, Granny (grandmother of
    Tony Jaconelli) 194, 228–9
anti-Semitism 236–40, 285–6
apprentices 11, 38–40, 49–51
Archer, Ian 217
abestos-related disease 27–9, 292–3,
    306
Asian community 324–33
        attitude towards East European
            migrants 335–6
        businesses 339–40
        immigration 324–32
        integration 344–6
Attlee, Clement 89, 282

back loans (pens) 4
Badesha, Karmjit 335–6, 340–41
Bailey, Elizabeth 271–2

Baird, Mr (neighbour of Bill Paterson)
    24–5
'Baldie' (shipyard worker) 50
Baldwin, Stanley 248
Baltic Fleet (gang) 207
Bans, Bishen Singh 329
Barbour, Jessie 101, 131–2
Barbour, Mary 72, 99, 100
Barbour, Mary (granddaughter of Mary)
    101, 131–2
Barrowlands: A Glasgow Experience
    (Naughton) 127
Baxter, James 63, 210–11
Baxter, Stanley 164, 165–6
Bell, Henry 10
Bellamy, Christine 98, 101
Benn, Tony 316
Bennett, Frank 127
Bennett, William 31–3
Berkeley, Monty 135, 143, 144, 236
Berkley, Delia 238
Berman, Philip 138–40, 142
Bernstein, Alec 143, 238–40
Billington, William 16, 241

Billy Boys (gang) 4, 184, 196, 224–7, 230–31
birthdays 78–9
Blake, George 49
Blochairn steelworks 24–5
Bob, Uncle (friend of Tommy Gilmour) 196
bonfires 115–16
bookmakers *see* gambling
books (reading) 162–3
Born Up A Close: Memoirs of a Brigton Boy (Savage) 68, 199
boxing 121–2, 187–9, 196
Boxing Dynasty: The Tommy Gilmour Story, A (Gilmour and Jeffrey) 188
Boyle, Jim (Oxfam) 341–3, 344
Boyle, Jimmy (reformed criminal) 183, 200–201, 207–8, 209
Brennan, Johnny 250, 251
Bridgeton 59
    see also tenements
Bridie, James 287
British East India Company 326–7
Brotchie, T. C. F. 57–8
Brown, George 311
Brown, Jackie 188
Brown, Les 221
Bruce Report 291
Bruce, Robert (engineer) 291
Bryson, Cathy 190
Bryson, Elizabeth *see* Gilmour
Bryson, Grandpa (father of Elizabeth) 190
Bryson, Matt 190
bugs, infestations 69–70
building programmes (tenements) 58–9
    see also housing schemes
Bygraves, Max 164
Byrne, Miss (teacher) 157

Cairney, Hugh 31, 45–6
Cairns, Mary 299–300
Calder, Boyd 17–18, 298–9
call-on (shipyards) 41–2
Calton Boys 231
Campbell, H. 197
Campbell, Jim 188
Capaldi, Mrs (Anderston Reminiscence Group) 76
Carlyle, Thomas 13
Carmont, Lord 232–3
Castlemilk 297–8, 299
Catholics *see* Irish migrants; sectarian conflict
celebrations 77–9, 115–17, 280–81
Celtic FC 214, 215, 219–22

Chambers, Charlie 115
Chaplin, Charlie (street performer) 117
Chapman, Deirdre 20
charities 75, 129–30, 341, 343–4
    see also poverty; welfare boards
Charles, Prince 322–3
Cheviot, the Stag, and the Black Black Oil, The (McGrath) 287
childbirth 72
children
    see also schools
    deaths 70–71, 271–2
    employment 83, 84
    evacuees 256–8
    illness and disease 70–71, 73–5
    play 109–15
    secretarian conflict 227–8
Christmas 77–8, 213
Churchill, Winston 168, 283
cinemas 168–9
class structure 180–83, 187, 189–91
clubs, youth 233–5
Clyde Valley Plan 295
Clydesiders, The (Munro) 48
co-operative principle 101–8, 122–3
    see also community spirit
Co-operative Society 101–4
Cocozza, Bertie 260–62
Cocozza, Peter (Pietro) 260
Cocozza, Rennie 260–62
Cohen, Ellis 80, 136, 137, 140–41, 145–6, 334–5
    on anti-Semitism 237, 285–6
    on markets 126–7
    on the Second World War 253–4, 255, 258–9, 278–80
Collet, J. 276
Collins, Chic 342
comedians 164–8
    see also humour
communism *see* socialism
community spirit 90–93, 119–22, 124
    see also co-operative principle
Como, Perry 164
concerts 117–18
Connell, John 70
Connolly, Billy 44, 53–5, 164–5
contraception 72
cooking 80–83
Cookson, Catherine 180
Corner Boys (gang) 206
corporal punishment (schools) 156–8
Corrie, Joe 286
Coyle, Gerard 27, 228
Crawfurd, Helen (*née* Jack) 99–100, 132
crime *see* gangs

Cromwell, Oliver 223
culture image (PR campaigns) 321–3
Cumbie gang 207
Curran, Joe 52

Daiches, David 137–8
Dalziel, James 174
Damer, Dr Seán 21, 87, 105, 119, 123, 231
dancing 118–19, 169–74
Davies, John 316
death 25, 46–7, 70–71, 272–3
  see also illness and disease
debtors' prison 5
Delftfield Pottery 111
detectives (shipbuilding) 310
Diamond, Joe 170
Dick, Crawford 78, 83–4, 84–5, 105–6, 156
Dickens, Charles 7
diet 80–83
Dinwiddie, Laurence 111
Dinwiddie, Robert 111
discrimination, sectarian 24–5, 29–31
disease see illness and disease
Dixon, William 27
Dixon's Blazes 27, 46
Docherty, Annie 117–18
docks 11, 34–6
Dollan, Lady Agnes 85, 99, 100
Dollan, Sir Patrick ('Paddy') 84, 100
domestic violence 201–4
Donnelly, Joe 118
Douglas, Robert 65, 67, 260–62
Doyle, Eddie 270–71
Doyle, Nicky 270–71
drinking 51–2, 197–201
Dromgoole, Dominic 288–9
Dudgeon, Brigadier 274
Dunkirk evacuation 258–9

East European migrants 333, 334–7
Easterhouse 301–3
Elizabeth, Queen (consort of George VI) 249
Empire Exhibition (1938) 249–51
England (football team) 215–17
Esther (friend of Elizabeth Bailey) 271–2
evacuees 256–9, 277

Fairfield Experiment 311–12
Fairfield shipyard 18, 40–41, 47–8, 53–4, 265–7, 309, 311–12, 318–19
Fairley, George 85, 157–8
Faley, Jean 59–60, 71, 91–2

family planning 72
fascism 236
Fergus, John F. 15
Ferguson, Sir Alex 40–41, 92
Ferguson, Martin 41
Fields, Ralph 166
Findlay, Jessie 98–9
First World War 242, 244
Fisher, Gregor 165
Flood, Pat 194
food 80–83
football 113–14, 214–22, 225, 263–4
foremen (shipbuilding) 11, 41–2, 310
Francis, Horace 277
Franco, General Francisco 143
'Fraud, The Evil of the Age' (Billington) 16
Fullerton, Billy 196, 225
Fulton, Rikki 167
Fulton, Sadie 130–31
Fyfe, Maria 33–4, 54, 96, 286–7
  on childhood play 109, 114
  on class structure 180–83
  on gangs 183–6
  on housing 88–90
  on the Second World War 254, 278, 279
Fyfe, Peter 125
Fyffe, William 323–4

Gaitens, Edward 46, 49
Gallacher, William 101, 104, 242, 243–4
gambling 142, 191–6
games (children) 109–15
Gandhi, Mohandas K. ('Mahatma') 330–31
gangs 183–7, 196–7, 204–11
  see also machismo
  code of honour 233–5
  dance halls 174–8
  insularity 212–13
  police tactics against 231–3
  protection rackets 191–2
  relocation 301–3
  sectarian conflict 224–7, 230–31
  youth clubs 233–5
Gangs of Glasgow (Jeffrey) 191, 206, 209
Garngad 25–7
General Strike 246–8
George VI 249
Gilmore, Maurice 192
Gilmore, Mrs (wife of Sam) 318
Gilmore, Sam 168, 309–10
  on gangs 177, 192, 225, 226–8, 230, 233
  on General Strike 247

on inter-union disputes 308
on sectarian conflict 29, 30
on work-in (shipyards) 18, 312–18
on working conditions 44–5, 312
Gilmour, Elizabeth, 'Lizzie' (née Bryson, mother of Tommy) 122, 187, 190–91
Gilmour, Frank (bookmaker) 191–2
Gilmour, Jim (grandfather of Tommy) 121–2, 188, 189, 190, 191, 192
Gilmour, Mary (grandmother of Tommy) 189
Gilmour, Tommy 121, 122, 187–91, 192, 194–6
Gilmour, Tommy (father of Tommy) 121, 122, 187, 190, 226
Glasgow: A Celebration (Hanley) 23
Glasgow Cross 3–5
Glasgow, foundation 1–3
Glasser, Ralph 46
Glassford, James 6
Godley, Janey 221–2
Gorbals 58–9, 290–91
see also tenements
Gorbals: The Way We Were (McAllister) 148
Gorbals Story, The (McLeish) 86–7, 162, 289–90
Govan 56–8
Govanhill 332–42, 344
Graham, Hugh Gardiner 16
Grant, Marald 129
Gray, Alasdair 270
Green, Arthur 192
Guild of Aid 129–30

'hairies' (women) 209–10
Hamilton, Irene 74, 77, 146, 213
Hamilton, John 34–5, 78, 146, 213
Hampden Park 214–17
Hanley, Cliff 23
Hardy, Thomas 7
Hargreaves, James 8
Havergal, Giles 287
health visitors 75
Healy, Mr (shop owner) 182
Heath, Doug 65–6
Heath, Edward 316–17, 318
Henderson, Meg 201
'Heroes' (Rawcliffe) 13
Hidden History of Glasgow's Women, The (King) 101, 129
'High Living' (Tierney) 294
high-rise blocks 291–5
Highlanders 19–22, 86–7
Hinduism 330–31

Hitler, Adolf 171, 215
Hoban, Mick 262
Hoey, Graham 95–6
Hogmanay 116–17
holidays 158–61
Holy Cross School 157–8
'Honest Poor, The' (Graham) 16
horses 146, 147–8
housing schemes 87–90, 296–301
see also tenements
humour 52–5, 163–8
Hutcheson, May 147–8, 151–6, 295
Hutcheson, Nan 152, 153
Hutt, Allen 133

identity, Glaswegian 323–4
illness and disease 70–71, 73–5
see also death
work-related 27–9, 33, 292–3, 305–6
Indian community see Asian community
industrial action see strike action; work-in
Industrial Revolution 7–10
insularity (communities) 212–13, 223
see also sectarian conflict
intellectual pursuits 161–3
internees 259–64, 284–5
Ireland 31–3
Irish migrants 22–35
Catholics 22–3, 24–6, 29–34
dockers 34–6
Protestants 23–4
religious conflict see sectarian conflict
Islam 330–31
Italian community 259–65, 284–5

Jack, Helen (married name Crawfurd) 99–100, 132
Jaconelli, Jack 263, 264–5
Jaconelli, Tony 110, 112, 173–4, 186–7, 193–4, 228–9, 259–60, 262–3, 264–5
James VII of Scotland (James II of England and Ireland) 223–4
Jeanneret, Charles-Edouard (Le Corbusier) 291
Jeffrey, Robert 188, 191, 206, 209
Jewish community 135–46, 235–40
anti-Semitism 236–40, 285–6
businesses 139–40, 142, 285
language 137–8, 141
left-wing politics 143–4
migrants 136–7
movement out of Gorbals 144–5
poverty 80, 141
job discrimination, sectarian 24–5, 29–31

Joe the Bull (gangster) 186
Johnston, Maurice ('Mo') 220
Jung, Carl 206

Kaur, Harbans 332
Kay, John 8
Kelly, Paul 25
Kendal, Jean 82, 110–11
King, Elspeth 101, 103–4, 124–5, 129
Kirkwood, David 14, 132–3
Knox, Betty 71, 75, 171–2
Kohli, Hardeep Singh 270

Labour Party 245–6, 282
Laird, Gavin 270–71
Lally, Pat 185
lamplighers 149–50
Lanark: A Life in Four Books (Gray) 269–70
Lane, Frankie 164
Lawrie, Marie McDonald McLaughlin
     (Lulu) 114–15
Le Corbusier (Charles-Edouard
     Jeanneret) 291
Lear, Anne 333–4, 335, 336
Lenin, Vladimir Ilyich 242, 243
Lennon, John 18, 314–15
Levy, Hannah Frank 145
Lipton, Thomas 146
Lipton's store 146
Logan, Jimmy 164
Long, H. Kingsley 96, 118–19, 185, 197,
     204, 208, 210
Lorne, Tommy 165
Lulu (Marie McDonald McLaughlin
     Lawrie) 114–15
Lynch, Benny 188

Maan, Bashir 22, 76, 339
McAllister, Ellen 148, 170–71, 172, 271
McArthur, Alexander 96, 118–19, 185,
     197, 204, 208, 210, 211
McArthur, Duncan 10
McBrearty, Richard 214, 215–16
McBride, Ella (fictional character) 210
McDonald, Agnes 102–3
Macdonald, Frances 151
MacDonald, Hugh 56–7
Macdonald, Margaret 151
MacFarlane, Colin 69, 114, 124, 162–3,
     201, 211
McG, P. 199
McGinlay, William 102–3
McGrath, John 161, 287
McGregor, Billy 172
McGrory Boys (gang) 206
McGrory, Jimmy 206

machismo 48–52, 198–9, 252
     see also gangs
McIver, James 126
McIver, Margaret, 'Maggie' (*née* Russell)
     126, 172
MacKane, David 289
McKay, Tommy 157
McKerrell, Miss (Anderston
     Reminiscence Group) 76
Mackintosh, Charles Rennie 151–2, 155
McLaughlin, Charles 59, 114
McLaughlin, John 157
Maclean, John 104, 132, 133, 161, 241–3
McLean, Rose 299, 300
McLeish, Robert 86–7, 162, 289–90
Macleod, Tazza 149–50, 151, 159–60,
     300–301
Macmillan, Harold 283
McNair, Herbert 151
McNaughtan, Adam 90–91, 294, 322–3
McSorley, Thomas 192–3
Major, The (street performer) 117
Malabari, B. M. 26
marches
     sectarian conflict 224, 229–30
     workers 249
markets 124–9
Marshall, Darkie 117, 118, 134–5
Matthews, Stanley 216–17
Maxton, James 104, 132, 242, 243, 246
Maxton, Tom 126
Men Should Weep (Stewart) 162, 287–9
middens 68–9
migrants *see* Asian community; East
     European migrants; Highlanders;
     Irish migrants; Italian community;
     Jewish community; Roma
     community
Milligan Boys (gang) 206
Milligan, Tommy 206
Milloy, John 250–51, 267–9
Milroy, Jack 164, 167
Mitchell, Ian R. 59
Moffat, Rita 106, 107, 108
Moseley, Hal 217–18
Mosley, Oswald 236
Moss, Michael 23
Mummey, Robert 203
Munro, Hugh 48
Murray, Chic 164, 167
Murray, J. A. C. 233–4
Mussolini, Benito 259

Napier, John 10
*Narrative of a Recent Journey of Six Weeks
     in Ireland* (Bennett) 31–3

Naughton, Nuala 127
Newton, Amelia 79
Night Song of the Last Tram: A Glasgow Childhood (Douglas) 260–62
No Mean City (McArthur and Long) 96, 118–19, 184–5, 197, 204–6, 208–9, 210–11, 212–13, 227
Noble, Mrs (striker) 99
Norah (victory celebrations companion) 280–81
Norman Conks (gang) 224–5, 230

O'Connor, Alex 35
O'Connor, Des 164
O'Donnell, Jim 53
O'Leary, Owen 23, 33
O'Neill, Daniel 33–4, 182
Orange Order 23, 224, 229–30
    see also sectarian conflict
Orr, Thomas 79
Osborne, John 289
overcrowding 4, 58, 61–5, 71–2, 337
Oxfam 341, 343–4

Page, Cathy 63
Pakistani community *see* Asian community
Pall, Gurdev 108–9
Paterson, Bill 1–2, 24–5, 161, 286
patter 52–5, 165–7
    see also humour
Pattison, Ian 164, 165
pawn shops 79
Peddie, J. Cameron 233–5
Penny Mob (gang) 207
pens (back loans) 4
People's Palace, Glasgow Green 92–3
Perrett, Eddie 140
Peter (newspaper vendor) 163
Petts, Peter J. 267
Pieri, Joe 168, 200, 222, 231–2, 284–5
Piratin, Phil 243
pitch-and-toss 192–3
play (children) 109–15
police 21–2, 195–6, 221, 231–3
Pollock, John 113–14
Pollok, Morris 58
potato famine (Ireland) 31–3
poverty 16–18, 26, 75–86
    see also charities; tenements
    birthdays and Christmas 77–9
    diet 80–83
    Jewish community 80, 141
Preece, Mary 79
pride, workers' 13–16, 48–9
protection rackets 191–2

Protestants *see* Irish migrants; sectarian conflict
public baths 65–6
public relations campaigns 321–3

Queen Elizabeth, HMS 12
Queen Elizabeth II, HMS 12
Queen Mary, HMS 12
Qureshi, Shah Abdul Najid 330

Rafiq, Fatima 332
rag women 124–5, 150, 288
railways 10
Rangers FC 214, 219–22
rate-fixing (shipbuilding) 42–4
rationing (Second World War) 279–80, 282
rats (tenements) 67–8
Rawcliffe, Richard 13
Rea, Joe 260
Real Gorbals Story, The (MacFarlane) 69, 114, 124
Red Road flats 292–3
Red Skirts on Clydeside (film) 98, 130
Redskins (gang) 191–2
regeneration and relocation 283–4, 290–303
    Bruce Report 291
    Clyde Valley Plan 295
    consequences 342–3
    gangs 301–3
    housing schemes 87–90, 296–301
    PR campaigns 321–3
    tower blocks 291–5
Reid, Jimmy 8, 16–17, 314–315
religion *see* Irish migrants; sectarian conflict
relocation *see* regeneration and relocation
rent strikes 17, 97–101, 245
Revolt on the Clyde (Gallacher) 243
Reynolds, Mr (teacher) 157–8
Ridley, Nicholas 18, 316
Riefenstahl, Leni 215
River of Memory: Memoirs of a Scots-Italian (Pieri) 200
riveting (shipbuilding) 38, 42
Roma community 333, 334, 336–8, 341–2
Roper, Mrs (Anderston, Reminiscence Group) 76
Ross, Norman 117–18
Rothesay 158–61
Rountree, George 69
Royle, Trevor 217
Russell, Dr J. B. 71

Russell, Margaret (*married name* McIver) 126, 172

Sacharin, Joe 240
Sacharin, Rosa 237, 240
St Kentigern (St Mungo) 1
St Mungo (St Kentigern) 1
Sattar, Abbdus 331–2
Savage, Hugh 30, 59, 60, 62–3, 68, 199, 310
Schier, Niklas 325–6
schools
    see also children
    anti-Semitism 238–9
    corporal punishment 156–8
    Scotland Street School 151–5
    sectarian conflict 227–8
    Sunday schools 131–2
Scotland (football team) 215–17
Scotland Street School 151–5
Second World War 251–81
    air raids 251–2, 254–5, 265–6, 269–79
    Dunkirk evacuation 258–9
    evacuees 256–9, 277
    internees 259–64, 284–5
    preparations 251–5
    rationing 279–80, 282
    Sussex sinking 265–9
    victory celebrations 280–81
    women workers 252–3
sectarian conflict (Catholic versus Protestant) 219–31, 235
    see also insularity; Orange Order
    football 214–15, 219–22
    gangs 224–7, 230–31
    job discrimination 24–5, 29–31
    marches 224, 229–30
    origins 223–4
    schools 227–8
Sense of Freedom, A (Boyle) 200–201, 207–8, 209
Serafini, Renzo 263–4, 284–5
Sharp, Alan 217–18
Shipbuilders, The (Blake) 49
shipbuilding 11–12, 36–55
    accidents 46–8, 305
    apprentices 11, 38–40, 49–51
    demise 305–19
    foremen 11, 41–2, 310
    industrial action 18, 308, 312–18
    origins 10
    patter 52–5
    Second World War 253
    types of work 36–8
    wages 42–4

work detectives 310
work ethic 14–15, 48–9
working conditions 15–16, 44–6
Sillitoe, Sir Percy 231
Silvestro, Rena 208
Simpson, Ronnie 219
Singh, Mrs Shewa Kaur 344–6
Skelly, Mr (teacher) 152–3
Skyscraper Wean (McNaughtan) 294
slums, *see* tenements
Smillie, William 273–4
Smith, Elaine C. 167–8
Smith, George (fictional character) 210
Smith, Marion 63–5, 72, 73, 74
Smith, Sydney 40
socialism 241–9
    see also trade unions
    development 241–6
    Jewish community 143–4
    Red Clydeside policy 133, 244–6
    theatre 161–2, 286–90
    women 129–33
Socialist Sunday School movement 131–2
Solomon, Judah 188
Soppitt, Eileen 256–7
Soppitt, Harry 256–7
Souness, Graeme 220
Spanish Civil War 143
Spence, Basil 292
Stalin, Joseph 283
Stark, Johnnie (fictional character) 177–8, 183–4, 197, 204–6, 208–9, 210, 211
Stark, Peter (fictional character) 204–5, 227
steelworks 24–5
Stephen, Alexander, shipyard 55, 308
Stephenson, Pamela 55
Steve (bouncer) 222
Stewart, Andy 20
Stewart, Ena Lamont 162, 287–8
Stewart, Tommy 40, 50–51
street performers 148–9
strike action
    see also trade unions; work-in
    before 1922 241, 244–5
    General Strike 246–8
    rents 17, 97–101, 245
    shipbuilding 308
    wages 144, 246–7, 252
    women 97–101, 144, 245
Struther, A. M. 275–6
Sunday schools 131–2
Sussex, HMS 265–9

Tales Beyond the Back Green (Paterson) 2
Taylor, Peggy 150
Taylor, Richard 317–18
tenements 58–86, 89, 94–124
    see also housing schemes; poverty;
        women
    building programme 58–9
    co-operative principle 101–8, 122–3
    community spirit 90–93, 119–22,
        124
    demolition 291–2, 296
    escaping 86–90
    middens 68–9
    modern-day 333–4
    nostalgia for 90–91
    overcrowding 4, 58, 61–5, 71–2
    pens (back loans) 4
    rent strikes 17, 97–101, 245
    toilets 66–7
    vermin 67–8, 69–70
textile industry 7–9, 241
Thatcher, Margaret 180–81
Thaw, Duncan (fictional character)
    269–70
theatres 161–2, 286–90
Tierney, Nan 294
tobacco trade 5–6
toilets (tenements) 66–7
Tongs (gang) 207
tower blocks 291–5
trade unions 16–17, 246–9, 307–8,
    311–12
    see also socialism; strike action
trams 247, 303–4
Turner's Asbestos Cement Co. 27–8, 306

UCS (Upper Clyde Shipbuilders) 312
Uddin, Shafiq 330
unemployment 84–5, 248–9
Up Oor Close (Faley) 71
Upper Clyde Shipbuilders (UCS) 312

Vaughan, Frankie 301–3
vermin infestations (tenements) 67–8,
    69–70
Vickery (stallholder) 128–9
Victoria, Queen 327
victory celebrations (Second World
    War) 280–81

wages 42–4, 144, 246–7, 252
Walker, Frances Kathleen 67–8, 86
Wallace, Joe 173
Walters, Mark 219–20
Warnes, S. H. R. 233–4
Watt, Sam 63
Waugh, Arthur 204
welfare boards 17–18, 79–80, 141
    see also charities
*We'll Support You Evermore: The
    Impertinent Saga of Scottish Fitba'*
    (Royle and Archer) 217
Whelan, Mrs (Anderston Reminiscence
    Group) 76
White, Miss (dancing teacher) 130
White, Norman 179–80
William III 224
Wilson, Harold 301, 311
Wilson, Sammy 188
Wilson, Thomas Scott 78, 134–5, 147,
    148–9
women 94–133, 344
    see also tenements
    co-operative principle 101–8, 122–3
    competitive pride 106–7
    cooking 80–83
    domestic violence 201–4
    gender roles 95–7, 155
    'hairies' 209–10
    markets 124–6
    rag women 124–5, 150, 288
    socialism 129–33
    strike action 97–101, 144, 245
    tram work 304
    wartime employment 252–3
Woodly, Jenny 98, 101
work ethic 13–16, 48–9
work-in (shipyards) 18, 312–18
    see also strike action
worker politics *see* socialism
workers' theatre 161–2, 286–90
working conditions 15–16, 24–5, 26–9,
    44–6
Wotherspoon, Ina 102
Wotherspoon, John 66

'Yairds, The' (Fergus) 15
Yates, Henry 13
Younger, George 316
youth clubs 233–5